THE SUBSTANCE OF ALL THINGS

THE SUBSTANCE OF ALL THINGS

SAM HARRIS

InkWell Management and Literary Agency
521 5th Avenue
New York, NY 10175

ISBN: 978-0-578-66878-9

For those who heal,
and those who allow themselves to be healed.

TABLE OF CONTENTS

PROLOGUE

Everything that came forever after was determined by my father's split-second decision to swerve. Only a moment before it happened there had been a kind of affectionate silliness and anxious laughter—his, half hiccupping, and hers, tinkling and soft and nervous.

Then the flash of the animal in fleeting light, solid and fixed, blurred by the downpour and the futile zigzag of windshield wipers, the eternity of the moment, knowing nothing can be done. There should be a way to stop time when these things happen—pull a lever, flip a switch.

The crash was relentless. The skidding, flipping, cartwheeling; the crushing of glass and metal mixed with the brittle snapping of my bones. I was flying through the air, my body flimsy and unmuscled, slammed and jolted; the foolish attempt to grab onto anything, the ripping away of every feeling of safety I'd ever known. Then absolute stillness.

I assumed I was dead. Then I felt my heart strike against my chest. *The only reason I'm alive right now is because death hasn't found me yet.* It was quiet but for the static chatter of the rain. *Shouldn't someone be moaning or calling out? Shouldn't I be calling out?* My eyelids fluttered to see steam rise, a fist of gray smoke in the red hue stretching out over the grassland. A constellation of shattered glass glistened across the dashboard in the moonlight. Then a sudden spewing, a hissing of air, something trying to escape. *I have to escape.*

I tried to pull myself up, but my hands were numb, limp. Just as I began to sense the sweat that covered me, I felt a pull at my foot. Then a hand, a cold hand, wrapping around my ankle, fingernails cutting into me. I heard short gusts of breath and I felt her swollen belly beneath me. *How can she be under me?*

"Theo, are you okay?"

"I don't know."

"Can you get out?"

"I don't know."

"George?" *Nothing.* "Help me, Theo."

"I don't know how."

"Try. You can do it, honey. You're my big boy. Try."

A low, aching pulse spread through my useless wrists and I climbed up with my elbows and twisted my body sideways and over her so that I could crawl through the broken window, snagged by the frame of jagged glass. I fell to the muddy ground with a thud and lay there, a minute, ten minutes, twenty? The metallic taste of blood thickened in my mouth like a rancid paste. *At some point I have to move.*

"Can you walk?"

"I think so."

"Run, Theo," she said. "Run and get help! The baby's coming."

As an adult, I've learned to take my painful memories and put them in a box alongside old photographs and forgotten keepsakes, tucked away on a high shelf and out of reach. It's not as if there's any point in remembering. Again. Any of it. Things happen, I know that. I've become expert at it. I can look at the facts; compartmentalize, assess, accept, and move on. The misfortune of that November night in 1961 is safely locked away, only rarely peering out—in sepia tones.

There was no way to know that night was merely a prelude to the summer, six years later, that would change everything, once more. I thought I'd put that behind me as well. What other choice was there if one is to live a full and contented life? But now, these decades later, I find myself at an insurmountable impasse, unfulfilled and discontent, and I am there again. It's the last thing I need now, these recollections, hovering, loitering, hanging on me in fragments like a movie out of sequence—always in color.

These cunning thoughts creep into my head like rampant vines, and I want to put them back in the box where they belong, but they no longer fit. And so, with some mishmash of apprehension and determination, I've decided to open it, fully, and write it all down. I hope that this—what shall I call it?— project, documentation, literary map—will finally make sense of the persistent angst that has slithered back into my brain. This process begins today.

I sit alone in silence, waiting for the appointment, tapping my crooked fingers on nothing, as if playing a clumsy piano concerto in the air. I look around the room and can't help but chuckle to myself. If an organized environment is the sign of an organized life, a sense of function and sanity, the therapist who inhabits this office must surely be stark raving mad.

Laminated diplomas and certificates hang crookedly against walls the color of cigarette ash. Two cheap looking wood-veneer bookcases stand side by side, the shelves empty but for a slackly stacked pile of unopened mail, a VCR wrapped in RCA jacks, and a worn black leather briefcase sitting atop, bridging the two bookcases like a choice.

Busy-looking papers are strewn across a walnut desk that is covered by a layer of dust interrupted by finger streaks, like a white-glove test never followed through; and to the side of a Queen Anne chair is a metal-based contraption supporting two glass shelves and two adjustable chrome arms bracing two iPads that can be swung in and out of position. An Apple tree.

A respectful knock sounds on the hollow door and I know it's time for my next client.

CHAPTER ONE

Nothing much moved in the heat if it didn't have to, even as early as Easter. Had Jesus been crucified in Dalton, Oklahoma in the summer of 1968, he might not have risen. I was twelve years old and I knew you could fry an egg on the sidewalk because I'd tried it, though I'd been unsuccessful in convincing my little sister to eat the thing. I couldn't understand why they said it was one hundred and four degrees but it felt like one hundred and thirteen. If it *felt* like one hundred and thirteen, why didn't they just say it *was* one hundred and thirteen? I wished my father's father's father had founded a town somewhere cooler, like in Colorado or Sweden, or at least a place where people say what they mean.

Withered cornstalks bore kernels black as rotted teeth, dogs panted in the shade of Blackjack oaks, and children stripped to their underwear and danced in spinning lawn sprinklers. Old ladies dusted themselves generously with talcum powder, which matted and caked by midafternoon when a cool bath and new coat of talcum was required. And in the evening, folks jimmied extension cords under screen doors and out to covered porches, setting themselves in front of oscillating fans as they reminisced about the numbing frost of the previous January, which had been the single subject of their discontent at the time. But if the town thirsted for something more, the good people of Dalton never showed it, nor would they leave it. For them, there was no finer place on this earth.

On the first Sunday of summer, a season dictated by the last day of school rather than a calendar, I hurriedly towel-dried a steaming cast iron skillet and a muffin tin, still warm to the touch, careful not to let them slip from my claw-knuckled grip. I couldn't afford to muss my navy slacks and crisp white short-sleeved shirt which I'd ironed prior to making breakfast, but was now slumped about the collar and shoulders as if it had just received sad news. I dried my hands and glanced at myself in the chipped-framed mirror hung crookedly by the back door, and saw the willow eyes of my father and the same thatch of brown hair, which was now slicked and comb-tracked, impervious to the breathless air and the trickle of sweat rolling down from my temple.

My sister, Lily, sat at the yellow Formica-topped kitchen table my father had proudly bought at a rummage sale for ten dollars. She broke the yolk of her sunny side up egg and crumbled a strip of bacon in a heart-shaped pattern on top, then sopped it all up with a yeasty split roll that she always said looked like a baby's bottom. Six-year-old girls said stupid things like that all the time, but from Lily it sounded introspective, like an art critic.

Our kitchen was a humble one. A chipped porcelain O'Keefe & Merritt stove sat heavily on the faux-marble linoleum-tiled floor; white cabinets that wouldn't completely close due to years of painting and repainting; a dull green-tiled countertop, lined with Sunbeam appliances—toaster, mixer, blender—that my mother had purchased at a Deal-For-A-Steal sale at Sears when I was five or six, I think. The other five rooms of the house were furnished like a disagreement. Among pieces that might be found in any lower middle class home were ornamental European antiques, scroll-legged and tufted, clunky and inappropriate, as if they had been accidentally lowered into our house by crane before the roof was attached. They had been passed down by the town's founder and my great grandfather, Jebediah Dalton.

My recollection of that summer is fraught with the soupy farrago of my predecessors, seen and unseen—the ghosts of my past. And no ghost loomed more portentously than Jebediah, who had been six foot and three inches in height and, from all accounts, magnetic, logical and frankly agreeable. He had grown up in Kansas supporting his mother and five siblings after his father suddenly died of "chronic trouble," according to the records. At twenty-one, Jeb was among the first of the Sooners during the Oklahoma land run of 1889 where parcels of property were given out, first-come, first-served. He hit a gusher on his first drill and the well began producing two thousand barrels of oil a day, making him a millionaire by age thirty. He purchased a quarter section of land to the east of Tulsa, where he founded the town bearing his name.

To pay back the fate that had made him rich, Jeb Dalton established a home for orphans, twenty-three of whom he adopted himself, and the Widow's Colony which provided free housing to young abandoned women with children, as well as a sanitarium for the mentally diseased and disfigured, and a school for the deaf.

In 1918, Jebediah died of a heart attack, leaving a wife and three children. The reading of his will declared that his fortune be left to maintain his various philanthropic institutions. Only a small stipend remained for his family, along with a house brimming with 19th century European antiques, a Singer Sargent painting entitled "Mrs. Fiske

Warren and Her Daughter Rachel," and a Hudson Super 6 touring car. All but the furniture was sold within the year.

I had come up in Dalton incessantly hearing of my millionaire great grandfather who had provided for everyone but his own, leaving his descendants with nothing but reminders of the injustice at every turn: Dalton High School, Dalton Refinery, Dalton Paper Mill, even a Dalton Lake with Dalton ducks and catfish and water moccasins.

Dalton, at least to me, seemed to be populated by the offspring of orphans, widows, the nervous and mentally diseased, and the deaf and the disfigured. I was among them though not by genetics.

It wasn't that my hands didn't work. When relaxed, my fingers curled slightly as if permanently holding a grapefruit. But I could grip and lift and even write if I turned my left hand at a right angle to my arm and grasped a pencil between my index finger and the middle one—the finger I could never fully extend for the pleasure of the gesture. There was no real pain, only the occasional cramp. I knew I would never throw a ball or swing from monkey bars, but that suited me just fine; I could do all I really needed to do. It was the origin of my affliction that preyed upon me now and then, but I had neither the desire nor the luxury to dwell on an unchangeable past. File away and forget, like a bad grade. I wished my father could have applied the same prudence to himself.

His name was Jebediah III, and he carried the striking good looks and solid stock of his forefathers but without the stuff of the preceding Jebs, and chose to be known by his middle name. That morning, he entered the kitchen with his distinctive limp, already dressed for work in his dark blue zipper-front coveralls with the name "George" stitched on his left breast pocket.

He mumbled a "Mornin'" and took his seat at the table, lit a hand-rolled cigarette, grabbed the *Dalton Courier*, which I'd laid folded at his place, and snapped it open, covering his face. I poured thick black coffee—*if you can see through it, it ain't strong enough*—into a dainty, only slightly chipped, ancestral China cup, and placed it on the table where it vanished behind the newspaper before the liquid settled.

The racket of scrunching gravel announced a visitor and an engine sputtered from the driveway just outside the back door. I nearly dropped the warm breakfast plate I'd just pulled from the oven and peeked out the window before placing it in front of my father. "She's here!" I said, and quickly tossed Lily's dishes into the sink. "I'll get these later."

My Aunty Li burst through the back screen door wearing a sheath dress the color of unripe bananas, a bit snug on her ample figure, a hat sprigged with silk violets, and a pair of blue kitten heels. A bundle of bracelets jangled as she waved. "Good mornin' ya'll! Isn't it a good mornin'? Hotter than a billy goat's bottom in a pepper patch, but the Lord waits for no man."

Auntie Li was a glossary of colorful, often too vivid, colloquialisms, and each one was presented with the conviction of an original idiom, swimming in its cleverness, though my sister and I had heard them all a thousand times. I found that the only way to endure her tiresome expressions was to finish her sentences in my mind, almost as a game, to see if I could match her tempo just right.

"Mornin' Aunty Li," my sister and I sing-songed. Lily rose from her chair to present a crudely sewn tutu made of pink tulle, dappled with paper crayon-colored stars, which we'd constructed together the night before.

"Take that thing off, Lily," said my aunt. "Jesus don't like spangly children in church. We're already late." I gave Lily a push and she raced out of the room. "George Dalton, what are you doin' goin' to work on the Lord's Day?"

My father lowered the paper and a puff of smoke escaped. "The Lord don't pay my bills, Lorelei," he quipped, turning the page and giving it a stiff shake. "And he don't fix cars."

Aunty Li plucked off a white cotton glove and nabbed a piece of bacon from my father's plate. "You don't mind, do you George? I could eat the leg off the lamb of God." *Oh brother.* She nibbled delicately to preserve her lipstick.

Lily rushed blindly back into the kitchen, attempting to pull a plaid tent dress over her sandy curls while carrying a time-worn big-eyed vinyl Kewpie doll with the remnants of drawn-on eyelashes and freckles, stuffed into a threadbare pink romper. Aunty Li smiled. "Now that's more like it, sugarplum, Jesus is happy now."

My father finally looked out from behind the sports section. "Lorelei, can you stay with Lily after church? I'm gonna be gone 'til supper and the shop ain't no place for a child."

"Yes, George," she exhaled, with a bone-weary sigh. "Darnell and I *were* gonna go to the movies, but when family calls…" She plucked another piece of bacon from the plate. "We were fixing to go to The Ritz to see *Charly* about that retarded man? I wanted to see *Funny Girl* with that Barbra Streisand but Darnell's already seen it. Three times! I said, 'Darnell, if you see that movie one more time you're gonna turn into a Jew!'" Aunty Li cackled and gave Lily a swift scoot on the bottom. "Get along, little missy, we gotta skedaddle."

My father pulled my sister to him and gave her a routine peck on the cheek. "Where's Joyce?" said Lily, and I clenched the doll in my fist and tossed it to her.

"You don't need to take that mangy thing to church," called out Aunty Li, but Lily was gone. She went for the last piece of bacon and my father cut her off mid-snatch.

"Have fun at church," he said with a wink. He knew how much I hated it and had promised I could stop going when I was thirteen. We scuttled out the back with a bang of the screen door. I'd no sooner made my way to the car when I realized I'd forgotten my Bible, which was more of a prop than anything else. I ran back in as the car idled, but when I reached the screen door, I saw that my father was standing, bracing himself on the chair with an aggravated sigh. The quiet of it stopped me in my tracks. Even though his bad leg bent his body into a slight stoop, there was a certitude about him, and I knew I would never stand as tall. He picked up his coffee cup and headed to the counter for a refill, but then lost his footing and lunged into the cabinet, catching himself just before the fall. "Goddam leg." And I decided that my Bible was not as important as just being gone.

I was barely in the car when Aunty Li threw it into reverse and stepped on the gas, pelting a spray of gravel. She dabbed her lower eyelid and checked her finger for mascara before ripping the car into drive. "Did we move to Africa and somebody forgot to tell me?" she screeched, lighting a Pall Mall with one hand and steering with the other. I rolled down the passenger window a crack. "Keep the windows up or you'll let the air out," she demanded. She blew the smoke into the air and grimaced, waving her hand—as if someone else was smoking and it offended her.

I sat quietly in the haze of blue smoke, testing myself to see how long I could hold my breath, and Lily flounced around in the backseat with Joyce. "We are gonna be late late late. Miss Sunday school and half the service," said Aunty Li, flicking an ash into the overflowing ashtray. "I got stuck behind that Selma Pritchett comin' in. If she drove any slower she'd be goin' backwards." *Flick.*

Aunty Li barreled into town and onto Dalton Boulevard, "boulevard" being a lofty term for the two-laned blacktop street, which was lined with a succession of two-story red brick buildings with nearly identical cement Greek cornices framing their flat roofs. She ignored the 15 MPH sign posted just past Daisy's Taco Hut, then flew by Pickle's Ice Cream Shack, and the newest mom and pop enterprise, Salmon Chanted Evening—a seafood restaurant. I knew it didn't stand a chance.

Aunty Li gunned the Impala to make the yellow traffic light. Realizing it was futile, she screeched to a stop, throwing Lily to the floor with a thud and a scream. I tossed myself over the seat in a flash. "Are you okay?!" I gasped. My heart raced and my body was suddenly engulfed in a cold sweat. I pulled my sister up to the seat and hurriedly examined her for any injury.

"I'm okay," said Lily, giving her doll a squeeze. "And so is Joyce."

"Theo, honey, calm down," said Aunty Li. "She fell on the floor, she didn't fly out the window!" She checked herself in the rear-view mirror and licked her fingers to smooth a stray hair. Her eyes fell on me, pale, the blood having rushed from my cheeks, then averted my gaze. *Flick.* "If we sit here much longer I'll need to put snow chains on my tires," she said, in a change-the-subject pitch. There was no opposing traffic and no one crossing the street. She glanced both ways and tore through the red light, gluing our backs to the seats. "Do you kids have your offering?" she prattled on. "I can't keep givin' you a dime here and a quarter there. Diggin' into my gas money. It's one thing for me to give up my Sundays but I have to draw the line somewhere."

Lily and I could feel it coming and sure enough it did: the story about Aunty Li's promising career as a singer with Uncle Darnell accompanying her on piano. About how she was told she had the voice of an angel and it was only a matter of time until she would be the next Connie Francis. About how she gave it all up to move to Oklahoma because she'd promised our mama she'd watch over us, take us to church on Sundays, make sure we got a good education. *Because family is family and a sister is a sister and a promise is a promise.*

When Aunty Li and Uncle Darnell first came to Dalton, I was sure it was only temporary. Church ladies regularly brought casseroles and cakes and compassionate, down-turned smiles, and it didn't occur to me that the casseroles and cakes would soon be delivered to the next families in need. Charity subsides. My father returned to the shop as soon as he was able and Aunty Li came to our house daily to take care of Lily. I wasn't sure why—I could change a diaper and make French toast and SpaghettiOs, even as I was still learning to use my hands.

When Uncle Darnell secured a job teaching music at Bent Fork High School thirty miles away, I knew they were never leaving. They made the permanent move from Marietta, Georgia, one of the few municipalities that General Sherman had spared on his march to burn Atlanta, and they'd returned only once for the November 12, 1965 Centennial celebration of the day that *nothing* had happened when Marietta was *not* invaded.

We entered Calvary Baptist Church mid-service. It was stark and white but for the eight stained glass depictions of the Miracles of Jesus on the high walls, and the pilled and moderately stained carpet, once the color of a No. 2 pencil. We sneaked down the aisle, skooching through the second-row pew to take our regular seats. The congregants were decked out in their Sunday best and the women were capped with flowered hats so abundant that a view from the mezzanine could be mistaken for a botanical garden.

Pastor Flynn was at the pulpit. He was squat and slightly hunched and always leaning forward, onward, with gray-white hair slicked back behind his ears. He paced in a constant motion that defied his age, with the scrappy carriage of a 1930s movie gangster. His face was wizened, thin-lipped, and bushy-browed, and his steely eyes could pierce a soul in two, or at the very least, damn it to hell. "I look around this great land of ours and what I see is the end of greatness," he preached, over-enunciating each word. "When God inspired our founding fathers to assure us freedom of speech, he did not mean that we should march in the streets and burn our draft cards and our flag. It's like my good friend George M. Cohan used to say. `You're a grand old flag!'"

In his younger days, Pastor Flynn had been a song and dance man. I'd been to his residence only once, just after my mother died, and I'd seen the photo on his wall—straw hat, beaming smile, hanging right next to Jesus—crown of thorns, somber. I realized I'd never seen Jesus' teeth.

I wasn't sure what Pastor Flynn had actually appeared in during his time as a performer, but I knew he'd lived in New York for a summer after the first World War, and referred to Al Jolson, Fanny Brice, Marilyn Miller, and Irving Berlin as his cronies. Word was that he'd had some divine inspiration in New York akin to Moses on Mount Sinai, but I'd always suspected something very bad must have happened in "Satan's Circus," as he called it, to lead him so hastily back to Dalton and into the arms of the Lord, because he never left again. Not even to Tulsa.

The pastor grew hotter. "When God inspired our founding fathers to promise freedom of religion, he did not mean we should allow godless Communists to take over our country. When God inspired our founding fathers to make all men equal, he did not mean we should riot in the streets and burn down neighborhoods in protest for Civil Rights. There ain't nothing civil about it!" Pastor Flynn held the Good Word high above his head like a torch, and the flesh-colored plaster crucifix above him looked down in approval.

Lily was already squirming, knees bobbing, as was always the case when we were too late to church to deposit her at Sunday school. Aunty Li rummaged through her purse, crumpled tissues spilling, whipped out a pencil, grabbed an offering card from the hymnal rack, and thrust them into Lily's hands. "Sit still and draw somethin'," she commanded.

"These acts of rebellion are not the reflection of social progress that the heathens of New York City and Hollywood would have you believe, no they are not. They are selfish and self-indulgent. Do not be bamboozled!" The pastor slammed the Bible onto the pulpit to punctuate his directive and the congregation jerked back in their seats as if stunned by a holy gust of wind. "Let Dalton remain untouched by a time when filth and treason is growing like a cancer. Let us exhibit the morals and values that we cherish. Let Dalton be a beacon of light to the nation! Can I get an amen!?"

I glanced down to see Lily crudely sketching Pastor Flynn with a crown of fire erupting from the top of his head. A snicker shot from my lips and Aunty Li knuckled my thigh hard.

Pastor Flynn carried on. "We are blessed this holy Sunday to have one of our fine brave boys home from the jungles of Vietnam. He is a hero. He is everything our country should be proud of. Sergeant Douglas Watson—Scooter, as most of y'all know him. Stand up, Scooter."

Enthusiastic applause greeted the soldier as he rose from the pew in front of us. He was short and muscular, his broad shoulders squared by his starched and pressed uniform. I was astounded at his striking profile, his prominent jawline, his sharp and slender nose, and closely cropped auburn hair. He appeared to be nineteen or twenty at most. *Not that much older than me*, I thought.

When he turned to face the congregation, an audible gasp stilled the air and the ovation trickled to silence. On fully half of his face was a raging scar, fresh and shiny, like swirling scarlet rivers, lumpy with jagged edges where it should be smooth. His left eye was red-rimmed and distorted and his mouth drooped as if melting.

He scanned the crowd, and when it seemed there would be no end to the resounding hush, he finally spoke. It was the voice of a boy. "It's good to be home." He shifted his weight and looked beyond the congregation to a far off place I couldn't know, and his lifeless eyes suddenly grew wide in a flash of panic. A woman I took to be his mother stood and placed her arms gently onto the boy's shoulders. "Come on, baby, it's okay. It's all gonna be okay." Then she tenderly guided him back to his seat.

Pastor Flynn immediately prompted the choir to stand, waving his arms up and up. The organ music began and the congregation sang along, weakly at first, but then gaining in morale:

I got my breastplate on
In the army of the Lord
I got my helmet on
In the army of the Lord
I got my sword and shield In the army of the Lord His
Truth is marching on!

When the service ended, the three of us milled to the glass-walled foyer, where the adults usually exchanged *heys* and *howdys* as Pastor Flynn shook hands and received praise for his sermon. But today it was all whispers as the young were shooshed out to the grassy churchyard for play.

The air was filled with the squeals of children and the drowsy hum of bumblebees coming from the zinnias that bordered the church, as if nothing out of the ordinary had happened. The girls gathered for jump rope and adolescent gossip, and the boys began a game of touch football. I found a corner of the yard and kept to myself.

Another boy, small and skinny as a rake, perhaps eight or nine, stood several feet away. He was new to Dalton, or at least I'd never seen him before. He was dressed a bit too stylishly, especially in the sweltering summer, in a sailor-style blazer and navy slacks. We didn't speak but recognized each other as brethren in our isolation.

The football suddenly landed at my feet. The boys stared at me, fixing me like a stickpin through a beetle, waiting for my next move. *What to do?* Petrified, I picked up the ball with both crooked hands, sweat beading above my upper lip. The small boy whispered, "You can do it, it's just a ball." It wasn't *just a ball.* My hands clenched tighter making the impossible more impossible. I gathered courage, held the ball in front of my chest, and punted it high and strong. I held my breath. Then the ball hit the rain gutter of the church and bounced, sailing over the roof and out of sight.

"Are you a retard? Why did you even try?" sneered Toby White. His voice was that of a rich boy, syrupy and superior. "You can't throw a ball with your gimpy hands so you kick it over the roof?" Toby was the leader of his pack, blond, with a stubborn cowlick at his forehead and a lock of hair flopping over one eye. He had a face that might grow into handsome, but was currently angular and red complexioned and oddly disproportionate for a fourteen-year-old. "You're dead, Dalton!" The girls swooned and the boys swelled with manliness. Toby nearly pounded his pathetic chest.

"Leave my brother alone!" shouted my sister.

Seconds hung like minutes as I was arrested in what would be my next move—a clever comeback or flight—when Aunty Li sauntered around the corner, the clank of her bracelets preceding her. I'd never been so happy to see her. "Lily, it's time to go," she called out. "Theo, you stay here and play with your nice church friends and just be home for supper."

"I'll walk you to the car," I shouted.

"Well, aren't you a gentleman, Theodore Dalton."

I took Lily's tiny hand in my misshapen one as a gesture of protection, but with the intention of using her as a barricade. After my aunt and sister were in the car, I fled around the other side of the church, off Dalton Boulevard, and across the back field.

I wandered along Saw Creek Road, a desolate band of tire-tracked, sunbaked clay that had once been a viable route before the interstate went in. The air was still, but for the occasional rustling of a redbud tree or when the grass moved to prove otherwise. I passed fields of wheat and sorghum and rolled bales of hay dotted the landscape like enormous spools of thread. I crouched to pick up a stone and watched an ant crawl quite decisively, then pause, then crawl in a different direction having changed its mind.

From a distance came the unmistakable snickers and howls of Toby White and his band of hoods. I quickened my pace and dust clouded at my feet. I could see them approaching through the violent shimmer of heat rising from the road like a fever.

Still unnoticed, I began running, searching for some place to hide, but the fields were bordered on either side by lazy lopsided posts connecting barbed wire. I spotted the old dilapidated house trailer, which I'd passed so many times before, but dared not go near. Everyone knew not to go near. But there was no other choice. A low-branched hackberry tree grew at its side and I dashed down the gravel driveway, found footing on the ledge of the trailer, and hugged the tree, my hands curving onto its craggy bark. I shimmied up, panic lifting me, until I found the first branch, and then pulled myself leg over arm over leg until I was out of view. The voices grew nearer and finally arrived at the end of the drive.

"Hey, soldier killer!" shouted Toby, pelting a rock toward the trailer.

The other boys joined in.

Communist!

Murderer!

Shoulda stayed at Leavenworth where you belong!

Prairie nigger!

They sniggered and puffed and spit.

I climbed higher. One limb, two, until I could go no further. I perched myself on a questionably sturdy branch and nearly toppled a nest cradling three fledgling sparrows covered in aimless, budding feathers. They sensed my presence and strained their fragile necks, opening their tiny beaks for food.

The boys neared the trailer in fits and starts, brave then cautious, and threw rocks that ricocheted against the metal siding. I slipped on the branch, rustling a shower of leaves to the ground.

"Well, look who's hidin' up in a tree?" hollered Jerry Carmichael, a gangly brute whose acne could not be discerned from his mass of freckles. I'd hated him since the first grade. "I think it's a squirrel."

Toby White shielded his eyes from the sun. "How'd you get up there, squirrel?" he said with a smirk, waving at me with his meaty paw. "Can't throw a ball but you can climb a tree? You been fakin' it the whole time?"

The boys began to toss handfuls of gravel at me, followed by small stones, then palm-sized rocks. I climbed higher, shifting my body to block the nest, taking the brunt of the fire on my back and calves.

"Stop it! Leave me alone!" I screamed, but the pelting continued. A rock flew past me and hit the nest, slaying one of the chicks. It lay twisted among bits of crumbled shell and twigs.

The blast of a shotgun rang out and echoed across the plain, and the punks stopped cold. I crouched low on the branch and peeked through the fluttering leaves, and I saw him. He was no folk tale, no apparition. He stood outside the screen door of the trailer holding a rifle. He was tall, but not the towering six-foot-five I'd imagined. He was Native American, dressed in worn jeans, which bagged on his spindly legs, bowed like new branches, and a frayed jean jacket vest with blue-inked tattoos pouring out onto his arms. A faded red bandana capped his head and his hair hung from beneath it in a long braid, shiny and smooth as black glass. A crescent scar sliced his left cheek from ear to mouth, landing at a cigarette that dangled from his lower lip. "Git outta here, you fuckin' delinquents!" The boys ran, but Toby paused to throw one last rock at the trailer before dashing after them. The man hocked a wad of spit and hollered up to me. "You can come on down now."

I froze. Trapped. I glanced at the nest. The remaining two babies were safe. Safer than me. I could hear my heart pounding and felt blood rush to my ears. I was prepared to stay up there for days if necessary. Suddenly from above, a bird, proud-breasted and determined, dove into a savage air strike, crying, screeching, its beak aimed at me like a missile. It circled and swooped again for its target and I felt the feathers of its cusped wing graze my cheek. I scrambled down and down, my bent hands skidding along the thick bark, scorching my palms, and jumped to the ground, landing hard. I grabbed my ankle and winced.

I looked up to see the man standing over me. His cigarette, burned down to its last puff, poked from the corner of his mouth and he squinted one eye in the smoke. His scar sickled along his cheek, dull and smooth like candle wax. "Don't mess with the babies. Mama's gonna protect her babies. Give her life for `em if she has to. Or yours." I stared at the man I'd heard tell of for as long as I could remember, waiting to see if he would take aim for the kill. Fear pierced the soles of my feet and moved up through my calves and thighs, through my spine, finally reaching my neck, my head, my eyes wide and my mouth open and frozen like a merry-go-round horse at the county fair. I jumped to my feet and attempted to run, but my ankle betrayed me.

"Slow down, son," the man said. "You're gonna make it worse."

I had no choice but to surrender to the pain. The man pulled me up and slowly walked with me as I leaned on his arm and hopped to the cinder block steps at his door. He went to a refrigerator planted outside the trailer, powered by a long extension cord snaking through a window. I anticipated a stabbing. Instead, he pulled out a tray of ice, cracked it into his bandana and returned to me to press it against my ankle.

"Sparrows come to this tree every year to nest and have their young, practically the same day, same branch, like clockwork," he said. "Just let the ice set there for a minute."

He adjusted the bandana and it soothed me. "Who are those assholes that pass by here every Sunday?"

I couldn't not smile. "Yeah, they are assholes."

"It's good they don't like you. Good you ain't one of them. Different from mean is good," he said. "Good is good." He gently rotated my ankle. "Just circle it around. That's it. Nothin' broken."

I stood, gingerly testing my ankle. "I'm better. I'm okay. Thank you."

"You got a name?"

"Theo. Theodore. Theo."

"Frank."

He reached out his hand and I shook it, anticipating the flinch that always accompanied contact with my deformity, but there was no trace of it.

I started slowly up the drive, distributing my weight more evenly as I walked, when a dented, snuff-colored Pontiac pulled up just off the road. It coughed for several moments after it was turned off, begging not to be turned on again. A wiry teenager, torn-jeaned and scraggle-haired, carried a box of groceries to the trailer with much apprehension. I figured he'd drawn the short straw at the Safeway. He reeked of skunk weed. I'd smelled it once before on Haskell Pierce before he got expelled from school. Frank gestured to his front step. "Right over here is good." The boy warily obeyed. Frank pulled a small roll of cash from his pocket and paid the boy, who grabbed it at arm's distance and pivoted away at a determined pace which quickened to a sprint.

The boy tripped over a row of nearly-buried cinder blocks, the remnants of the foundation of a house, and fell at my feet. "Fuck!" He winced and plucked an enormous shard of brown glass, probably from a shattered beer bottle, from deep in his forearm and covered the wound to stop the bleeding, to no avail. Frank started toward him. "Shit!" the boy hollered, scuffling to get to his feet. The crazy man was coming! I helped him to stand and when I let go of his arm, his eyes widened and he jerked himself away from me. "What the ...?" he said, looking at me glassy-eyed. "I'm okay." And he resumed his gallop to the car, peeling out and leaving a cloud of dust in his wake. I started away.

"Hold it, boy!" I turned to see Frank coming toward me. I was panicked, certain his kindness had been a decoy, and that this was the moment of my death. When he reached me, he paused, as if considering what he was about to say, or if he should say it. Finally, he spoke. "I saw that."

"Saw what?"

"That boy's arm was cut pretty bad, then it stopped bleeding when you touched him."

"So?"

"You reckon that was coincidence?"

"Huh?"

"That happen before? Somebody gets better after you touch 'em?

"I don't know."

"You think about it. I reckon it has."

"I gotta get home."

I headed for the road and Frank called after me. "Hey boy! My calculations are that those fledglings are gonna fly from the nest in a week. Every year like clockwork. Come Sunday when those assholes are chasing you, you should stop by and watch if you want."

"Thanks for the ice," I said, and hurried away as if late for something, anything, somewhere. It was then that I heard the man chuckle.

Session 1

A second knock sounds. I draw in a long breath and survey my office one more time. Even the artificial plants sitting on the windowsill look dead. "Come in," I say, forcing an invitational tone, and pull myself to a respectable sitting position.

The door clicks and swings inward, grazing the arm of the leather sofa. *I need to move that away just an inch or so.* My new girl stands in the doorway. The third in as many months. I've always hated it when someone refers to an employee as their girl. *My girl will call you. My girl will send that right over.* But I can't remember her name. She rests her shoulder against the jamb with an ambiguous lull that suggests she can't remember mine either. Or doesn't care to. I sense that she'll be gone by the end of the week.

"Dr. Dalton." I'm wrong about her not remembering my name but I still don't think she'll last. "The building manager said the air will be back on before lunchtime."

"Thank you ..." *person ... girl ... whatever your name is.*

She bows away, revealing a woman standing awkwardly in the frame of the door, clutching an oversized white leather purse in front of her like a shield. She is a new patient.

"Good morning," I say. "Please come in."

"Good morning," she answers, but she doesn't smile when she says it.

I stand and extend my hand, but she nods in lieu of a handshake. I nod back. Whether she is appalled by my deformity or just very private, I am grateful for the detachment. I close the door behind her and sit in my chair, then swing the metal arms of my iPad contraption toward me so that I can glance down at my notes through my readers and still see her over the top. She takes a seat across from me and brings her bag to her lap, hugging it tightly as if I might nab it.

I flip my mental switch, ready to begin.

I consider myself good at my job. Very good, in fact. Or I was at one time. I knew I had the gift, the indirect gift, to heal. To lead to healing. To dredge through complicated lives, tragedies, stumbling blocks, bullshit, blaming, forgiving; people attempting to divest themselves of the barnacles of their pasts, or embracing them as justification for whatever unhappiness brought them to me in the first place. I'd say it's about fifty-fifty. But whatever passion that had initially drawn me to this profession is now somehow lacking. Something has shifted, but I don't know what else I would do if not this. It seems a little late in life for a plan B. Or plan C.

"I'm very glad to meet you," I say.

"Yelp."

"I beg your pardon?"

"That's how I heard about you. Yelp."

"Oh, of course. I didn't know if you were ..."

"Yelping? Why, doctor, it's only our first session. I don't usually yelp until, I don't know, session five, session six." I acknowledge her wit with a smile.

The initial session can be excruciating for both me and them—unbalanced, like a first date where only one person talks and the other asks all the questions. Not that I have any desire to talk about myself, certainly not at work, even aside from the unprofessionalism. I don't care much to talk about myself in general. Ironic, I think, being a therapist who knows the power of expressing oneself, but it's not my thing.

I take a moment to study the form she filled out in reception: forty-two, no hospitalizations, no major illnesses, no drugs, some pot on occasion. Nothing out of the ordinary. There is an elegant harmony to her face—moon-shaped with high-sitting cheekbones, pale pink lips, and the soft pucker of a dimple, just the one. A wrinkle at the bridge of her nose connects her wide chocolate eyes. Her shoulder length hair is a weighty sable, ribboned with strands of silver as if etched with a soft white pencil. She probably weighs three hundred or so pounds and is dressed in a nearly floor length, billowy midnight blue skirt and a blousy ivory linen top that covers her arms completely, but is cut low enough at the neckline to expose the very top of her cleavage. Give her an apron and she could be serving Kaltenberger in a Bavarian beer garden.

"So. What brings you here?"

"Oh, no reason. I just thought I'd pop in for some therapy," she smiles or smirks, I can't tell which. "I mean why not?"

I laugh politely. She eyes me, then fidgets. She leans forward as if to leave but then leans back again. Pause. "I'm unhappy with my life. Is that what you want to know?" She's edgily defensive and we're only two minutes in.

"Good."

"Good? It's good that I'm unhappy with my life?"

"No, I mean good for saying it. It's a good place to begin. When did you start feeling this way?"

"I don't know. Over time. Things have gotten worse."

"What things?"

"Feelings." She places her purse tightly against her side, ready for a quick exit. "I hate that word. It's so banal. Like the corny song."

"What kind of feelings?"

"I tend to isolate," she states flatly, as if delivering a fiscal report.

"In what way?"

"I spend my time alone. I don't leave my house much. I don't like to be in public." *Fact, fact, fact.*

"Have you seen other therapists?"

"Yes."

"Have you been diagnosed with anything in specific? Agoraphobia?"

"Haphephobia," she says clinically. "Are you familiar?"

"Yes."

"Hmph. Have you had any other patients who've had it?"

"Yes, one."

"What happened? Were they cured?"

"I know that we made progress but he ..."

"A man? Your patient was a man?"

"Yes."

"But he what?"

"He stopped coming and I don't know if he sought other treatment."

She leans forward and back then forward again, rocking herself to a stand. "Sounds like I got off at the wrong station." She reaches the door and turns the knob.

"Please sit down," I say, wondering if I should just let her go. I already regret the effort.

She pauses and lowers her forehead against the door. Her shoulders rise with a sharp inhale and deflate with a slow release. She goes back to the sofa, unsure of her decision.

"Let's just take it one step at a time." I speak softly. "How long has it been?"

"How long has what been?"

"Since you've been touched by another person."

"In the elevator on the way up here. A woman brushed against me."

I can't tell if she's joking or if she considers this an accurate answer. "I mean since you allowed yourself to be touched."

"I don't know…years."

"How many years?"

"I don't know."

"Try to remember."

She swallows and folds her hands in her lap. "It wasn't all at once. I didn't just wake up one day and think *I don't want anyone to touch me.*" Her breath stutters into an anemic laugh.

"Rough guess."

"I don't know. Fifteen years?…Fourteen years," she says definitively. "I was twenty-eight. I remember because it was the day after my birthday. At least that's when I realized it had happened. Over time. That touching was…that touching was uncomfortable. At first anyway—just uncomfortable."

"Was there a specific moment? Some sort of incident?"

"Shit, I knew I was going to have to do this. I just didn't think it would be right out of the gate." I can see that she is questioning, once again, whether to go or stay. And she stays. For now. "I was standing in line at Target," she recalls. "And I dropped something, a brush I think it was, and a man reached down to get it and when he handed it back to me his hand lingered on mine and I remember jerking back. And I realized that I'd avoided being touched for such a long time already. It was the first time I consciously knew it."

The heat crawls across my forehead. But California heat isn't the same as Oklahoma heat, thank God. When a drop of sweat rolls from my temple I wipe it away with the claw of my misshapen hand, and it is all I can feel or think about. "And now?" I carry on. "You said at first it was just uncomfortable. What does it feel like now when someone touches you?"

"It hurts." She stares as if challenging me with her condition. Daring me. As if I might just tell her she's more than I bargained for when I got my license to practice.

"Can you tell me about your previous therapy?"

"Well, that's tricky. I've had, let me think, four therapists, not counting you. But it's never been very productive."

"Why is that, do you think?"

"Lousy therapists. Or because I don't tend to stick with it. Therapy and diets. Not my strong suits."

"It can be tough, I know. We'll go at whatever pace we need to go."

"I'd like to come twice a week. If I'm going to do this I want to get it done as quickly as possible." She is determined but resistant, like standing in the jump door of an airplane ready/not ready to skydive.

"It doesn't really work that way."

"Can I come twice a week or not?"

"Of course," I say. "Just check the schedule with my receptionist." I settle back in my chair and pull my iPad contraption closer. "I'd like to know more about you."

"Like what?"

"Let's start with what you do for a living?"

"Phone sales from home. You know the TV commercials for everything from non-stick pans to miracle pillows to medical alerts? I take the calls. I go on a shift and log into the system and talk talk talk. If they want a pair of compression socks, I sell them a dozen. It's all in the voice." Her tone shifts into a higher register, efficient, engaging. "Do I sound friendly, doctor?" she demonstrates. It is a sound that comes from an entirely different person. "I bet you'd think I was twenty-five." And then it's gone; she drops the octave. "That's what they want, you know. They want everybody to be twenty-five."

"So, would you say that you've found ways to live and function without having to..."

"Be with actual human beings? You bet. It's not so hard, Doc. No one needs to actually meet anyone anymore."

"You can call me Theo."

"I like Doc. Anyway, very little personal necessary. Ironically, less in a big city. You can get anything online, right? Amazon.com is like Chinese food – you order and twenty minutes later it's at your door. It's really kind of freaky. Like they're just around the corner. From everybody!"

She makes me laugh. There is a warmth about her despite her attempt to conceal it. "And even when I have to go out," she continues, "it's easier than you'd think, not touching. You'd be surprised how little touching is actually necessary."

She waits for my response, but I say nothing. I don't tell her I know what she says is true and that I've relied on the same culture. And that every time I'm required to shake hands, even after all these years, there is a scramble of split-second fear in anticipation of the surprise of my deformity—the way people jerk their hands back and then try to cover their embarrassment with a distracting comment. Then there are those who see it coming and hold on a little longer to let me know they aren't judging me, as if saying *some of my best friends are crippled.*

The room is silent. I realize she's waiting for me to speak.

"What do you do for pleasure?" I'm looking for a way into anything.

"I eat. Surprise! Actually, I take that back—I wouldn't call it pleasure. I don't really enjoy it when I'm doing it and I certainly don't enjoy it after I've done it. And now you're going to ask me why I do it if I hate it."

"No, I wasn't going to ask you that."

"I've been in therapy before, Doc, remember? You're going to tell me I stuff my feelings with food and I'm not going to get anywhere as long as I'm not dealing. And that when I lose the weight I'll be more emotionally available."

"No, not at all. In fact, I don't think you should be thinking about dieting or losing weight or anything of the sort."

She stops cold and I wait for one of her clever remarks, but none come. She just sits. The air conditioning kicks in with a soft thump and I can feel it blow through the vent. Thank God. She folds her arms across her chest. I move on.

"Where did you grow up? What was it like to be you as a kid?"

"And away we go!" She's armed and ready once again.

"Away we go where?" I say.

"With the tormented childhood. The neglect, the abuse, the emotional and psychological torture. Spare me."

"Was it?"

"Was it what?"

"Tormented?"

"Everyone had a rotten childhood, right, Doc? I mean that's what keeps you guys in business. Someone to blame."

"I'm not here to blame anyone. I, we, are here to identify things that may have caused you to make certain choices, consciously or subconsciously. Everyone wants to be happy. And you told me you came here because you're unhappy.

You don't like the way it is now. You want to change that. I'm here to help. This is a safe place, I promise." I offer a soft smile and she returns the expression.

"Okay." She stills herself.

"Okay."

She pulls her arms around her body, hugging herself, her fingers growing long, and sits silently for a full minute. Is she remembering? Preparing? Editing?

"My childhood was pretty normal, I guess. I grew up in a little town in Florida. Apalachicola. Sounds absolutely Ozarkian, doesn't it?" She laughs. It is a big hearty laugh.

"What about your parents?" I ask.

Sigh. "My mother was...efficient. Quiet, subservient, but in charge. She made me do my homework and brush my teeth and help with the dishes. Is that good enough?"

"How was she subservient?"

"She was old-fashioned. She did what she had to do. She didn't complain. She read ladies' magazines. She had a glass of wine on Christmas and New Year's. The brownie-baking type. She would definitely be called a mousy housewife. And she wasn't, how do I say this—warm and fuzzy. She was efficient. Did I already say that?"

"You did."

"Well, that sums her up." She makes a sound in her throat. "And she would have keeled over if she had to spend a single minute in this room."

"You mean she'd oppose therapy?"

"Well, yes, but I really mean this particular room. Dingy. What a mess. Really, Doc, it looks like a burglar ransacked the place but couldn't find anything he wanted."

I don't take the bait. "How was your relationship with her growing up?"

"Not close," she laughs. "She lived in a bit of a dream world. I think she was jealous of my relationship with my father."

"How so?"

"He was, what would the therapy jargon be—emotionally available. A lot more than she was. More than she was capable of being. And I think a part of her hated that—her own incapacity. I was definitely daddy's little girl. I know, cliché." She rolls her eyes but I can feel her settling. "My mother never made a fuss over me the way he did. Like she thought it would have been too much to come from both of them. Like she had to balance it or something. I mean she showed up at school plays and football games when I was cheerleading, but she didn't ever praise me. She was quiet but tough in that way."

"You were a cheerleader?"

"Hard to believe, right? Yes, my freshman and sophomore years."

"And not after that?"

"I got fat. Nobody wants a fat cheerleader."

"What's your relationship like with her now?"

"She's not with us anymore."

"I'm sorry. When did she die?"

"She's not dead. Alzheimer's. Final stages. She may as well be dead. Once in a while there's a glint in her eyes that makes me think she recognizes me, but very rarely. It's pathetic really. If that happens to me I hope someone just shoots me."

"So, she lives in LA?"

"Yes, I moved her here to a care facility in the valley."

"What about your father?"

"He's actually dead," she says, and gathers herself.

"I'm sorry."

"Lung cancer. It was a long time ago. I'm okay with it now."

"What was your relationship with him like?"

"He loved me more than anyone ever loved me. Or ever will I suppose. He was generous and kind and he always made me know that I was special."

"When did he die?"

"When I was twenty-three."

"How about siblings?"

"No. I mean yes, but not for a long time. I had an older sister who died when I was seven. She drowned."

"That's terrible."

"She fell out of a motorboat when she was thirteen and she drowned. They found the boat on the shore with the engine still running."

"That's a lot to take for a seven-year-old."

There is a slight tremor in her cheek. "It was a lot, yes. People don't know how to talk to a kid that young after a tragedy. My parents sent me to school the next day, probably to get me out of their hair. And after the funeral we didn't talk about it anymore."

"What a lonely, confusing time that must have been for you," I say.

I think of my mother. I think of my hospital room in the days after the accident, the cold quiet of it, knowing that she was gone and my father might soon be, and the only one left in my immediate family would be a baby sister I'd never met. I remember globby tapioca and how it jiggled on the spoon and made me want to vomit. "You get what you get and you don't get upset," my Aunty Li had said, force feeding me. Nasty tapioca, a dead mother, the expectation for a child to just—carry on.

"I'm sorry you had to go through so much grief and pain alone with no explanation," I say, hoping she can sense the common ground that my professionalism dictates I not share. "Children should never have to experience that kind of loss on their own. No one should." At closer look, her eyes are not brown, a deep hazel maybe, but I don't want to stare long enough to find out. I look down to my notes. "You haven't mentioned your husband."

"I don't have a husband." She works her tongue around her teeth.

"You're wearing a wedding ring."

"Oh, that. I got it years ago at a pawn shop for twenty bucks. You can figure that one out, can't you, Doc? I don't want to appear available. As if my weight and my age aren't enough of a deterrent. I mean there might be some poor schlub and that's his thing: fat middle-aged women who can't be touched. Probably a whole club for them, I bet, if you Google. What about you, Doctor? Are you married?"

"No."

"Have you ever been?"

"No."

"Why not?"

"I'd rather talk about you.

"Where are you from, Doc?"

"Oklahoma."

"I knew it was something like that. It's like you try to hide it, but sometimes the accent slips out. Like the way you said, `I'd rather talk about you.' You said, 'Odd rather talk about you.'" She smiles slyly. "The past is hard to let go of, isn't it?"

"Excellent segue." She's trying my patience. "Have there been past relationships with men?"

"How do you know I'm not a lesbian?"

"Are you a lesbian?"

"No."

More and more I regret asking her to stay. And it appears that she's testing me to decide if she will. "So back to the question," I say. "Have there been many men in your life?"

"Wouldn't that involve touching?"

"Before."

"A few. Two or three. Three."

"Did you date in high school?"

"Some of it."

"What do you mean?"

"Well, I was thinner then. And pretty. Can you imagine that, Doc?"

She is pretty now, but I know better than to say so. She takes a deep sigh that I already realize is characteristic of a detour into the facts of her life. Straightforward. Unattached.

"When I was sixteen I had a boyfriend. His name was Rick and he was sort of a rebel. He smoked cigarettes, pot. Very handsome. Daddy didn't approve, he hated the guy. Said he was trouble. And what do you know, Rick is in jail now for manslaughter! I mean for real. He married a girl we went to school with and two years later he shot her. You can't make this shit up. Could have been me! Daddy was right. About pretty much everything. He saw things other people didn't see."

"Like what?"

"He could read people. He knew who was good and not good. For me."

"How so?"

"I'm not sure, he just knew. He had a sense."

"What about after that?"

Sigh. "When I was sixteen I started putting on weight. My mother had me tested and they said it was a thyroid problem."

"Did you, do you take medication for that?"

Pause. "Yes. Hmm."

"What?"

"I took something for it back then, for a few years. But then I just stopped. Or I guess my mother just stopped giving them to me. I haven't really ever thought about it. That's weird, right?"

"Is it?"

"And then my skin started breaking out and my hair started to get greasy. Hormones. It was embarrassing."

"So this affected your dating life?"

"No shit, Doc, all those degrees on the wall really paid off."

I hope she can relax soon and rid herself of this snide cat and mouse game. It's annoying. "And after high school? Other relationships?"

"One man. I don't really want to talk about him."

"That's why you're here. To talk about things."

"I know I'm going to. I'm just saying I really don't *want* to. He was an asshole. It was after college and I was working at a U-Haul and he was one of the guys that cleaned the trucks."

"What was his name?"

"Link. Short for Lincoln. He was very sexy in his blue coveralls. He had a confident kind of smarmy attitude and it was very appealing. And he was handsome. Way out of my league."

"How was he an asshole?"

She reaches beneath the neckline of her blouse and kneads her shoulder. "He had a way of finding the perfect moment to say something condescending or offensive. Not just about me, about everybody. He'd make you feel like you were the only one he was confiding in. Comments about people. Like you were on the inside. He thought he was superior to everybody else. He was a bully."

"How long were you together?"

"A year-ish. But I never believed we were exclusive, even though he said we were."

"Why did you stay with him?"

"I wasn't exactly top choice for men," she snickers. "Sometimes you take what you can get. And, like I said, he was handsome and sexy. And he had a confidence. And that was a big deal for me." She is finally chipping at the barricade.

"How was he condescending?"

"He called me fat. Which was a fact, so I accepted it. He told me no one else would have me. Which was a fact, so I accepted it. And he said he loved me in spite of all that. Which was not a fact, but I accepted it." Silence. "He was my first real boyfriend who I had sexual relationship with."

"And how was that part of your relationship?"

"More sex than lovemaking. He could be rough."

"How do you mean, rough? Did he hurt you? Physically?"

"Once or twice."

"Once, or twice?"

"Or more." She is matter of fact. She pulls a tissue from her purse and blows her nose. "I don't want you to think all my relationships were bad."

"I don't think anything one way or another."

"I went to a community college thirty miles from my house, so it didn't make sense to leave home. So, you know, I didn't really get the dorm experience at a big university where everybody parties and has sex with everybody. There was a boy I knew from drama class and we got to be friends. Good friends. And then we moved in together in my sophomore year."

"What was his name?"

"Sergio."

"Tell me about him."

"He was handsome in a kind of odd, non-traditional way. He was Latino, exotic looking, and he was funny and sweet and kind." I hear the memory in her voice, faint. "And gentle. He was gentle. I think he reminded me of my father." And she is back. "There you go, Doc, I've answered your next question. I was seeking someone like my father, right? Isn't that what people do? Seek out their mothers and fathers?"

"Tell me more about Sergio."

She relaxes her shoulders and lets her hands fall weak-jointed at her sides. "We laughed all the time. We were always singing in the car with the radio cranked full blast. We would hold hands. We messed around a few times, but he turned out to be gay. Gee, I bet you didn't see that coming."

"How did you feel about that at the time?"

"I don't know. Disappointed, I guess, but I think I knew. I didn't blame him. His father had thrown him out of the house when he was like, sixteen, and I think he was trying to prove something. We stayed close after he told me. He was my best friend all through college."

"Are you still in touch?"

"Not really. Christmas cards. He came to town a few years ago and wanted to get together but, you know..."

"What?"

"I didn't want him to see me. What I've become."

"What have you become?"

"I don't like to be touched! What was I gonna say at our little reunion? `Hey Serge, great to see you! Don't get too close, okay? When people get near me I panic and I get this feeling of impending doom. And if they touch me it burns, Serge. Like fire. Pretty cool, huh?'" The expression she pulls is pinched with anger and absurdity.

"Do you think it's possible that if it was someone you really loved, who really loved you, that perhaps touching wouldn't hurt?"

"I'm not willing to take that chance." Her chin quivers and she stills it.

"I can understand that. And how frightening that can be."

Minutes go by. Then she speaks softly to the air. "People drift away." She collects herself and I don't know if she's going to go further or just move on.

When she does neither I say, "Who in your life has not—drifted away? What's the longest relationship you can remember?"

Her shoulders spill forward and she lets out a breath. "My father never did. He was the only one. The only constant. My mother was never really there, not after my sister died. I mean she was there but not present." She shifts. "Daddy knew that about her. Her vacancy. And I think he felt like it was his duty to make up for that. He told me how much he loved me all the time. How special I was. And he told me that no matter what, he would love me more than anyone else ever, ever would."

"And that made you feel special?"

"Of course it did."

"Do you think it's fair for a father to tell his daughter that no one can love her as much as he does? Not a friend or a boyfriend or even a husband?"

"Well, he turned out to be right, didn't he, Doc?"

"Or did you make sure he turned out to be right?"

She stares at me smugly. Like ice. "All I know is that he was there for me. And he needed me too. And if you'd had to live with my mother you'd understand." She looks at her watch and I know she's hoping our time is up. "What? What do you want me to say? She was a bitch, okay? When I was in high school, I snuck out one night to meet Rick and I got caught sneaking back in. And the next day she put a padlock on my bedroom door and locked me in at night. And Daddy yelled at her and he said she couldn't treat me like a prisoner so she hid the key from him. I had to knock on the door to go to the bathroom! And this went on for two months and finally she gave in to my father. She was a terrible mother and I hated her." She throws up her arms, triumphantly. "Bingo! Jackpot! I hated my mother! How many times have you heard that one, Doc? Are we done?"

I glance at the clock. "We have ten minutes."

"I think we're done."

Her lips curl into a confident smile and she rises as if we'd just split the check after a casual luncheon. She grabs her bag and starts for the door, but when her hand reaches the knob, she turns to me. "They said you were skilled," she says, softly.

"I'm sorry? Who?"

"Yelp. The yelp reviewers. They said you were skilled and, what was the word? ... thorough. That's it. Skilled and thorough," she says, with a sure nod. "I don't want warm and fuzzy, Doc. I'm not the type. I want skilled and thorough."

Skilled and thorough. It sounds like the mission statement for a law firm.

"Do you want me to leave the door open?" she asks.

"Open is good." And she goes.

I sit with myself; unpleasant company. *Skilled and thorough.* As I've grown older, I've learned to wear empathy like a doctor's white coat, so that I can take it off at my discretion, so that I am not depleted by the constant, consuming grief of others. I've learned that while it was compassion that drew me here, it was compassion that would sink me if I stepped into a patient's world of ache and affliction for even a fraction of a moment after their allotted time was up. I knew that it would devour me bit by bit and tear its way into my susceptible heart until there was nothing left. Balance, I've told myself. But now it occurs to me that the years have eroded my soul into a detachment that has separated me from my work and beyond—from the world at large.

I realize I have less and less patience for the long process typical of therapy. Most therapists want to hang onto clients for years—bread and butter—endless layers to peel. I'd rather turn them over, bing-bang-bam, tie a pretty ribbon around it and move on, no applause please. Perhaps that's why I often fantasize about being at the center of emergency calamities: earthquakes, tsunamis, uncontained fires. I watch them on the news and wish myself there, where I could be the superhero and save people. Maybe I should have become a medical doctor.

Crisis have always been a touchstone for me. People in need, immediate, specific. Crisis present the opportunity for a tangible, concrete plan, which can be enacted with a realistic and accomplishable goal. Addiction, a death, a divorce, I'm your man. Cool and collected. I'm the sort of person you'd want on a bus if you were pregnant and suddenly going into labor. The only catch—I'm not really a public transportation kind of guy.

CHAPTER TWO

The violet morning sun peeked through my bedroom window, shining brightly enough for me to screw up my eyes and turn away to bury my face in the covers. It was already Sunday and the prospect of church made me groan. Suddenly, a pillow clocked me in the head. My father stood in the doorway, hooting, holding another pillow above his head, and he lobbed it at me. I threw it back, narrowly missing a lamp, and bopped my father in the belly. Lily ran in shrieking and jumped into his unexpecting arms with delight. Pillows flew.

When my father laughed, his disposition of despair and resentment evaporated; affection and goodness emanated from him like the sun, and my sister and I basked in it, never knowing how long it would last. He chased Lily around the room and tossed her on the bed. I jumped on his back and he spun me round and round, lifting away gravity. He lost his footing and I flew onto the bed as my father fell to the floor, grabbing his bad leg, grimacing. Lily and I stared in apprehensive silence.

"Goddam leg." My father pulled himself up and limped toward the door. "Just one goddam day. One goddam day."

The game was over. My father hobbled away, leaving Lily and I frozen on the bed. We heard him in the hallway, yelling to himself. "I get it, okay?! I goddam get it!"

Lily sat quietly, deflated amongst the pile of pillows. It was what she knew. I wanted to cry for her. And for him. I wanted him to take us both in his arms and pull us close. I wanted to push my face hard into his chest and let him stroke my hair and kiss my sister sweetly on the forehead. And I wanted to hit him, to hurt him. But I knew that none of those things would happen.

I muttered under my breath, "One goddam day."

Lily gasped. "I heard that. Takin' the Lord's name in vain. I'm tellin'."

"You can pray for me at church!" I grabbed a pillow and popped her on the head. "You children are never ready on time!" I said, mocking Aunty Li in a high falsetto. "God hates lazy children. Anadele Pettigrew had to send her children to the penitentiary because they was so rotten!"

Lily grabbed a pillow and popped me right back, screaming with satisfaction at her aim.

I avoided Pastor Flynn's sermon by offering to sweep the fellowship room in the basement of the church and set out donuts and coffee. I would have re-roofed the building if it got me out of the sanctuary. I meandered my way home, cutting through the field by way of Saw Creek Road as I always did, dragging a stick behind me in the dirt, making tracks like a sidewinder. I thought I could actually hear the searing air hum but then I realized it wasn't the air at all. Toby White and his mutts were following at a distance, howling and passing around a cigarette. But they were not distant enough.

"Hey chickenhands," Toby called out through cupped palms. "I'm gonna pound you, asshole."

The other boys joined in, quickening their pace.

"Skuz!"

"Cripple!"

"Asswipe!"

I ran and the boys gathered small stones and heaved them as they gave chase. When I reached Frank's trailer I dashed around back and shielded myself behind a dilapidated Ford pickup, once the color of blood, but now faded into a rusty shade of pink. I grabbed a chunk of broken cinderblock with the idea of heaving it at Toby's throat. Self-defense would surely stand in a court of law. But the boys came to an abrupt stop at the driveway.

"I ain't goin' over there. That crazy fuck has a gun," said Ned "Hammer" Pullman, a particularly swarthy boy who'd been smacked in the face with a hammer when he was five, leaving him with the flat-nosed features of an unskilled boxer.

They yapped, "Soldier-killer!" and swaggered on.

Once safe, I inched from the hiding place. I knew I should go home but I was curious about the man with the tattoos and the scar and the gun and the bandana full of ice. Frank. I crept to the front window of the trailer, carefully spying, and saw Frank's back as he heated canned soup on a hotplate. He turned and I ducked out of sight just in time. I sneaked under the window ledge and to the tree. It was quiet. No sounds of birds.

"They're gone," came a voice from behind, startling me. Frank was standing several feet away with a dishtowel flung over his shoulder and a cigarette flapping from his mouth as he spoke. "Flew off this mornin'."

A man the color of molasses stopped plowing the parcel of land next over and leaned against a fence post. "Mornin', Mr. Kotori," he called out, and wiped his brow and waved his straw hat to cool his glistening cheeks.

"Mornin' Mr. Lewis. How's that sweet girl?"

The man took a swig from his canteen. "Was better yesterday, but took a turn today. Vida's got Missus Walker over with some spirits and camphor oil."

"I'm thinkin' of ya'll. You take care now."

I spotted something wriggling in the grass in the shade of the tree and went to get a closer look. A baby bird lay on the ground, struggling and injured, one wing sputtering. I crouched down and stared at it thoughtfully. It was plump and neckless, brown and gray and white breasted, flecked with spots. Its black eyes glittered. And it was broken.

Frank walked over to me. "Mama's gone. Babies gone. This one don't have much of a chance."

"What if I take it home?"

"That baby's got a bad wing, son. Fell outta the tree. Not much a person can do except put it out of its misery." He waited an uncertain moment, then kneeled down beside me. "Not most people, anyway."

I bent closer to the fledgling.

Frank said, "Go on, pick it up."

I was unsure, but I cocked my head and shyly gathered up the baby bird and cradled it in my palm. It was soft and ticklish.

Frank crouched down by my side. "Now imagine the bird flyin'."

"What?"

"Put your other hand over the little bird and imagine it flyin'. Go on boy. Fly in your mind. Be the bird." Frank's gaze was confident.

I was confused and wary, but I trusted him somehow. The shape of my malformed hands cupped the bird perfectly. I closed my eyes and concentrated. And I imagined: *The bird is perched on a branch. It flutters and shakes and takes flight. And then I could see through the bird's eyes as it soared over the trees and fields, up and down and around.* I felt a tingle in my fingers and I opened my eyes with a sharp intake of air and lifted my hand. The baby bird sat quietly, then jiggled and quivered and stood in my palm. It got its bearings and hopped onto my arm, and then it flew away.

I gasped, open-mouthed.

Frank stood and wiped his hands on the dish towel. "I told you, boy. You got the touch. Special gift. Only seen it once before in my life. You get to know a person when there ain't a lot of people to get to know."

I shook my head, casting it off. "It's just a coincidence. I couldn't have …"

"You wanna find out?" Frank said. "Come by here tonight after the sun's down and we'll just see."

Confusion pounded my brain. "I can't. I gotta make dinner and get my sister to bed."

"Fair enough. If you change your mind, I ain't going nowhere."

Chapter Three

As I prepared dinner, I couldn't resist glancing again and again at my hands, tautened and crooked and magical, and I imagined the baby bird shivering in my palm. Lily set the kitchen table with sterling silverware left by our great grandfather, plastic dinner plates, white with blue daisies at the rim, paper towels for napkins, and ice water in mason jars, though she was too short to reach the freezer for ice trays, so I handed them to her as I plated supper. Lily loved to pull the lever on the metal trays and watch the cubes pop and crunch. Even at that hour, it was as bright and hot as noon, and using the oven seemed downright tortuous. I was nervous, distracted, clumsy.

"What's goin' on with you?" said my father.

"Nothin'," I replied, and I knocked over a glass, shattering it on the floor. Lily screamed and jumped to her chair. "I'm sorry," I said, gathering the largest pieces.

My father glared. "You're a regular butterfingers tonight, boy."

Lily was barefoot, so I carried her to the living room then rushed back to sweep up.

My father said, "I don't know what's goin' on with you but you're about to tell me."

"Nothin'. I'm just—I'm just tired, I guess."

"From what?" he attacked. "It's summer. You got no school. You got no friends. You're hangin' around this place all the time doin' this and fixin' that like a goddam housewife."

I kept my gaze down, sweeping. Then, under my breath, "If Mama was here …"

My father jumped up from the table, knocking his chair to the floor. "What did you say?" He grabbed me by the arm and gripped it hard.

"Nothin'. I didn't say nothin'."

He kicked the chair away. "You reckon I like this? You reckon I like workin' my ass off tryin' to take care of you and your sister and this shithole all by myself?" I heard Lily scamper up the stairs and shut her bedroom door and I hoped she couldn't hear. "Don't give me any of this 'if Mama was here' bullshit," he bellowed. "Your Mama made a *choice* not to be here, you got that?! A *choice*! And I'm the one's gotta deal with it. So take a good look around, son. Ain't nobody else here but me. I'm all you got!"

For a single moment, my father's eyes flashed anguish and a nearly undetectable apology, which betrayed his anger. But he would not give himself to it. He would have stormed out of the kitchen but his bum leg diminished the power of his exit. I knew it was one of the things he hated most—the inability to feel strong. But he could still slam a door and that's what he did when he reached the top of the stairs and his bedroom.

I hurried to Lily's room and found her sitting cross-legged on the bed, sullen, already in her pink pajamas and covering Joyce's drawn-on ears with her cupped hands. "Joyce is kinda sad right now."

"I see," I said, leaning in to the doll. "Joyce, don't you pay Daddy no mind. He's just bein' cranky. He don't mean it."

"Yeah, he don't mean it," said Lily, reassuringly.

"Supper's ready. You want me to bring you two a plate?"

Lily shook her head. "Me and Joyce lost our taste buds."

I pulled back the covers and patted her pillow. "Then it's time to get you both to bed."

"Theo, my head hurts." Lily said. "Will you make it better?" She crawled under the crisp sheets I'd changed just that morning. I switched off the overhead light and turned on the dim Cinderella bedside table lamp, giving the room a warm consoling glow, then sat beside my sister and she laid her head in my lap. The crooked shape of my hands was a familiar touch for my sister, stroking her thick curls down to the scalp and rubbing her forehead in silence. She especially liked her earlobes gently tweaked and tugged, and she sighed to my touch, lost in thought. "Hey Theo?" she said softly. "I asked Daddy how come there ain't no pictures of Mama in the house."

"What did he say?"

"He told me he didn't want me to miss someone I didn't never know."

I knew it was more likely that he was trying not to miss someone he did.

"What about you?" she said in a hush. "Do you miss her?"

It wasn't an easy question and I took my time before answering. "I think," I started slowly, "sometimes I miss her somethin' awful. And sometimes I have to think real hard to remember what it is I'm missin'."

"Think real hard now, Theo. Tell me what Mama was like."

It was times like this that I was better able to conjure a memory, as if my sister was the magical gateway to a fading past. "Well, she was funny and sweet. And pretty. I think her hair was a kind of unusual color, not brown, not blonde, not red, and she tucked it behind her ears, but it would fall down when she bent over to kiss me. And she was silly."

"And what else?"

"Well, she always seemed certain of things." I pressed my fingers against Lily's temples. "She was kind. Like the time I was ridin' my bike and I ran smack dab into the garage door and I banged my head real hard and she cleaned me up and laid all curled up next to me and tickled my hair just like I'm doing with you now. And she sang to me."

"And you were better?"

"Mama always made everything better." Lily and I were still.

"What was Daddy like?" she asked.

"Different from now. He used to spin me around with my arms out like airplane wings, then he'd set me on the ground and I'd be so dizzy I'd wobble around like a drunk old man." Lily laughed so hard she snorted, which made her laugh all the more. "And he'd save all his change in a mason jar and every couple of weeks we'd sit at the kitchen table and roll the coins into little brown wrappers and then go to Tasty Freeze and get ice cream."

"What flavor?"

"I always got chocolate and Daddy got strawberry. And he told me to never throw away a penny. He said you could throw away other stuff that might even be worth somethin', but never a single penny. And if we was walkin' and we saw one on the sidewalk, he'd say `Find a penny pick it up, all the day you'll have good luck.'"

"That sounds like a good idea," said Lily, as if taking notes.

"You know, Bug, Daddy loves us bundles but it's a lot for him. That's why we gotta help out as much as we can. We gotta be good."

"I try my best to be good."

"I know you do."

Quiet. Then Lily whispered, "My head feels better now."

"I'm glad," I whispered back.

I kissed my sister on the forehead and left the room, closing the door lightly. I thought of all the times I'd rubbed her head when it ached and how it always got better. And I remembered the previous winter when the church kids were sledding down the big hill and Dickie Haney crashed into a tree and everyone was sure something had to be broken, but when I helped Dickie up to his feet, he was just fine. There were other times that felt like good luck or a close call. And I made a decision. I checked the crack at the bottom of my father's door to make sure no light was spilling through and I listened for his snore. Then I tiptoed to the front door and sneaked out of the house.

It was a starless night, but the moon carved a bow shape through the blackness. Careful as a thief, I made my way down Jackson Street and hopscotched the shortcut through Mr. Lafler's vegetable garden and sprinted to the field out back. Once on Saw Creek Road, I slowed my pace and took in the lonely open plain and the smell of long-ago cows. When I reached the top of the driveway, Frank stepped out of his trailer, putting on his jean jacket.

"You ready?" he said, as if expecting me.

I nodded, unsure of what I was supposed to be ready for. I walked briskly, trying to match Frank's broad stride.

"Where're we goin'?"

"To see if we can help somebody."

It must have been a mile. The cicadas came alive in a staccato chant, jubilant or cautionary, I couldn't know which. When we reached a small hill, Frank lifted a rusty strand of barbed wire and I crawled under, then he used a post to brace himself and hopped over. We trod through a cluster of blackberry bramble, careful to avoid the prickly thorns, and came out the other side.

Before us was small settlement of rundown clapboard houses with wood-shingled roofs, set on chalky red clay earth. Colored Town. It was a dismal place. There were no streetlights, only the flicker of televisions from inside houses. A man, black as slate, wearing overalls hanging by one strap and mud-caked infantry boots, sat on a tree stump and spit a stream of tobacco juice a good three feet when Frank and I walked by. I knew white people didn't come here.

I was scared. I didn't know Frank that well. Or really at all for that matter. My father didn't know where I was. I could be kidnapped or worse, and no one would know. "*Sad. Sad. Sad. But that's what happens when boys disobey,*" I could hear my Aunty Li say at my funeral.

Frank and I climbed the creaking steps of a wooden porch, gray and splintered and patched with planks of newer wood. One of the posts holding up the porch roof had been replaced with the narrow trunk of a tree. A clothesline was nailed to it and draped to the next porch in the space between houses. A bicycle with one wheel leaned against the wall, and I wondered if it was meant for repair or just that no one had bothered to get rid of it.

Frank knocked on the door and the man who'd been plowing the field next to Frank's trailer answered. Mr. Lewis. "Evenin'. This is the boy I was tellin' you about. Name's Theo."

Mr. Lewis said, "Howdy, young man. Come on in."

"Pleased to meet you, sir."

I entered the house. My breath was high and shallow and my heart fluttered inside my chest like a moth caught in a spider's web. *What am I doing here?* Mr. Lewis led us through the front room; tidy and furnished with mismatched wooden chairs of varying size. Embroidered pillows sagged against a high-backed scrolled sofa with the carving chipped and gouged. A weathered guitar lay on its side, its shape like a woman in repose, and a stack of record albums lay strewn on a side table—Jackie Wilson, Aretha Franklin, Elvis Presley. There were two pictures on a recently painted white wall, hung loosely on wire so that the tops leaned out: A photograph of what seemed to be extended family—the men in smart, long-hemmed, striped suits; the women, fancied in magentas, cyans, and canary yellows with matching hats and gloves, and a dozen snappily dressed children smiling, making faces, covering eyes—Easter I suspected. Next to it, a picture of Jesus, pale complexioned, with long, straight, light brown hair and soft blue eyes—the same one that hung in Aunty Li's house.

On wobbly legs, I shuffled toward the dim light that bled from beneath a doorway. We entered the small bedroom with barely enough space for the double bed and two cots that were separated by hanging sheets drawn back and tied with red ribbon. Two boys, one about Lily's age and the other a little younger, sat on the cots and stared at the back of a slight, kerchiefed woman I guessed to be their mama.

"Vida, this is the boy. Theo." said Mr. Lewis.

She turned to me, her hazel eyes distressed and her eyebrows crooked with worry. A baby lay back in her arms, breathing short and ragged. The child's skin was the same cinnamon blush as its mother's.

"Thank you for comin', Theo," she said, her bottom lip trembling until she bit it hard. "We done tried everything. Went to emergency at St. Francis and they made us wait five hours just to get seen. Cece got better then she got worse. Medicines ain't working." She shifted side to side, rocking the baby. "Curtis fetched a doctor from town, a Dr. Wallace. Never been to our parts before." She shook her head side to side like a metronome. "Was here all of fifteen minutes like he was gonna catch a virus and turn colored. He give us more medicine and Cece got better but then she took sick again. Sicker this time. I know Dr. Wallace ain't comin' back." The woman started to cry but pushed back her tears. "My baby cain't breathe. She don't eat. She got a whistle inside her chest like a kettle on the stove."

I pulled Frank aside and whispered to him desperately. "You shoulda told me. I can't do this. I ain't no doctor."

"Yes, you can, son. Just like you helped that baby bird."

"This ain't a bird."

"Don't make no difference. A life is a life."

"How am I supposed to do something I don't know how to do?" I said, terrified.

"You just be still and let it come to you. You can't go chasing it down."

"But what if…"

"Just imagine," said Frank in a hush, taking me by the shoulders. "Just like you did that baby bird flying, you imagine this baby healthy. You imagine this baby breathing. You let all that imagination go through your hands."

"And then what?"

"I don't know. You'll know better'n me. Go on, boy. Be brave."

Nudged by Frank, I slowly inched my way to Mrs. Lewis and she placed the child in my arms. A band of fear wrapped around my chest and squeezed, making it hard for me to breathe. I was shaking so hard I was afraid I might drop her, and I realized I hadn't held an infant since Lily was new. I placed my crooked hand on the baby's chest and closed my eyes, making soothing sounds of breathing in and out slowly, openly. And I imagined, just like Frank told me to: *The baby is lying on a soft pillow, gurgling and smiling. She is reaching up toward something. From the baby's eyes I can see her grab for a crudely sewn doll with button eyes. Mr. and Mrs. Lewis smile from above her. Mr. Lewis tickles her and Mrs. Lewis says, "Stop it, Curtis, you're gonna make her spit up!"*

Suddenly, I felt a twitch in the palm of my left hand. Just the slightest tingle, a prickling really, so that I couldn't quite discern if the feeling was painful or stimulating—like when water is so hot on the skin that it might be cold, the distinction cannot be made. Then my right hand twitched, sparkling to a tickle that felt like a fortune-teller following the lines of my destiny with a fingernail. The current splayed to my fingers, tiny jolts of something—something charged, even voltaic. Then came a hotness. I felt my hands releasing, my fingers stretching and elongating, and I remembered when they had felt this way so long ago. Before. But there was something more—a feeling inside of me that couldn't be located in my physical body, as if a door which had always existed but had always been locked suddenly opened, slowly, to a secret place, and whatever was within engulfed me like a color I'd never seen; a feeling almost too large for my body, and my knees buckled at its enormity, but I would not fall. I knew that something beyond myself was happening like a dream and I dared not peek for fear that it would end.

I heard a gasp. *Vida? Elijah? Frank? Not Frank.* The sound had emitted from my own mouth—a sharp intake of air—and it startled me and I opened my eyes. It was no dream. My hands were free and my fingers long and limber, *like a pianist's,* I thought. But when I looked at the baby she lay still, with only the whites of her eyes visible through her hooded lids. For a moment I thought she was dead. *Have I been healed for the life of a baby?* Then she took the smallest breath. Then another, and another, staggered. She coughed and her breathing steadied and her eyes fully opened. A crooked smile slowly crept over her lips and spread to a gummy grin. She reached up to her mother. I looked to Frank and he gently nodded.

And then I could feel my hands growing taut and cramped, withdrawing into what I knew. And the blaze that had filled me began to blur and sneak away, and the door to the secret place softly closed.

Vida Lewis took her baby to her breast and rocked her back and forth, tears falling. Mr. Lewis leaned in and hugged me hard. It was the first time I had been hugged by a Negro and I hugged him back. He rushed to his wife and child and Frank led me out. I was weak and confused and astounded, even more so than the others.

As we padded back through the field with only the lurching song of cicadas in the air, Frank put his hand on my shoulder with a strong reassuring pressure. I wasn't really sure what had happened, or how it had happened, or why. *Has the baby really been healed?* I wanted to embrace and reject whatever this was. But my hands had been restored for just those moments, I knew that for sure.

Frank patted my shoulder. "I knew I was right about you. I think you been doin' this a long time without even knowin' it. Not `til now, when you put your mind to it."

My chest felt tight. I coughed. Then again.

"You git on home now," he said. "This night air'll give you a cold."

SESSION 2

The woman sits quietly, knees together, hands flat on her lap, as if she's waiting at a bus stop. "What's that around your neck?" she asks.

"It's an arrowhead. Cheyenne. It belonged to a very dear friend. I've had it since I was a boy."

"Things can be nice. Comforting."

The sky outside is almost black; thick rolling mounds of darkness, unusual for California at any time, but especially in the summer. The crackle of new rain comes and we both stare at the specks of water tickling the window. Rain in Los Angeles is a rare phenomenon, something to pause for, and it almost always goes as quickly as it comes. A memory threatens to take me, but a cannon of thunder jolts me back to the session.

"I'm sorry," I say. "Yes, this necklace is one of the only things I have from my childhood, and it means the world to me."

"I still have a box of stuff Daddy gave me when I was little. It's wooden with a carved heart on the top. I don't know if he actually carved it but I always imagined he did. It was my treasure box—matchbooks, foreign coins, a rabbit's foot, stuff." A burst of lightning slashes the sky like distant fireworks. She flinches. "Where I grew up there were so many thunderstorms. All the time. Especially in the spring and the summer. I think Apalachicola, Florida might be the capital of thunderstorms, I'd have to look that up. They'd sneak up on you and last for thirty minutes or so, day or night. Mostly at night when everyone had gone to bed."

"We had them where I grew up in Oklahoma, too," I say. "They terrified me when I was a little kid. I used to hide under the bed." *Until Lily was old enough to be terrified herself, I remember, and it became my duty to squelch my own fear in order to assuage hers.*

She tilts her head to the side and shifts her eyes to the floor. "It rained like this at my sister's funeral. I remember I was wearing these black shiny shoes that were too small for my feet because there hadn't been time to buy new ones, and I remember I couldn't wait to take them off. And then we got to the graveside service and it was pouring and my father held a giant blue umbrella over me and my mother, the kind for golfing, and my shoes were soaking wet and tight and squeaky and I thought maybe I'd never get them off my feet. That I'd have to wear them forever."

Her face softens with a sort of sweet melancholy and I can almost see her, the little girl, standing in the rain. Suddenly, she regains composure. "Afterward, we went back to the house and everyone was there—the neighbors, people from church, my grandfather and grandmother on my daddy's side. And it was just so, so sad. I'd been to one funeral before that—my grandmother's, my mother's mother. She died when I was four, but I remember her funeral, bits and pieces. I remember sneaking to see her in the casket even though my mother told me not to, and how she didn't seem real at all, all waxy, her cheeks rouged like polka dots. There was no doubting she was dead. And afterward at our house with everybody there it was sad, but people laughed and told jokes about her. There was a sense of celebration.

"When my sister died, of course it wasn't the same." Her words fade to a quiet that nearly demands privacy. "I was only six, but I knew this was different—a different kind of sadness when a child has died. There's nothing to say. I remember overhearing our pastor tell my mother that God must have needed an angel. And even then, I knew it was bullshit, and I thought, if God is so great, why didn't he just make an angel instead of taking my sister?" Anguish flashes beneath her steely expression. "People patted me on the head and my mother made sure food was always out. She never stopped moving. My father just sat on the sofa and smoked."

I can't help but travel in my mind to a memory of nothing, when there had been no proper funeral for my mother. Not with me in the hospital for days and my father for weeks, and Lily being passed from family to family until Aunty Li and Uncle Darnell had driven from Georgia. "Next month," everyone had said, but it never came.

She slips away once more. I fear that she will push down whatever she's seeing and I want her to remain where she is. "What are you thinking about? Right now."

"I'm trying to remember my sister. I think she's become more of a childhood character than an actual person. You know, like Cinderella or Snow White. There was a big age difference, seven years, and I was so young when she died." She looks around at the room, studying it. I think she's going to comment again on how hideous it is but then I realize she's searching for something.

"She loved to read. She was always reading. And I think she passed that on to me. I read a lot, mostly fiction. And I write sometimes. Poetry."

"I'd like to hear some if you're comfortable with that?"

"I'm not."

"What else do you remember about her?"

"I remember playing dress up with her. Well, she dressed me up." She pauses, quizzically. "And my mother ... She and my mother would dress me up."

"You seem surprised."

"I just don't usually think of my mother in a—a fun way."

"How so?"

"She and my sister and me. We had ... fun together. Girly things. Making cookies. Making crafty things. Making messes." She finds no joy in this discovery. "She was different before."

"Before?"

"Before my sister died."

"How so?

"She was ... happier."

I think of my father before my mother died. I'd never known him without resentment, but there had been a tenderness that my mother had seen in him and nurtured, and without her there, he had no one to remind him of his softer parts.

"And then what happened?" I ask. "After?"

"It was like she left us. Daddy and me. It was like she just disappeared."

"That's pretty tough for a little girl to understand, isn't it?"

Her voice grows soft as a whisper and her eyes gather water at the edges. "Yes."

"And it's a mother's responsibility to be there for the child who's alive, isn't it?"

"Yes."

"And she didn't do that for you, did she?"

"No." She clenches her teeth and her eyes dry. An unfulfilled promise of tears.

"She fed you and clothed you and made sure you were at school on time but she didn't do what she was supposed to do. What do you think she was she supposed to do?"

"She was supposed to love me."

"She was supposed to love you."

"But my daddy did."

"Yes, he did."

Rain pummels the window. I can see that her mind is aflutter with specific details and she is allowing herself to fully experience a memory. "That day, after the funeral, after everyone had left, my mother cleaned up the house and went to bed. She didn't come to kiss me goodnight, she just went to bed. But my daddy came to my room and he held me. He promised me everything would be all right. And I could smell the cigarettes on his breath and on his clothes." Her head bows and her chest folds into itself, hollowed. "And he wept. And he told me he was broken. I remember those words, *I am broken.* He curled himself against me and he made me promise I would never leave him. And he slept next to me through the night." Pain splinters her voice. "And I knew that he was there for me, and that I would be there for him too, even if my mother wasn't."

"That's a lot of pressure. One parent who cuts herself off emotionally and another who's making you responsible for his emotional wellbeing."

"It wasn't like that."

"It's not a child's job to comfort a parent."

"It wasn't a job," she insists, angrily. "I wanted him to know I loved him too. Because, unlike my mother, when you love someone, you're supposed to show it."

CHAPTER FOUR

The morning after the Lewis's, I felt empowered and powerless, somehow more and less myself. I was distracted as I scuffed down Jackson Street with Lily skipping along beside me. Monica Johnson lived five houses up in a one-story house with white, wood-grained aluminum siding. The front door was painted a royal blue to match the shutters and trim, and ruby red azaleas bloomed across the length of the front porch. On the Fourth of July, Monica joked that she didn't need to hang a flag out front because her house was already patriotic.

We let ourselves in as we did every morning during the summer months. My father paid Monica five dollars a day to keep Lily during the week so I wouldn't be stuck with my sister until school started up again.

"We're here, Miss Monica!" I called out, and Lily ran to the kitchen to fetch a glass of extra-sweet Cherry Kool-Aide Monica always had at the ready.

"Good morning!" said Monica, carrying in an overflowing laundry basket and dumping it on the sofa.

Monica Johnson was petite and nearly always wore a uniform of Capri pants, an untucked button-down shirt, and ballet flats. She reminded me of Laura Petrie on "The Dick Van Dyke Show." Her features were small and pointed, with large expressive blue eyes, framed by her nearly black hair, which was pulled back into a ponytail. That Monica was divorced had been quite the scandal in Dalton. She was one of two women I knew who had been married and were now single without being widowed.

Monica had moved to Dalton only three years prior from somewhere north, along with her daughters Missy and Lilly. Lily loved that there was another Lilly, a springy and daring four-year-old, whose name was spelled with two *l*s in the middle rather than her one. She called her Lillytwo as if the name was one three-syllabled word. The only reason Lily had agreed to stay at Monica's house instead of being with me all day was that she'd convinced herself she was there to watch over Lillytwo. My sister ran to find her and a scream of joy could be heard in the living room.

Then there was Missy, Monica's sixteen-year-old daughter. I thought she was beautiful in a wrong way, though I'd never say so. Like her mother, Missy had dark hair, which she wore free and wavy with a strand or two always falling over her fiery almond-shaped blue eyes. Her lips were perpetually pouted and one eyebrow always seemed to be arched, as if she was harboring a secret that she might tell, but only under very specific circumstances. I was thinking about her when she appeared, leaning against the hallway wall, wearing a skin-toned camisole that fell and floated beneath her breasts, and a pair of baggy cotton drawstring pajama bottoms. She always spoke in unseparated thoughts. "Hi Theo Mom where are my gold stud earrings?"

"They're on the kitchen counter where you left them, and where I told you not to leave them," said Monica.

"I'm meeting up with Carla and Robin to go shopping and can I borrow the car and did you see what I did with my brown purse with the buckle not the brown one with the snap?" She swept a lock of hair from her eyes but it fell right back to its original spot.

"Yes, no, and be back by six o'clock for dinner. Here! You're having dinner here!"

Missy expelled an excessive sigh, as if the world would end from the vastness of her obligation, and she whipped around and back into the darkness of the hallway. The spit of the shower began and I wondered if she was naked yet.

"Theo," said Monica, who was trying to figure out how to fold a fitted sheet just like I did every time I folded a fitted sheet. "See those two boxes by the TV? Can you please take them up to the attic? You just pull on that rope hanging in the hallway and the stairs will fold down."

"Sure thing, Miss Monica." Monica never treated me less-than because of my hands, and I liked helping out as a kind of surrogate man of the house when something needed to be done. It beat doing the woman of the house stuff in my own home.

I pulled down the staircase and carried up the boxes, stacked one on top of the other because it was manlier that way, and climbed to the attic. A wall of heat hit my face, even more stifling than that outside. I ducked so as not to bang my head on the ceiling and placed the boxes in the corner. Light streaked through chicken wire-covered vents and a million particles of dust danced in the thick air. I wondered if it was like this everywhere all the time but could only be seen when beams of light pierced through darkness.

I stood under the peak of the roof and surveyed its contents: boxes sealed with tape marked "winter clothes" "Christmas" "Doug pictures," and open boxes of stuffed animals and a plastic jack-o-lantern and a violin. Suddenly I felt like a thief, prying into the private world of the Johnsons.

I'd long been tempted to sneak into our basement, which was strictly off limits. I'd been down there only once since my mother died, when I'd heard my father fall, and I'd dashed down the steep wooden stairs skipping two at a time. I found him in a heap on the cement floor, holding a wedding dress amid opened boxes of photos and clothes. Women's jackets and pants and hats. I knew they were my mother's things and I wished I could touch them. "Get the hell out of here!" he'd growled. "And don't ever come down here again or I'll tan your hide!"

Hey Jude. Don't bring me down ... The song slapped me out of my reflection and I climbed down the stairs and sprung them back into place.

The sound of song and shower spray grew louder as I got closer. Missy's voice wasn't half bad. The door was slightly ajar, five or six inches, enough to make me stop and peer in. The bathroom was filled with the heavy haze of steam, which gathered and ran in droplets down the inside of the distorted glass shower door. Behind the fog was Missy, her head tilted back and her breasts thrust forward, blurred enough to be a dream but more real than anything I had ever seen.

She lathered her hair, twisting and piling it on top of her head. She turned in my direction and I pulled away from the door, my heart pounding. When I peeked back in, Missy shifted to profile and grabbed a bar of soap and rubbed it over herself. First her long neck, then her shoulders, outstretched arms, then over the jut of her collarbone and down to the roundness of her breasts.

I felt the press against my jeans. This had been happening more and more in the most inopportune places with no relationship to where I was or what I was doing: riding my bike, doing homework, eating lunch, watching *Animal*

Kingdom, making meatloaf, folding towels, it made no sense. But this was different. I knew exactly why it was happening and I hoped I wouldn't burst before I could tear myself away. But I wasn't ready to tear away. Not just yet.

Then Missy pivoted to my direction and placed her finger on the foggy glass door and began to write, backwards, from her right so that it was readable from the outside:

H I T H E O. And she pressed her lips against the glass and kissed it.

I ran.

"Goodbye, Miss Monica," I shouted, as I bolted through the living room and out the front door. I flew down the street, untied shoelaces sailing behind me like comet tails, past my house and around back of Mr. Jacobsen's shed, and unzipped my jeans and exploded onto the woodpile stacked against the wall.

CHAPTER FIVE

"**B**eloved, I urge you as sojourners and exiles to abstain from the passions of the flesh, which wage war against your soul." Pastor Flynn closed his Bible and canvassed the crowd, seeming to meet eyes with everyone in the church. If he was powerful when he was enraged, he was more powerful when he whispered. "Free love. That's what they're calling it. That's what they would have you believe. I have witnessed the sin of `free love' first hand in the bowels of degradation, in Satan's Circus, and let me tell you, free love has a high price. A very high price indeed. This is not an evolution of society, it is enslavement to our lowest, most animal impulses."

Aunty Li smacked her lips and leaned into me. "Honey, you are too young for this sermon. You really should be in Sunday school."

"I'm almost thirteen, Aunty Li," I whispered. "I hate it in there with all those little kids, and Miss Patsy is an idiot."

"Hush your mouth, Theodore Dalton."

"I'm not going back there."

"Suit yourself," said Aunty Li, and gave her attention back to Pastor Flynn as he preached about one of her favorite subjects: the sins of the flesh.

The minister adjusted his glasses and flipped to the next bookmark in his Bible. "Colossians three, verse one: `Put to death therefore what is earthly in you: sexual immorality, impurity, passion, evil desire.' Brothers and sisters, I don't know how much plainer God can get."

I felt the swelling in my pants. *How could this be happening? How could a sermon on the wages of sexual sin actually make me hard?* I covered my lap with the church bulletin and when I was sure Aunty Li couldn't see, I slipped my hand under it to adjust myself. My aunt reached into her purse for her handkerchief and nearly caught me. "Theo, you shouldn't be here. I am telling you to go to Sunday school until the offering." I didn't budge. "You are stubborn as your mama was," she said, and dabbed her moist hairline with the hanky.

I wanted to go but I couldn't just get up and walk out; everyone would see the bulge in my pants and I couldn't very well cover myself like Adam and Eve in the Garden of Eden.

Pastor Flynn didn't need his Bible for the next scripture quotation. "Romans chapter eight, verse five: `The mind that is set on the flesh is hostile to God. Those who are in the flesh cannot please God.'"

What if it was true? Then I was surely headed for eternal hellfire without question. I began to sweat. Then profusely. I was sure all eyes were on the clammy kid in the second pew. And of course they would know why. I reeked of immorality.

I forced myself to turn around to see the congregation. Everyone was focused on Pastor Flynn and I breathed a sigh of relief. Then I saw her. Missy Johnson. She was sitting with her mother and Lillytwo four rows back and she was fixed on me, smiling with a saporous twist, her eyes dancing with wicked mischief. She shook her hair so that it bounced against the shoulders of her cherry-colored blouse. And then she licked her lips.

"You're right," I said to Aunty Li, a bit too loudly. "I shouldn't be here." I jumped from my seat and scooted through the pew, damn the consequences. I raced out of the sanctuary and into the bathroom where I leaned against the cool tiled wall. I splashed cold water on my face and steadied my breathing. Then I went into a stall and tried to pee but my gears wouldn't switch that easily and the angle of my stream would have been disastrous even if I could.

I forced myself to think of the time I saw old Mrs. Delilah Patterson's saggy, wrinkled breast fall out of her house dress when she was weeding her geraniums. Just the one breast. Her skin was like crumpled wax paper and the weight of the thing bobbed and swayed from her narrow chest like a pendulum made of chewing gum.

That seemed to do the trick.

I made my way down the hall to the Sunday school class and joined the other kids sitting cross-legged in a semi-circle on the checkered rug. Leading the circle was Miss Patsy Carmichael, who was what some folks might call slight but what Aunty Li called downright rangy. *She's so skinny she'd have to stand up twice to cast a shadow.* Miss Patsy had a broad forehead and high, emphatic eyebrows that gave her the permanent look of having been startled. Her nose was stubby and red-tipped as if she'd just run smack-dab into a strawberry. She spoke with a sort of animated anticipation usually reserved for ghost stories around a campfire. "So Cain was a farmer and Abel was a shepherd. And they both made their offerin's to God, but God liked meat more than he liked vegetables and Cain was real jealous so he said, `Hey Abel, wanna come play out in the field?' And Abel said, `Sure, Cain, that'll be fun,' and so they went to the field and Cain killed his brother."

Buddy Parks squirmed on the rug. "It's hot in here. Can we shut that window to keep the air in?" Buddy had a year-round mass of coagulated, gummy snot creeping down from his nose that crusted on his upper lip, and he wiped it on his shirtsleeve.

Miss Patsy was agitated. She hated interruptions when she was in the middle of a Bible story—they messed with her rhythm. "That window don't close, Buddy. Jesus was in the desert for forty days and forty nights, I think you can sit here for thirty minutes." She turned back to the class with a smile. "And then God was madder than a wet hen, and he sent Cain away to wander around so he was the first wandering Jew, like the plant, `cause he was evil and Abel was good and that was that, plain and simple."

"Yeah, evil and good, plain and simple." It was Toby White, my archenemy, sitting directly across from me, taunting me under his breath, spitting at me with his eyes.

Miss Patsy leaned in for the big finish. "And Cain lived to be seven hundred and thirty years old and his children lived on to spread evil on the earth but everything came out in the wash. God works in mysterious ways." Miss Patsy smiled as if to say *and they lived happily ever after.*

People were always saying that. *God works in mysterious ways. Everything turns out for the best.* I didn't believe everything turned out for the best. Too much had turned out for the worst.

"But how could God choose one brother's offering over the other if everybody is one of God's children?" It was the new small boy I'd met/not met in the churchyard, who seemed smarter than the others, or perhaps it was just that he was wearing a bow tie.

Miss Patsy was exasperated. "Fathers get mad at their children all the time. Who in this room has not got a whippin' from their Daddy?" No one budged. "But then everything is okay," she chirped. "And how many of you have heard your parents say, `This hurts me more than it does you?' Well, it hurts God to punish his children, even if they're evil, like when He killed all the people in the world by drowning everybody except Noah and his family. But then He felt real bad and He made a rainbow as a promise he'd never destroy all the people again and it all turned out for the best."

"'Cept for the people got drowned," said Buddy Parks in a whisper, pinching a glob of snot from his nose and mushing it into the carpet.

Then the new boy said, "Ain't a rainbow a scientific thing? Water drops in the air with the sun makin' a spectrum of light." I was right, he was smarter.

"You can make one with a garden hose," I added. "Did it myself just yesterday."

"Theo Dalton's sayin' he's God, Miss Patsy!" jeered Toby.

"I ain't sayin' no such thing!"

"You are an instigator, Theodore Dalton! You could argue the tusks off an elephant!" Miss Patsy yawped. "And you are tryin' my patience! God don't like ornery children, no sir, not one bit. Now you march yourself right back out of this classroom and straight to the sanctuary. You need a big ol' shot of Jesus into that thick head of yours."

I headed out of the room as Miss Patsy continued with the rest of the class, shiny and bright. "Okay now, for our art project, I brought in some barberry brush and we're gonna make crowns of thorns for everybody!"

I was glad to be out of this hellhole. Miss Patsy was a moron.

After church, in the play yard, the new boy and I were once again on the outs, united in our separation. The boy offered his hand and I shook it, trying to stretch my fingers to some kind of normal. I'd never shaken hands with another kid before and he didn't seem to mind. "I'm Henry Hardy, but you can call me Hen. That Miss Patsy is a bitch." Kids didn't normally say words like *bitch* at first introduction. I knew I liked him right away. "We just moved here. I'm thirteen years old but I know I look eight."

"I'm Theodore Dalton. You can call me Theo. I'm almost thirteen and I reckon I look almost thirteen."

"Dalton, like the town?"

"Exactly like the town."

"My daddy works at Phillips Petroleum and we have horses."

"My daddy works at Pappy Ray's Same Day Auto Repair and we don't have no livestock at all."

Just then, Toby strutted over to me, practically nose to nose, closely followed by his henchmen. "If I was Cain and you was Abel," he sneered, "I'd have no trouble at all killin' you." His boys broke up with laughter.

A man, older than Aunty Li but younger than Pastor Flynn, wandered near the play yard, seemingly lost. He was long-faced and saddle-colored, and he was weeping uncontrollably, discombobulated, searching. "Lillias Jean where is you at? I'm here just like I promised."

Toby rallied the boys. "It's crazy `lijah Brown!"

They joined him in the chant:

"Don't know up from down.
Turns up here and turns up there and all around the town."

A dilapidated Chevy pulled up and parked catawampus at the curb. A younger man got out and raced to Elijah Brown. "Hey there, Papa," he said gently, pulling his father away from the play yard. "I been lookin' all over. Time to go home."

The old man's eyes were desperate. "Your mama said she'd meet me here. I gotta stay and wait."

"I know. It's okay, Papa. We're gonna go on home now. Mama will find us at home. Nettie's made you a chocolate cake."

Elijah seemed to find some comfort in this. "Nettie, she make a fine chocolate cake."

"Yes, she do," said his son, and he led his father to the car. He passed me on the rise of the grass up from the sidewalk and I saw him glance at my hands. "Hey, ain't you that boy went over to Curtis Lewis's house?"

I scanned the faces of the other kids to make sure no one had heard, and then I nodded.

"My name's Kevin Brown, and this here's my Papa, Elijah. Can you help me with him?"

I said yes, and we each took Mr. Elijah by an arm and walked him to the car and more importantly, away from Toby. I held the old man's head down to keep it from hitting the doorframe.

"I sure hope he's gonna be okay," I said, and I started away from the curb.

Kevin said, "I thought you was gonna help."

I was confused. "What? I did."

"No, I thought you was gonna *help*."

Then I knew what he meant. "No sir, I don't really..."

"Nigger lover!" Toby hollered from the yard. The gang of boys stood at his side. Lily looked on. Henry looked on. Then I turned and got in the back seat of Kevin's car. Henry smiled at my bravery, but the truth was that I wanted to do it. I wanted the feeling in my hands again. Even if just for a few moments.

We drove to the same neighborhood I'd visited at the Lewis's. It wasn't nearly as scary as in the nighttime, but looked even poorer in the light. We passed the Lewis's house and I saw Miss Vida nursing her baby girl on the front porch.

We arrived at Mr. Elijah's house, which could have been mistaken for the Lewis's or any other for that matter. Kevin told me that his father had the dementia. "He walks into town. He takes off on the bus. One time I found him at Darrell's Café all the way over in Cushing. I don't know why they let him on the bus, they knows him. Everybody knows him. He goes wanderin' all over town lookin' for my mama. She been passed away near on five years."

When we entered, Kevin got me a mason jar of sweet tea and I swallowed a great gulp, then held the moist, cool glass to my forehead. Kevin said, "It started out small, forgettin' where he left things, a hammer, his pipe. But now it's everything all the time. I worry he gonna git hit by a car."

I led Mr. Elijah to a time-worn easy chair, faded red velvet with a button back, all but one button missing. A tall, glass-doored China cabinet caught my eye. It was filled with baseball memorabilia: faded game tickets, a cap frayed at the bill, a trophy with the nameplate illegibly tarnished, a team photo. "That's my daddy's stuff," said Kevin. "Played for the Black Spiders in the Negro League." He pointed to the photo. "That's him. 'King Kong', they called him, `cause he could pitch two double-headers in a weekend." Kevin opened the case and pulled out a signed ball. "Don't touch the writing," he said, handing it to me gently. It read `K.K. – Play ball! Jackie Robinson.' "He give it to my daddy hisself in Brooklyn, New York. See here's the bus ticket."

I looked to Mr. Elijah and thought of all the things that must be swirling around in his head; a lifetime seen and done. I placed the heel of my hand against the bridge of his nose, my fingers brushing his forehead, and closed my eyes hard, asking for entrance into the man's hope. He breathed. He immediately calmed. Then the feeling came again—the twittering, shivering itch that both stung and caressed my hands and moved through my fingers, elongating them into a reach. And I imagined: *Mr. Elijah sitting on the front porch reading the sports section of the paper. Singing at church. Then through Mr. Elijah's eyes: winning at checkers. Seeing the smile on Kevin's face.*

My hands withdrew to what I knew. I opened my eyes and Mr. Elijah shook his head like he was trying to shoo a fly off of his ear. He didn't seem to know where he'd been, but he was clearer now, more curious, more at peace. Kevin gaped. Mr. Elijah held his hand out to his son. "Such a fine boy you turned out to be," he said. "Your mama's looking down on you so proud."

I told Mr. Elijah he should take a nap and he'd feel even better. He patted me on the shoulder and headed out of the room. "Sweet dreams, Papa," Kevin called after him.

Then I said, "I guess there ain't much point in sweet dreams unless you wake up."

Kevin walked me to the porch. "I don't got much to pay you."

"I don't want no money." I smiled. "But I will take another glass of that sweet tea, if it ain't too much trouble."

Kevin went back into the house, leaving me on the porch. A chipped rocking chair creaked in the tease of a breeze. The smooth wooden seat was worn into shallow valleys and I guessed it was shaped by years of Mr. Elijah's behind. I took in the scope of the treeless, narrow clay street, and the row of houses built of wooden slats, roofed by piece-meal shingles with tar paper sneaking out from beneath them. I wondered if the colored kids from my school lived there and I figured most likely. They'd just been admitted to Dalton Elementary two years prior and I only knew them by name. They mostly stayed to themselves, and it occurred to me that we had something in common in an odd way—it wasn't that they only fit inside their own circle, it was that they didn't fit outside of it, and outside was a lot of space not to fit into.

Kevin returned with the tea. "I'll take you on home now."

"Aw, that's okay. You stay here with your daddy, I know my way back. I still ain't sure how all this works but I reckon you should stay with him."

"Anybody messes with you," he said, pointing a finger, "you tell 'em you was at the Brown's place and they gotta deal with me."

"I'll be all right," I said, and I gulped the tea and wiped my mouth with the back of my hand.

I started home, a bit disoriented. I looked up at the cloudless sky, clean and smooth as a second coat of paint. The thorny prick of the blackberry bramble was a welcome landmark. A line of blood striped my arm like a red pencil mark and as I smudged it off, I got an idea. I found a rock, large and flat enough for sitting cross-legged, and I shifted to settle myself. I interlaced my fingers so that my palms pressed together and I closed my eyes and filled my lungs with the still air and I imagined: *gripping the handlebars of my bike with confidence, tossing a baseball to no one in particular, writing—how I dreamed of writing cleanly, comfortably so that my words could come almost as quickly as my thoughts.* But there was no tingle or mysterious stretching. I felt nothing. I opened my eyes and my hands remained crooked and ugly.

SESSION 3

She is late. Or maybe she's changed her mind about the whole endeavor. Her final words in our last session have haunted me. *When you love someone you're supposed to show it.* I need to call my sister. It's not as if we're out of touch, but our conversations have become perfunctory. How is my work going? How is her art going? How are the kids? I always think of them as younger than they actually are. I miss her. Not so much the person she's become—the mom her, the wife her, the painter her. I miss *her*. The sister who knows more about me than anyone on this earth. Perhaps I'll call later, but then I don't know what I'd say. I'm not so eager to tell her that I'm writing down our past. She seems to have put it behind her much better than I. Maybe I'll call on the weekend.

There's a knock on the door. "Come in!" My receptionist opens it and leans against the door jamb. She always seems to be leaning on something, as if she doesn't have the strength to completely support herself. It's a millennial thing. The millennial lean. When she quits, I'll hire someone older who can stand up straight like a person.

"Hi, Dr. Dalton..." She smiles vapidly.

"Hi..." I smile back...we smile at each other..."Can I help you with something...uh..."

"Stefani," she reminds me.

How could I have forgotten? Her first words to me when I interviewed her were *I'm Stefani with an "f"* as if the whole phrase was her name.

"Can I help you with something, Stefani?" *with an "f,"* I finish in my head. It's got a ring to it.

"Well, since you have a break with the no-show, is this a good time to talk about me taking off next Friday? My boyfriend got tickets for Maroon 5."

"The concert is during the day?"

"No, but I have to get ready."

"For the whole day?"

The woman appears from behind Stefani with an *f*.

"I'm sorry I'm late." She sits with a thud and dabs her forehead with a tissue crumpled in her fist.

"Can I get you some water?"

"No, I'm fine." *Pant.* "I took the stairs." *Pant.* "Too many people on the elevator." *Pant.* "Fat *and* haphephobic are a nasty combination." *Pant.* "It's ironic, isn't it?"

"What's that?"

"That a person who's afraid of being touched is someone no one wants to touch. And yet I'm the one running up three flights of stairs! I mean that's a real kick in the pants, isn't it?"

I pretend to look over the notes on my iPad contraption to give her a moment to settle. She waits for my attention.

"How was your week?" I say, trying to measure her mood.

"Fine. The same. Most of them are the same."

"How is work?"

"Busier than usual, I guess. A lot of people have fallen and they can't get up." She laughs at her joke, but it doesn't float like a laugh. There's no joy in it, just a barren sound filling the air.

"The last time you were here we talked about your sister's death and how your mother and father handled it. Have you thought any more about that time? How *you* handled it?"

"Yes."

"Go on."

"I have something bigger to talk about." She looks down at the floor and then back at me, setting her eyes to mine with a resoluteness that I recognize means she's about to make a prepared speech. "I don't think I need to keep coming here," she says. The truth is I don't really *desire* to be touched. It's not like something is missing, I just want to stop worrying about it. I think sometimes you have to just accept certain things as the way they are and you deal with it. Like your hands must be to you."

No one ever refers to my hands. It's always the elephant in the room. And I'm grateful that she doesn't think of them as taboo.

She goes on. "My problem is dealing with it. And this isn't helping me." She lifts her chin and points it at me. "So today will be our last session."

I am shaken and I hope she can't see it. "Okay. Why did you come here instead of just calling?"

"Because I thought it would be the right thing to do. I thought I owed you that. You've been very kind. I'll give you a good review on Yelp."

She is so adept at hiding her broken insides. I want to tell her she's fooling herself. "I'm sorry to see you leave," I say instead. "I think you're just beginning to get comfortable here and you told me you've started therapy several times in the past and you tend to quit not long after you've begun."

"It sounds to me like I just need to stop starting." Her sarcasm falls flat.

"Well, you're here today, so shall we use the time?"

"At a hundred and fifty an hour, you bet. How was your week, Doc?"

"Please call me Theo."

"Okay ... Theo. How was your week?"

"Actually, my week sucked," I tell her. "Not sleeping so well. Probably drinking a little too much to sleep. I'm at a bit of a roadblock in my life and I'm trying to figure it out."

I've never done this before and I know better, but I am stung by her abrupt breaking-off of our work together and I somehow want to take back the reins, ethics be damned. I can tell she's astonished by my honesty, my unprofessional honesty, but she maintains the same neutral look I like to think I've perfected in my work.

"I'm sorry," she says, with a playful smirk. "Maybe you should try therapy."

"Well, I try it now and then, but I tend to quit just as I get to the good stuff." I can play too.

She laughs. "Maybe we should switch seats. Unless you're more comfortable sitting behind all your machinery. I took psych in college and I'd say you've got some pretty thick walls up." I don't interrupt her. If it really is her last session, she needs to say this. If it's not—she needs to say this. "I think you've got some issues, Doc. Theo. Tell me about your mother."

"She died when I was six."

"That had to be hard."

"It was."

"I hope you had a better transition team than I did when my sister died."

"Not so much. My generation didn't have the tools for that kind of thing. Not where I grew up anyway."

"How about your father?"

"What about him?" *I can't believe I'm doing this.*

"Still living?"

"No."

"What was he like?"

"He was rough. It was complicated. As an adult I can see it more clearly, but it was confusing as a kid."

"Siblings?"

"Yes, a sister. She's a painter. Lives in Colorado."

"Kids?"

"Yes, three."

"You have three kids? Nice."

"No, my sister, sorry, I wasn't clear." I feel muddled.

"Okay, you. Kids?"

"No." I shift in my seat and sit back. "My turn. How is *your* sleep?"

She pauses and glances at the clock. She's deciding what to do. She softens and finally speaks. "Look. I'll admit these sessions have given me things to think about. I've been remembering things. Not things I didn't know, but specific things. About stuff I thought I knew. Does that make sense?" I can't tell her that our sessions have also sparked in me details of memories I thought *I'd* known; impressions strategically labeled and meticulously filed away. "But it's not the direction I want to go," she says. "I'm still leaving."

"What are you remembering?"

"Bits and pieces." *The sigh.* "Like I was thinking about the time my parents took me to the fair. It came to Panama City every year and we always went. Daddy would pull us out of school for the day because the crowds were smaller during the week, so it was a real adventure, like playing hooky. I was always jealous of my sister because she was tall enough to go on the big rides. And I would stuff wads of toilet paper in my shoes and stretch my body as long as I could, but I was still too little. Until that year. I'd measured myself for months before, and I was sure I'd be tall enough to ride the Screamin' Eagle with my sister. But then she died." She moves her lips silently, as if she's afraid the words won't come out properly. "And when the fair came a month or so later, my mother didn't want to go. She said I shouldn't miss school. My birthday was coming up and I remember Daddy telling her we needed to do something fun for me and it was just second grade and it didn't matter if I missed one day. She was against it, big time, but he insisted. I'm sure he wanted things to get back to some kind of normal." She stops.

"What is it? What are you thinking?"

"That word. Normal. It's such a stupid word."

"How so?"

"Because normal isn't determined by what somebody else thinks or even what most people think. Normal is personal. Your hands are normal to you. Normal is what you know. It's whatever you're used to." She lets herself drift in the thought before catching herself. "You can write that down and use it on another patient, Doc! My parting gift to you."

"You were telling me about going to the fair."

"Right, yes." Her lips quirk upward into a shy, faraway smile. "It was really hot, I remember, and as soon as we got there, Daddy got us Koolies. You know, those icy, sweet slushy drinks? Cherry. And Daddy and I stuck out our red tongues and my mother said we looked disgusting. And we spent the entire day going on rides and going to the animal exhibits. There was a petting zoo and a goat tried to bite my hand." She smiles at the memory. "My mother didn't go on any of the rides. So it was me and Daddy—including the Screamin' Eagle. That was a really big deal. I remember the force of the wind in my hair and against my cheeks and thinking `my sister did this and now I'm doing it too.' And I remember feeling guilty that I was having fun without her there. But Daddy was determined to make it a great day." She disappears in thought again for a moment, and then returns. "That's it. That's what I was remembering."

I sense there is something more, just out of reach. "What else?"

Sigh. "And we went on the Ferris wheel and it stopped at the very top and I thought we were stuck because we were up there so long, and Daddy took my hand and he said it would be all right and that he would never let anything happen to me. And I wondered how he could save us if we suddenly dropped or if we were up there forever. And he told me that if we had to, we would fly. And I believed him. And I knew I was safe with him. And so we just stared out at the view and all the people from so high above them. Just me and my daddy. Holding hands. On top of the world. And I could see my mother on the ground below with her arms crossed, staring up at us like we were staying up there on purpose. I couldn't see her eyes but I could feel her anger, her goddamn quiet anger, all the way at the top of that Ferris wheel."

She closes her eyes as if remembering the picture, the feeling.

"It's okay," I tell her.

Her eyes flash open and she attempts a smile. "That's it. My angry mother. I'm done."

I know she's not done. "Go on. Take your time."

She looks up and she waits and she ponders, and then she speaks, softly, like she's reading the words she says on the ceiling.

"And then my daddy took my hand and placed it on his thigh. Very gently. And after a minute he pulled my hand up higher. I could feel the hardness in his pants and I didn't know what it was. And he said, `That's it, baby girl. Daddy loves his baby girl.'"

Chapter Six

I was grateful for the stillness of the empty house. I lay on
my bed, clasped hands behind my head, and traced the
tiny cracks in the ceiling with my eyes. It needed a coat of
paint but I wouldn't say so or I'd be the one who would
have to paint it. My temples had continued to throb since
I'd left Mr. Elijah's, and I went to the bathroom and swallowed two aspirin. Then two more. There was a knock at the
front door and when I answered it, I found Henry Hardy,
still dressed from church.

"You wanna hang out?" said the boy.

"How'd you get here?"

"I walked."

"How'd you know where I live?"

"I asked."

"Where'd you come from?"

"Church! You saw me there."

"I mean before that. Before Dalton. I ain't seen you
`round here 'til a week ago."

"Dallas."

"I ain't never been," I said.

"It's just like Dalton except not at all," laughed Henry.

I couldn't tell if he was commenting on Dallas or Dalton.
Dalton, I supposed.

"How come you come here?"

"We get relocated a lot, my daddy bein' an oil man. Before Dallas it was Midland and Cutola before that. We got a place just outside of town but we probably won't be here more than a year or two no matter how much my mama says it's gonna be the last time. Hey, you wanna stand here all day asking stupid questions or do you wanna hang out?"

"Okay, I guess," I said.

We ambled down the street and I stuffed my hands in my pockets. I usually kept my hands in my pockets when I was just getting to know someone, to make them feel more comfortable with me, or make me feel more comfortable with myself. And then Henry put his hands in his pockets as well, perhaps so that we were the same.

Henry said, "I thought what you did back there at church was really cool. Helpin' that man to his car and goin' with `em. Toby White is a total jackass. Racist asshole."

"With any luck, him and his idiots will all be in juvie by the time we graduate high school."

Henry laughed, then asked seriously, "Where'd you go? With that colored man?"

I was quick. "To his house to get some fresh corn from the farm where he sharecrops. My daddy loves fresh corn."

I plucked an empty coffee can from a trash can at the end of a fractured cement driveway and we took turns kicking it down the street.

"Who's that lady who brings you to church? I can tell she ain't your mama."

"She's my Aunty Li. My mama's sister."

"Where's your mama?"

"She died."

"I'm sorry."

"Me too."

We headed across the field and stopped by the ancient remains of a battered chain-link fence that protected nothing, overtaken with honeysuckle the color of baby chicks. We plucked buds off the scrub and cut the tips with our fingernails and sucked out the sweet syrup.

"My mama's alive but she's a nutcase," said Henry. "Treats me like I'm seven. Everybody treats me like I'm seven but my mama *knows* I'm thirteen but she still treats me like I'm seven."

"Have you always been small?"

"No, I used to be six foot tall when I was five but I shrunk down as I got older." Henry snapped his head to me, one eyebrow raised. "What kind of a stupid-ass question is that?"

"Sorry," I muttered.

"Don't be. I don't want people actin' like I might break."

"Me neither."

Henry paused and then said it. "You mean `cause of your hands?"

"Yeah," I said, my eyes glued to my feet.

"Well, if you won't break, I won't break," said Henry, and he knocked me to the grassy ground. I smiled and hopped to my feet and charged toward Henry, taking him down, and we wrestled, arms and legs tangled like two cubs testing their premature virility. Finally exhausted, we lay in the grass, our chests rising and falling in short gusts as we stared up at a changing sky—careless fleecy clouds scudding across a palette of timid blue.

"If you don't mind me askin'—how do you do stuff you gotta do? With your hands I mean?"

"It was tough at first, but you just do," I said, grateful for the easy way he asked. "You figure it out as you go. Ain't much of a choice, really."

"I mean, like, can you jerk off?"

"What?"

"It's a fair question."

"Yes, and shut up."

"I knew a three-legged dog once. His name was Reverend Jones. Got along just fine … 'til the coyotes got him!" Henry laughed so hard I thought he would choke. He punched me hard on the shoulder and I punched him back harder.

"My daddy's got *Playboys* hid behind his tool rack in the garage," he announced, feigning no particular importance. "First thing he did when we moved into the new place."

"Can I see?"

"For fifty cents."

A June bug circled and zigzagged and landed on my leg until it had somewhere else to go. I snagged a stem of prairie grass and chewed on it and its sweetness tasted like watermelon.

"Do you ever look at the clouds and see things, like think of things?" asked Henry.

"Sure. Everybody does that."

"Like that one over there looks like big titties."

I searched. "Where?"

"There," Henry pointed. "You can even see the nipples. I'm a titties man."

"Good thing," I added, "'cause that's about as high as you can reach on a girl."

"Well, at least when I reach 'em I can squeeze 'em!"

"I can squeeze just fine, thank you very much." I surveyed the clouds and said, "That one over yonder looks like a horse."

"I see it. A horse with titties."

"Shut up, pervert!"

Our laughter blended with the soothing rustle of the grass.

"Hey, wanna come to my house and ride real horses?" asked Henry.

"Sure, I guess." I'd learned not to get too excited about doing anything until I knew I could do it.

Henry jumped up. "Well, I don't wanna put you out."

I looked at him seriously. "One question: Do they let you ride on top of the horse or does it pull you along in a little red wagon?"

"You're a dead man!" yelled Henry and dove for me, but I averted his attack. I bounced up and ran with Henry in pursuit, dodging, finally tackling, rolling.

The summer will be a good one, I thought.

SESSION 4

She's been a no-show for the past three sessions, but she's paid by credit card for each one, so her name remains on the schedule. Yesterday, I asked Stefani with an *f* to call and check if the woman is coming in, but she'd only been able to leave a message. I called her myself and left my private cell number—*which I never do*—but there had been no response. Still I wait.

Just as I have the prior two weeks before her scheduled appointed time, I brush my teeth in the office, swish the last bit of bottled water in my mouth, and spit into the trash can. I blow onto my palm and test my breath for the stench of cigarettes, and then spritz Eau de Lacoste onto my jacket. I've promised myself to quit the monsters a thousand times but until that magical day happens, I don't need to remind her of her father. I glance in the small mirror hanging by the door and am reminded of mine: the same strong jaw and erudite nose, but with the graying hair he would have worn had he lived to be my age. I smile at the thought that he would have made fun of my hair, nearly shoulder length and scraggly at the ears. My father only approved of two haircuts: the side-part pompadour and the crew cut. Even in his final weeks and days, he would ask me to moisten his hair with Vitalis, still thick and wavy, and comb it into a scoop.

When thirty-five minutes have passed, I finally admit to myself that she's not coming. My heart sinks at the knowledge that I cannot fix her.

There is a knock and Stefani with an *f* pokes her head in the door.

"She's here."

I sit up in my chair briskly to appear busy and make notes on my Apple tree iPads, one finger at a time. "Yes, sure, tell her to come in." I wipe beads of sweat from my upper lip.

The woman enters. "Hi," she says, tentatively. I think of standing but decide it's better not to. She takes her regular side of the sofa and plants her purse beside her. It is her territory and she assumes it with surprising ease.

"It's good to see you," I say, undecided whether to pepper my words with forgiveness or admonishment, so they just come out as insipid. I pull my iPad contraption closer toward me. "I'm glad you decided to come back. I was concerned."

"I wasn't sure I was going to. I needed a break."

"Well, you're here now, that's what counts." I'm eager to get past this clumsiness and proceed.

"I made a list," she says, pulling out a folded sheet of yellow legal paper.

"What kind of list?"

She stares at me for a moment, then drops her head to one side. "My grocery list, Doc. Let's see…" she says earnestly, scouring the page. "Six boxes of Ho-Hos, twenty-seven bags of Ruffles, five Hungry Man frozen dinners." She returns her eyes to mine. "What kind of list?" she laughs. "Listen, I can't go through every episode of my—history, with you expecting me to cry and wail and re-live every moment. I'm not a crier. So I made a list. I broke it down to ages and … evolvement—I don't know what to call it."

"I'm not sure this is the best way to …"

"It's my way, Doc. This is the way I'm going to do it."

"You have to trust me."

"I'm happy to leave." It is an ultimatum.

"I don't want you to leave." *I don't want her to leave.* The thought of it hits me unexpectedly hard. I'd spent the better part of two weeks hoping she would return.

"Okay then, here we go." She unfolds the lined paper and retrieves a pair of reading glasses from the outside pocket of her purse. "I tried to break it down by age, but I'm not always exactly sure, so this will be approximate." She snaps the page and smooths it on her lap. "Okay then," she repeats, then reads: "When I was seven, after the Ferris wheel, my father would come to my room at night on a pretty regular basis, a few times a month." She looks up at me. "At first it was just him asking me to touch him—there— through his pants. Then he started taking it out and asking me to hold it. He taught me how to masturbate him and he would direct me as I went—faster, slower, harder."

She goes back to the page with no emotion whatsoever.

"When I was about nine, he started touching me. He would rub his hands together to make them warm and he would massage me between my legs. Then he would use his finger." She leaves the page. "The first time it hurt so badly, but he said, `Shhh, it only hurts for a little bit,' and he was right. He took his time. He would ask me if I was okay. Sometimes if he'd go too deep I would cry out a little but the sound of the rain would cover it up."

"The rain?"

"He would come to me when it rained. During the thunderstorms."

"So that your mother couldn't hear."

"I need to stick to my list, Theo, no sidebars," she says, matter-of-factly. She returns to the page. "He started using things, pencils, a carrot, I don't know what else, I didn't look." *Next.* "When I was about eleven, he would ask me to put my mouth on it. On his penis..."

"I need to stop you."

"I'm not finished," she announces, and goes back to the list. "I was thirteen when he put himself inside me."

"Stop!" I am surprised by my outburst. I've never raised my voice to a patient. I collect myself. "I appreciate that you've... recorded all this. That you've gone there and thought about these things. But you need to slow down. I'm asking you to talk to me about it, more than the facts. What was going on in your head, your heart. What you felt as a little girl."

I think of the damaged people I helped when I was a boy, and how wounds on the outside were so much easier to heal than the ones on the inside. More specific, more easily located. She wears her internal wounds like a scab, ripped away, only to reform again and again until they scar.

"What do you want me to say, Theo?" Her condescension drips from my name. "That he hurt me and brutalized me? He didn't. He was kind and loving. He never forced me. He loved me. He told me it was what all little girls did who loved their fathers. He told me this is what my sister did when she was a little girl. He told me it was our bond, Daddy and Daddy's girl. He gave me little treasures and I kept them all in the box he gave me." She touches a heart-shaped locket hanging around her neck. "He gave me this. He'd given it to my sister. He made me hide it and told me not to tell my mother because she'd be jealous. I knew how I felt about her, and I felt sorry for him for having to be married to her. She was so cold. And he was so broken. He told me so. I knew he needed to feel better. And he let me make him feel better. He let me heal him."

The word punctures my heart.

"And I enjoyed that." She holds my eye for a long antagonistic moment, defying me to say anything. "Yeah, there was a part of me that enjoyed it, Theo," she spits. I try to contain the gasp that wants to burst from me. "It felt good to take care of him. Boy, the child abuse people would love that one!" Suddenly she is a hurricane of a thousand impressions. "I know that's supposed to be wrong. It's wrong on every level—psychologically, physically, legally. And I've read about all the horrible monsters who did this to children. The fathers and the priests and the uncles and the neighbors. All the adults who abuse their power and their authority and how sick that is."

There is bravery in her defensiveness, and I want to tear away the blame she heaps upon herself. I start to speak but she cuts me off.

"And I've looked for myself in all the literature, and the websites, and the organizations. And I'm not in there. I'm not there!" she bursts. "Unlike you, when there was a thunderstorm I *didn't* hide under the bed! I didn't cower or shut my eyes and think of ponies or flowers." Then quiet again. "I *loved* my father … and after, sometimes he would cry. Just sort of whimper and cry." Suddenly, she stares at me as though I'm judging her and I soften my gaze to assure her that I'm not.

"I know what you're thinking," she says. "Incest."

"I wasn't thinking that."

"It wasn't incest," she says defiantly. "We weren't lovers. There was nothing romantic about it. It was deeper than that."

I want to push my stupid fucking iPad contraption away and go to her. I want to hold her. I want to heal her brokenness. It's the first time I want to use my—my gift—if it still exists—in such a long time. Wondering if I can. Knowing I can't.

She pushes her readers up on the bridge of her nose and returns to the list, taking a deep breath. "Okay then, let's see, where was I?" she says, coolly. "Touching, fingering, sucking, fucking, I think that about covers it." She refolds the paper and puts it in her purse like a receipt after a purchase. "Oh! I didn't tell you this. He never kissed me on the mouth. He didn't look at me as some kind of lover any more than I did him."

I don't know what to say. She has timed her prepared announcement to finish precisely at the end of our shortened session. But I am unprepared. Just when I think that my years of experience have braced me for any admission, no matter how shocking, I find myself unable to offer the kind of solace or, at the very least, decorum that my profession demands. It is not the confession itself. I've heard it all. It's rather her total lack of empathy for herself, of having spoken these words, most certainly for the first time, with no sense of relief, no sorrow, no heartbreak, no human aftermath. Only absolute defiance. I find myself oddly jealous of her ability to disconnect; the ability I have sustained for so long, but am no longer able to muster in my own life.

"As much as you may feel it, you are not alone," I tell her. "You are not to blame. You are not responsible. You are not guilty. I can't fix this. I wish I could, but I can't make it go away, this painful, confusing thing. But we can get through it to a better understanding if you'll allow it. I promise."

She is armored in her laser stare.

The success of my work has been predicated on my ability to guide the path of discovery without becoming a part of it. And though I know I can't show more compassion for her than she does for herself at this particular moment, I find myself blinking to dry my eyes.

CHAPTER SEVEN

The air in Frank's trailer was thick and stale with the smell of ancient cigarette smoke and fried eggs. I sipped a Mountain Dew while Frank sat in his Lay-Z-Boy and cleaned his fingernails with a jackknife.

The place was a lot to take in. The walls were papered in a faded brown floral print that might have been popular in the early 1950s when the trailer must have been new. The shabby hem of a checkered curtain brushed the metal-framed windowsill. A Winchester rested solidly on a gun rack next to a crookedly hung framed print of a Paris café. On the adjacent wall hung a wooden frame housing a grainy black and white photo of two soldiers in baggy fatigues, netted helmets and worn combat boots, laden with necklaces of grenades, and canteens strapped to their belts. One I took to be Frank, grime-faced and smiling, all teeth. The young men each hung an arm around the other's neck and, with their other hands, held up a captured Nazi flag. A corner of the photo was burned and curled, and at the bottom was thick handwriting in black grease pencil: 36th Infantry, Panther Division. Ravenoville, France. 6 June 1944.

I didn't want Frank to catch me staring so I sank into the harlequin-print couch with pieces of stuffing peeking through the ripped seams. A wagon wheel-shaped coffee table was covered with folded newspapers, a book of

Rumi poems, and a red glass ashtray with "The Golden Nugget" written on the side in Old-West lettering. Beneath the clutter were the black blots of ignored cigarettes and white rings from sweaty beer bottles. I noticed craters in the window glass from BBs that had attempted to shatter them. And on a side table next to Frank was a harmonica, a bowl of peanuts circled by scattered shells, and a book titled "The Seven Rites of Cheyenne." It was a jumble of rummage that could have been a collection of precious memories in another setting with a gallon or so of Formula 409.

Frank and I silently watched the news on a snowy console black and white TV. Bobby Kennedy was dead, and his brother, Teddy, was delivering his eulogy:

"My brother need not be idealized, or enlarged in death beyond what he was in life; to be remembered simply as a good and decent man, who saw wrong and tried to right it, saw suffering and tried to heal it, saw war and tried to stop it."

"Breaks my fuckin' heart," said Frank. "Such a good man. He was gonna win, too. Civil Rights. End this fuckin' war, and the one even bigger than Vietnam—between the past and the future. Change is hard, Theo. Whole goddamn country's strugglin' to grow up."

I looked at the peanuts out of the corner of my eye and wondered if I could shell them with my hands or if I'd have to do it with my teeth. Frank stared at the TV and then turned to me. "I want you to have this." He cleaned off the jackknife and closed it with a pop and handed it to me. "This ain't for nothing but whittlin' and cuttin' kite string and such. But it's also for havin' when that boy and his flock of pricks come after you."

I shook my head. "I wouldn't, I mean I couldn't…"

"You don't do nothin' with it. Just let 'em know you got it. They're the kind of boys that only feel good when they're hurtin' somebody else. The kind that grow into men who hunt for the sake of the kill. Bein' cruel satisfies something in them. And if that's the only language they know, then this jackknife shows `em you mean business. Like that gunshot scared the holy shit out of `em. You never know when a knife's gonna come in handy."

I begrudgingly pocketed it. "What's that around your neck?" I asked.

"This, my friend, is a genuine Cheyenne arrowhead from my ancestor tribe. My daddy give it to me when I went out on my own. He said it'd bring me good luck and protect me." Frank held up the necklace to give me a closer look. "There was a time when I guess I shoulda worn it a little more often!" he said with a burst of laughter. "But now I never take it off."

I glimpsed at the World War II photograph and saw the necklace plastered against his glistening chest. Below it on a cloth-covered TV tray, I spotted a photo in a tarnished silver-plated frame of a slightly older Frank in full dress uniform with a woman and a baby. I studied it intently. "That your family?"

"Yes," said Frank.

"Where are they?"

"France." Something flickered in his black eyes—sorrow, remorse—but it disappeared before I could identify it.

"Do you see them?"

"No."

"Do you talk to them?"

"They ain't much interested in talking to me."

I knew not to pry any further.

Footage of Rose Kennedy flickered on the TV set. She looked as if she was sleepwalking. Frank scooped up a handful of peanuts and began to shell them. I watched. *It's just stupid peanuts. Take some!*

"This fella that's got two names, this Sirhan Sirhan fella," said Frank. "One person can change the world for good or for bad. You know, it's possible to assassinate the future. Or heal it. Works both ways."

"I ain't an idiot," I said. "I know what you're tryin' to say."

The television suddenly blared with the low-low price of the Veg-O-Matic, the barkers voice as rabid as an auctioneer. *It slices! It dices!* Frank turned down the volume. "And what's that, smartass?"

I leaned forward. "That I can change the world, and for anyone I help, they might be somebody who changes the world. Like you think if I was in Los Angeles at that Ambassador Hotel, this Sir Ham-whoever is the bad guy to take Kennedy out, but I could be the good guy to bring him back. Well, I ain't ready for that!"

Frank laughed. "I didn't say nothin' of the sort." He laid the handful of shelled peanuts on the table and I knew not to say thank you.

"Then what? It's all confusing. And weird." I sighed. "I don't even know how it works. Or even if it really works. What if they're better for a while but it don't stick, I don't know what happens after. What happens after the bird flies away? Maybe it falls out of the sky. Or what if Mr. Elijah gets up from his nap and goes out lookin' for his dead wife again?"

"I understand why you want to know, son, it's natural. But the truth is it ain't none of your business what happens after." He found the two-button TV remote and hit *off.* Nothing happened. He tried again. Nothing. "Damn it. When you hit a switch, it's supposed to work." He aimed and hit the button again and again. Finally, he got up, groaning, and walked the four feet to the TV and switched it off.

"You sure you don't need a rest after walkin' all that way?" I said.

"Ain't you a regular comedian. The point is it didn't do what it was supposed to do. Biggest human dilemma."

I looked at him quizzically and spit out the stringy strand of a peanut shell. "Turnin' off a TV is the biggest human dilemma?"

"Yup," said Frank. He trod to the tiny kitchen area and plugged in a hot plate. "When we do somethin' we have a pretty good expectation of what's supposed to happen." He went outside to the refrigerator and returned with a block of Velveeta, Wonder Bread and margarine, talking all the while. "When you hit the TV remote it's supposed to work. When you flick a light switch a light's supposed to go on. And we reckon it's supposed to work that way for everything." Frank placed a cast iron skillet, greased with time, on the hotplate and began constructing the sandwich. "You want a grilled cheese?"

"No, thanks."

He slathered the bread with margarine and tossed it in the skillet. "The trick is to give what you got and not hitch yourself to what you reckon is *supposed* to happen after, like there's just one thing possible." He flipped the grilled cheese and smashed it with a spatula. "Action without the hitch. That's the ticket. *A* plus *B* don't always get you to *C*. It might take you to *D* or *M* or someplace better than *C*. Some place you couldn't have even imagined. You get what I'm sayin'?"

"*A* plus *B* might be *M*? No, I don't."

"What I'm sayin' is you put it out there, you say 'yes', and you don't know what the hell's gonna happen. But if you say 'no', you know damn well what's gonna happen. Not a god-dam thing. So you take the chance. You say yes, and what goes on after your part ain't none of your business." Frank paper-plated the grilled cheese and plopped down in his Lay-Z-Boy.

"But I *have* been sayin' yes," I argued. "Even to stuff I want to say no to. And I don't even know what I'm sayin' yes to! I don't know if any of this is real."

He took a bite of the sandwich and chomped, "You sure you don't want one of these? I make a mean grilled cheese."

"I ain't hungry." I was frustrated that Frank could talk and cook and eat and that one didn't seem any more impor-tant than the other.

"One time when I was seven I was so sick," I said. "I had the flu. And it was my birthday. And I didn't want my daddy to cancel my party so I *made* myself be well. I forced myself well. And as soon as that party was over I was sicker than I was before. In bed for three days. The truth is I wasn't never *not* sick. I just fooled myself into feeling better. But it wasn't real. It couldn't last."

Frank stuffed most of his sandwich in his mouth and tossed the rest in the trashcan, grabbed his jacket and fum-bled through a junk drawer, locating a key. Crumbs littered his shirt and his speech was garbled. "Come on, boy, we're takin' a ride."

"Where to?"

He swallowed and held a knowing finger in the air as he headed outside. "To see what's real and what ain't. Get in the truck."

We made our way to the ramshackle pickup and I tugged at the stubborn passenger door with my full body-weight. Finally, it gave with a creak. "I don't take this old girl out too often," said Frank. He turned the key and the truck sputtered and hacked and fired up and edged forward with a crawl and then a gust.

Once we reached the neighboring town of Skiatook, Frank pulled the truck into a newly-mowed field that had been converted to a temporary parking lot in front of a large canvas tent, like the kind used for livestock exhibits at the county fair. Rhythmic organ music and waves of fervent shouting could be heard from within. A placard at the entrance read "TENT REVIVAL!" in large block letters.

God's Hand Ministries!
Salvation and Divine Healing!
Reverend Jimmie Dale Oldman
Evangelist of Antlers, Okla.

I'd heard about such healing crusades. They frequented the small towns of Oklahoma, occasionally landing in Dalton, but I'd never been this close. *What are we doing there?! Did he bring me here to get my hands healed? Did he bring me here to heal these people?* "I ain't ready for this. I can't…"

"Hold your horses, son. We're just here to watch," he said, and guided me into the tent with his hand on my back.

There were two hundred or so people inside and enough folding chairs to accommodate them all, but few were seated. They were dancing, weeping, waving, capering all around us. Some lay in the aisles motionless, slayed by the spirit. Frank and I stood at the back of the tent behind the congregation. The charismatic preacher, Brother Jimmie Dale Oldman, laid hands on a man who fell back into the waiting arms of a woman in a white robe gathered at the waist by a thin rope.

"Hallelujah, Lord! Lead me to your next disciple," rallied the preacher.

Brother Jimmie was swollen. The kind of fat that, from the size of his wrinkled blue and red-checkered suit, indicated that he'd once been much thinner and hadn't bothered to get a new one, or that there had been a catastrophic dry cleaning mishap. He was bald but for a ring of matted hair dyed ebony black, ending on each side behind his large flat ears, which sat perpendicular to his head like a saucer broken clean in half and glued on. He sweated and dripped and dabbed his forehead with a white hand towel. A handkerchief would not have been sufficient.

Brother Jimmie hurried onto a small raised platform and pulled an envelope from a fishbowl. He held it to his forehead and closed his eyes tightly as if telepathically reading its contents. "Yes, Lord, I see a woman. A woman in pain. Lucifer has stricken her with arthritis in her back and her legs. Lord, she wants to give herself to you in the name of Jesus. Her name is Betty."

A woman screamed, "That's me! I'm Betty."

Brother Jimmie blubbered up the aisle, pulling the long microphone cord behind him to the third row where Betty sat, conveniently on the end, as Brother Jimmie would not have been able to squeeze through the people without disastrous results and the potential necessity of more healings.

"God's ears are open to the righteous!" he preached. "What has the devil cast upon you, Betty?"

The woman swooned. "My back and my legs, just like you said, Brother Jimmie."

"Your back and your legs!"

"My back and my legs."

"Your back and your legs!"

"My back and my…"

"Thank you, Betty." He turned her chair to face the aisle and knelt down. He lifted her legs straight out in front of her, grasping her ankles, and one of the white-robed helpers held the microphone in front of Brother Jimmie's mouth. "Betty, the devil has invaded you and made your heart and your body outta whack. You are unbalanced with the Lord. That's what's causing your pain, Betty. Your left leg is longer than your right. Can you see that, Betty? Can I get a witness?" People from several aisles moved in closer to get a look and I strained to see between them. "Do you see, Betty's left leg's an inch shorter than the right?" Brother Jimmie asked.

I can see it, Brother Jimmie!

Yes, Lawd, yes!

It's a good full inch short than the other'n!

Brother Jimmie prayed. "Oh, Lord of all things, restore this woman to herself so that she may live in your everlastin' light. In the name of the Father, the Son and the Holy Spirit, I command you to heal this woman! Heal!"

The spectators watched in anticipation and I stood on my tiptoes to see Brother Jimmie hold Betty's ankles in his hands, jiggling them slightly. And Betty's left leg started to grow! The organ underscored the miracle and accentuated Brother Jimmie's every move.

"Can you see it?" he said to the throng that had swarmed around the healer. "Can you see the miracle of the Lord's work? Betty's right leg is getting longer before your eyes! Can you feel the glory, Betty? Can you feel God's healing?"

Betty's face gnarled into a pained joyful scrunch and she waved high up to Jesus as though he was taking off on a jet plane. "Jesus, sweet Jesus, I can feel it! I can feel the power through my body!"

"Stand up, Betty! Bend down, touch the floor! Lift your knees up in the air!" Betty performed the calisthenics requested, then swayed forward and back, and suddenly began speaking in a quick endlessly-syllabic gibberish in an accent that one might hear at a Turkish bazaar.

"She's speaking in tongues," I whispered.

"No shit," said Frank.

I found myself edging forward for a closer look. Brother Jimmie was repellant and intoxicating at the same time. I looked down at my clawed hands. *If I can't heal myself, maybe he…* Frank pulled me back by the shoulder and his heavy hand rested there.

The organ resumed a joyful noise and the people danced as Brother Jimmie made his way through the noisy crowd, one lamb of God after another, casting out the devil, defeating heathenism, popping foreheads with the heel of his hand, each falling back into the arms of one of his helpers as they received the spirit. There was a salesman with bursitis. A schoolboy with bronchitis. And a long-nosed farmer in overalls with no shirt and a train engineer's cap whom Brother Jimmie diagnosed as having "a devil in his belly." He led the man to the small stage. "Where's my table?" he said, with the hint of admonishment. "I need one of God's Servants out here now!" *So that's what they're called.* One of them rolled out a rickety table draped with a cloth that brushed the floor.

"This man is riddled with demonitis! Corrupt with temptation!" Brother Jimmie laid the man back onto the table. "Tonight, God has asked me to do a holy psychic surgery." Brother Jimmie unsnapped the buttons on the man's overalls so that the bib could be pulled down, exposing a pale bloated stomach. He raised his index finger high into the air, as if to make a point, but then it seemed more like an antenna when it shook as if the preacher was receiving an electrical shock. He brought his finger down swiftly and made a slicing motion across the man's belly, and blood trickled down from it. The congregation shrieked in awe. Brother Jimmie raised his hand into the air again and then lowered it, appearing to immerse his entire hand through the incision and into the man's body. The crowd held their collective breath. Brother Jimmie dug around and then pulled out globs and clots of small dripping organs. He lifted the coagulated evidence of evil, and ribbons of blood stretched and plopped into a metal bowl held by one of God's Servants. "Behold the cancer!" Brother Jimmie decreed. "God has removed the evil from this man and he is pure!"

I watched with astonishment and the throng cheered. A God's Servant cleaned the blood off of the man with a water-soaked cloth and Brother Jimmie sat him up to show that there was miraculously no sign of the incision. "God finishes up the job clean, no stitches required!" The man shouted that he was relieved of the pain! I looked to Frank for some measure of what was and was not real, but got nothing.

Brother Jimmie next received a message from God for someone in a wheelchair, stricken with multiple sclerosis. A scrawny, filthy, raggedly dressed man identified himself, and one of God's Servants wheeled him to the stage. Brother Jimmie laid his hands on the man and commanded that God relieve this lost sheep from his burden.

Then he whipped around behind the wheelchair and threw it forward with a violent surge, tossing the man to the floor. "Get up! I command you to stand in the name of Jesus!" The man slowly pulled himself to his feet, wobbly but standing. He took small uneven steps but was soon able to lift his knees, and moments later was running in circles. He sprinted around the tent in laps and music accompanied his accelerating speed like an organ at a baseball game.

Brother Jimmie continued to heal at random, spiritually sensing various maladies. I was transfixed. Suddenly, I saw a woman deep in the crowd dressed in jungle colors so bright that I was surprised I'd not spotted her before this moment. "Shit! That's my aunt and uncle!" My uncle Darnell looked out of place, clearly overdressed for the event in a tasteful crested navy blazer and narrow striped tie, done in a classic Windsor knot.

Aunty Li pushed Uncle Darnell past and nearly over an old woman on crutches toward Brother Jimmie. I knew that she'd complained of my uncle's "digestive affairs" in the past but I couldn't imagine she would go to this extreme for his recovery. *It must be something else.* Uncle Darnell seemed reluctant, but stepped up to Brother Jimmie and braced himself as his forehead was popped by the heel of the preacher's hand, and whatever part of him the devil had penetrated was surely restored. He turned to Aunty Li and held her, wiping away her tears.

When the service was over, Brother Jimmie reminded his devotees that God's Hand Ministry desperately needed their tithing so that many more could be healed and saved. Cash only. The crowd began to disperse.

"We gotta get out of here before they see me!" I whispered, as Frank and I ducked into the departing crowd, pushing our way through to where we'd come in. Just outside the entrance we passed several of God's Servants standing under large signs—Love Gifts for God's Hand Ministry—where people lined up to give their money. We lost ourselves in the herd and scurried out to the field of parked cars.

Confident of our escape, I suddenly saw a glimpse of Aunty Li's jungle dress in the crowd only a few feet away.

"There they are!" I said. A sea of headlights ignited like rays of interrogation, all searching for me. Frank pushed me through a canvas flap at the side of the tent.

It was the backstage area, dark but for a caged pendant light casting shadows behind stacked boxes and trunks. When my eyes had adjusted to the dimness, I spotted the wheelchair folded up on the sawdust-covered floor. The surgery table had been rolled into a corner and was still wet with blood. I saw that two metal pans were attached to the back, one half full of the "evil" which was nothing but bloody chicken gizzards and livers. And the other was filled with blood, who knew from what animal?

Voices approached and Frank pushed me behind a tower of trunks. The scrawny disheveled man who'd been healed from multiple sclerosis was accompanied by one of God's Servants, a woman in the white robe that was her uniform. She clomped through the sawdust in nurse's shoes the color of Band-Aids. The man held out his hand and she pulled a crumpled bill from her pocket and tucked it into his hand. Then she handed him a brown bag twisted around the shape of a bottle. "God bless you," she said, and the man snuck out the back of the tent.

"Still not sure if what you do is real?" whispered Frank.

We drove back in silence. The engine rumbled with an occasional grunt as each pothole bounced us as jarringly as a galloping horse. The headlights shined only upon what lay immediately before us, into nowhere, then the road finally smoothed into a black ribbon once we reached town. As we came upon Judson's Drug Store, I saw the woman known as Vinita sitting cross-legged in her usual spot on the sidewalk.

Vinita wasn't her real name. No one knew her real name. A faded daisy-speckled house dress draped from her mopey shoulders. Her spine curved to such a degree that it pitched her to one side, and she leaned forward on one elbow with her fist under her chin, the stub of a cigarette jutting from the drawn lips of her toothless mouth, as if contemplating the current political climate.

She'd appeared just after Easter, when rumors floated that she'd been a patient at the asylum for the insane in the nearby town of Vinita, hence the nickname. Nobody knew what to do with her, she being the only homeless person anyone in Dalton could remember. So, like a stray dog, she'd been reluctantly accepted as a fixture of the town and was given scraps of food and spare change when it seemed convenient, or stepped over when it seemed more convenient. "Any change?" she would mew. Only those words to each passerby. "Any change?"

"Can you pull over?" I asked, and we slowed to a stop at the curb. I jumped from the high seat of the pickup and approached the woman, careful not to startle her. She looked up at me and blew out a puff of smoke that hung around her face like a chiffon veil. "Any change?"

I pulled a quarter from my pocket and leaned to her gently, slowly, as if toward a terror-stricken animal. When she took the coin, I held onto her hand, not letting go. The woman was stunned and tried to pull away, and I thought it must have been a long while since anyone had touched her. But when she looked to me, she surrendered to a kind of peaceful composure. I closed my eyes. And I imagined: *The woman is shopping at Judson's. She is clean, neatly dressed, and straight-backed. Then through her eyes: she is giving money to another version of her past on the street.* When I opened my eyes, the woman was gazing gently at me. "Thank you, boy, for the quarter. God bless you," she said, in a voice that scraped the air like a rusty garden gate. I thought I saw the memory of a smile but decided I was wrong. Frank gently tossed the remainder of his pack of Lucky Strikes out the window and Vinita scooped it up and nodded her gratitude.

I climbed back into the truck and we carried on. The engine grumbled as if it had been taken advantage of. After some time, I said, "It's more of a quiet thing."

We continued down Dalton Boulevard, past the imposing bronze statue of my great grandfather, pedestaled on a dull patch of grass in front of the Dalton Library. His face looked downward on all who passed, bearing an expression that fell somewhere between stalwart and annoyed. His veined hands were disproportionately large and thick, and they rested on the heads of little bronze children, none of whom were his.

Finally, I whispered, "Is it true?"

"Is what true?"

"Did you do what they say?"

"Depends."

"On what?"

"On what they say." Frank turned off the boulevard and rolled onto the back road. "But probably."

SESSION 5

Most of our time is spent on nothing. She carries no emotional fallout from our last session, as if it had never happened. She talks about episodic television and how much she hates reality shows. She talks about baseball. The Cubs. While I don't want to be considered a friend, I recognize that her condition has prevented her from having many, if at all, and so I listen and laugh, hoping that this is all part of making her comfortable enough to get to the next level.

"What about you, Doc? Who's your team?"

"I don't really follow baseball." I look ruefully at my hands, then cock my head and shrug with a playful arch of my eyebrow. "Never played."

"Woops, right, sorry." Her tone is laconic, but without judgment.

"Don't be," I say slyly. "Soccer would have been my sport if they had it when I was growing up. Lots of feet action, no hands. I would have been a superstar."

My quip gives her permission to say, "Were you born with your hands like that or did something happen?"

She asks the question everyone wants to ask but doesn't dare, and I am grateful. She leans forward intently to listen. It's one of the things I most admire about her—her freedom to get to the point, almost to a fault.

111

"They were damaged in an accident when I was a boy."

"That's rough. I'm sure it wasn't easy. Kids can be cruel."

"So can adults."

"Ah! Excellent segue, Doc!"

"The thing about my hands is that they were visible. No secret there."

"Oh, come on, I'm sure you have secrets. I'll even bet there are secrets *behind* the hands." She waits. "Am I right?"

Her audacity is staggering, as if I might actually answer—as if we were old friends having a heart to heart after one too many. I pull it back. "Of course I have secrets. We all have secrets. I'd rather talk about yours."

"There it is again, the accent," she says, with a laugh. "It just pops out. '*Odd* rather talk about *yurs.*' I think it's sweet."

"I realize it's easier to avoid talking about your own experiences," I say, "but you're really doing good work here. So, I'd like to ask, did you ever tell anyone?"

She sighs her signature sigh and I know she's ready to begin, even though we have little time left. "I knew not to tell," she says. "I thought of it more like a secret bond than a dirty secret. For a long time anyway." She pauses and I don't know if she's about to say something she's planned to tell, like the list, or if it is occurring to her at this moment.

"There was this one time I came pretty close," she says. "There was a doctor."

"You talked to a doctor?"

"Well, no, not exactly. I'd started having my period when I was twelve. And I knew from health class what it was."

"Not from your mother?"

"No," she laughs. "When I started, she saw blood in my panties and suddenly sanitary pads appeared in the bathroom."

"But she never talked to you about it?"

"No, but I wouldn't have expected her to. And when I was fourteen my period was late. Really late. Like two months. And one day I started bleeding. A lot. And really cramping. And I kept having to excuse myself from science class to go to the restroom. And it wasn't just blood, there were ... pieces. Of tissue. Clots. And I was terrified I was dying. And I told my friend, Teresa, and she made me go to the nurse's office and I told her what was happening, and she called my mother and told her she needed to get me to a gynecologist right away. So my mother took me to this doctor, and she sat in the waiting room while he examined me.

And then he took me into his office and shut the door and told me to have a seat across the desk from him." She conjures up the room and I can see that she is there, her struggle pulling down the corners of her mouth. "And he told me that I'd been pregnant and I'd miscarried. And he said he had to tell my mother because I was a minor. I begged him not to. I told him she would kill me. I told him I would kill myself. But he insisted he had an obligation to tell a parent. And I told him to tell my father instead. So he did. He called him right then and told him."

"And what did he say? Your father."

She sits up, straight-backed. "To the doctor? I don't know, it was all on the phone."

"To you, what did your father say to you?"

"He didn't say anything."

"And what about your mother? What did you tell her?"

"I told her I was fine. That it was just a heavy period and I would probably spot for a few more days. The doctor told me that. And he told me not to do any sports for a week or two. And I should just take Advil for cramps."

"And you didn't tell anyone else?"

"Of course not."

"And after that?"

She looks to the window and breathes out into her words. "After that my father started using condoms."

CHAPTER EIGHT

"Tallyho!" said Henry, before I could even get the front door fully open. I looked past him and saw a woman leaning casually against a new perfectly pale blue Cadillac DeVille. She was wearing a perfectly pale blue shift dress, short by Dalton standards, with a delicate gold chain draped at her waist. She had thick auburn hair that was bubbled on top and covered by a nearly transparent, perfectly pale blue, bird-themed silk scarf with kiss curls reaching out to her high cheekbones. Her heavy bangs were swept to one side and fell behind enormous white-framed sunglasses. She looked just like Audrey Hepburn. I wondered if she'd purposely planned to color coordinate with her car and, if so, did the outfit match the car or did the car match the outfit? I could imagine a stable of automobiles in every color, one chosen each day according to whatever Henry's mother decided to wear.

"You boys ready?" called Mrs. Hardy. She opened the back door with one arm raised high as if presenting a new washer/dryer set on *Let's Make a Deal*. Henry and I ran and jumped inside and I was extra careful not to get my dirt-caked Keds on the leather seats. Mrs. Hardy took her place behind the wheel and said, "Hold onto your hats!" even though we weren't wearing hats. She pushed a button on the dash, a motor hummed, and the roof of the car dislodged itself from the frame and began lifting up up up, as if we were going to be ejected into outer space. The roof reached its full height and then retracted like the accordion of a great giant.

"I am honored to be chauffeuring an ancestor of the founder of this fine town," she said. She stepped on the gas a bit too enthusiastically and we were off. She rifled through a small stack of eight-track tapes in the passenger seat and slid one into the deck. I'd only heard tell of these magical cartridges.

And here's to you Mrs. Robinson.
Heaven holds a place for those who pray.
Hey hey hey.

She yelled above the wind and the music. "I am so happy Henry has found a friend. Of course he had so many friends in Dallas but here we are in a new town. In a new world practically. Or an old world I should say," she laughed, loud and throaty. I strained to hear her as she rattled on. "I just love it. The fresh smell of the earth to greet you in the morning. And manure. And burning oil. Earth and manure and oil, it's divine! And the people are so friendly."

"Glad to have you in Dalton, ma'am," I screamed.

"Henry tells me your father repairs cars," she screamed back.

"Yes ma'am."

"What a noble profession. I mean what would the world be like without cars?"

"He don't make 'em, ma'am, he just fixes 'em."

"Well, isn't that the same thing? It doesn't matter who makes them if they don't work. Why I'd say your daddy's job is *more* important than the men who make the cars. We'd all be walking or riding horseback or taking one of those rickshaws they use in China. A noble profession, indeed. Henry's daddy works at Philips Petroleum. Sits at a desk all day, that's what he does. Doesn't work with his hands like your daddy."

I wished Henry's mother would stop trying to make me feel better about being poor. Her car was worth more than my house.

"Do you work with your hands, Theodore?"

Henry dropped his head and shook it, smiling to himself.

"Um, no ma'am," I said, stifling a titter. "That would prob'ly be a bad idea."

"Mr. Hardy is at home and he can't wait to meet you, Theodore."

"You can call him Theo, Mama," Henry piped in.

"I like Theodore," she argued. "Sounds downright important, like Theodore Roosevelt or Theodore Dreiser, of course he was a socialist. Or, what's the name of that baseball player, Ted ..."

"Williams," Henry informed her.

"What?" she yelled and swerved to avoid a squirrel.

"Ted Williams!" hollered Henry.

"What?" hollered Mrs. Hardy.

"Ted Williams!!" we hollered back in unison.

"Yes, Theodore Williams, that's it! Theodore, are you gonna be president or a socialist or a baseball player?"

"Yeah, Theo," Henry said. "You gonna be a baseball player?"

"I don't know, Henry," I replied with a smirk. "Are you gonna be a basketball player?" And then I knuckle-punched Henry on the thigh. "I don't reckon I'll be any of those things, ma'am."

"Well, whatever you do, Theodore, I'm sure it'll be something real important."

We arrived at the circular drive of a ranch house and pulled under a carport where Mrs. Hardy screeched to a stop. The house was built of large sandstones, puzzle-pieced together by zigzag lines of mortar connecting like a map. The A-frame entrance featured large windows from floor to ceiling and I could see the sparse elegant furnishings, even with the glare of the sun. My reflection in the glass made me appear as if I was inside amidst the furniture and I pretended myself there.

Mr. Hardy came from around the house to greet us. He was tall and thick and wore untarnished cowboy boots with silver tips. I wondered how Henry could have come from such a strapping man. Introductions were made. He offered me a handshake and I extended my hand and he took it without looking, recoiling a bit but recovering quickly. I felt sorry for people taken by surprise.

"I've got the horses saddled up around back," he said.

"Now Henry," pointed Mrs. Hardy, "You know the rules. And you know how I feel about you riding. It's dangerous. You are no equestrian, young man. You could get hurt. Or maimed. People get killed on horses every day."

"Mama, you're being dramatic," said Henry.

"Well, I'd rather be dramatic with a live child than undramatic with a dead one."

Mr. Hardy stepped in. "Let him be a boy, Margaret. He's not made of glass."

Henry and I walked behind the house to a stable, my head craning so hard to survey the vast property that it might have twisted off. Two proud horses were dressed for riding. Henry offered me the black one. "Thunder is a good horse. Don't let the name scare you. He's real gentle."

I placed my foot into the stirrup and attempted to hoist myself onto the horse but it took me three tries. Henry's horse, Rain, was tall. Henry wasn't. But he'd invented a complex system of stepping and shifting and twirling himself to mount, a feat that nearly demanded applause.

I'd been on a horse only once before, when I was five, and we'd visited my father's brother, Uncle Bob, in Fayetteville. But Bob had passed away the following year when lightning struck his house and burst through the TV, electrocuting him as he watched *Gunsmoke*. I'd not had another opportunity to ride since.

"Keep your heels down and your head up," Henry instructed. "Wrap the reins just once around your hands. Be a leader but be gentle. Ask him for what you want."

Henry gave Rain a lively nudge and I did the same, following Rain's confident gait away from the stable and into the endless field before us. In no time at all, we increased our speed from a walk to a trot to a canter to, within the hour, a gallop that exploded into a freedom I'd never known. Thunder's sleek muscles pulsed, his hooves pounding the earth in a blur of motion. The oppressive air became cool and crisp. I lifted my chest to the wind and I rode, bound by nothing, surrounded by trees and grass and room to journey, like a vagabond with wings.

Thunder overtook Rain to lead the way. I saw the land rise before me and prepared for the ditch that was surely behind it, not knowing how or when to prompt Thunder for the jump. I closed my eyes and felt the massive animal lift from the earth and fly, high, in an arc, suspended in the air for seconds that felt like minutes, or a lifetime if I could remember it.

Thunder landed gracefully and sped on. I turned my head in time to watch Rain halt before the ditch and throw Henry over her head and onto the ground in a heap. I instinctively pulled the reins and jumped off the nickering horse and ran to him. "Are you okay?"

Henry was as angry as a whipped dog, covered in silt and pebbles that had planted themselves into the heels of his hands. "Shit!" he blasted.

I noticed a cut on his knee, visible through his slashed jeans. "My mama's gonna tan my hide," he said, "after she sends me to the hospital for surgery and a blood transfusion and a wooden leg."

I reached out to place my hand on the cut, but Henry pushed me away. He got to his feet and dusted himself off. "I don't need no help, thank you very much. I ain't five."

"Absolutely not—I'd take you for a solid seven."

"Shut up!" he growled, and spit on his hand and wiped the dirt from his mouth.

We walked our horses to McAffee Pond and tied them to a rough-leafed dogwood. "This is the spot," I said. "Everybody knows it's here but it still feels like a secret."

Henry surveyed the area and placed his hands on his hips and nodded as if he was shopping for real estate. "I like it."

We kicked off our shoes and lowered our feet into the still water, smooshing our toes in the cool mud, and then sat quietly on the bank and chewed on reeds and tossed stones in the water.

"Don't pay no attention to my mama," Henry said. "She's always apologizin' for everything. She feels guilty that she came from nothin' and got somethin' and thinks everybody's gonna hate her if she likes what she's got."

"I think she's nice."

The afternoon sun was back to its old tricks but the shaded cover of the dogwood and the soft moist moss beneath it was like spitting in its eye.

"Toby White is an asshole," said Henry.

"The whole gang is assholes."

"But you know what? They're gonna be assholes for the rest of their lives. And we won't never be."

I puffed my chest and said, "I'm gonna be president or a socialist or a baseball player. And you! You could be a jockey!"

"Go to hell, Dalton!" said Henry, and we punched each other's arms, rocking side to side like a seesaw.

"You mean go to hell, so I can join your little tea party with Toby White?"

Our energy came and went in bursts and stillness. We laughed the kind of laughter that falls into the air and settles into nothing, but there was conversation in our silence. Then, "Do you believe in miracles?" I said tentatively, not sure I dared to go this far.

"You mean like God miracles?" asked Henry.

"Maybe. I don't know. Just miracles."

"Well, I never much reckoned God chooses who to save and who to let die if that's what you mean. Everybody prayed for my Aunt Velma when she got cancer and if she'da lived they would have said God saved her, but when she died, they said God had a plan." He spit on his bloody knee and rubbed it with his finger. "Made me think it don't work both ways. If He gets credit for savin' somebody then He's gotta take the blame when they don't make it, so I reckon it's none of His business either way. If you ask me, people are always prayin' for miracles all the time. 'Lord, let the Cowboys win the Super Bowl!' when there ain't a snowball's chance in hell!"

I laughed. "My Aunty Li'll say it's a miracle if she gets a good parking space. Or `Thank you Jesus,' if carrots are on sale at the Safeway." I pried a stone from the mud with a sucking sound and tossed it far into the middle of the pond. Henry picked up another and drew his arm back to beat my distance. "But I mean, you know, real miracles," I said. "Things that happen that there ain't no explanation for."

Henry became quiet on this. "You mean like Jesus and the lepers kind of thing or some statue of the Virgin Mary crying tears of blood? One: maybe. Two: no way. You?"

"Same. One: maybe."

A pair of blue jays chased each other through the branches above us. A caterpillar crawled around to the bottom side of a poison oak leaf. A squirrel chattered. It was the kind of quiet that boys can only tolerate for so long.

"Last one in licks Toby White's asshole!" called Henry, and we stripped down to our underwear and jumped into the pond, splashing and dunking each other, cherishing the summer day.

It was still light when Henry and I headed back to the house and the sky was melting into sundown colors, red and purple and gold. We concocted what we believed was a palatable story to explain Henry's cut in which we'd been running from a swarm of bees and had headed for the pond to escape them, and Henry had tripped and fallen, tearing his jeans and cutting his knee, but we'd made it just before being stung to death, and our swollen bodies would have been discovered days later, floating on McAffee Pond among tadpoles and cottonmouths. It sounded plausible. Of course there was the threat that Henry's mother wouldn't allow him to go outside again without a beekeeper's suit and veil, but we knew we had to take that chance. Anything but being forbidden to ride.

We arrived at the stable and led Thunder and Rain inside. Henry showed me how to loosen the girths and run the stirrups up and we let the horses cool down before unsaddling them. I saw three other horses in the stalls. One lay in a bed of straw.

"That's Girly-Girl," said Henry. "She birthed a foal last week, but it was stillborn. Girly-Girl wouldn't leave its side until Daddy and the vet took it away. She ain't been the same since. Won't eat nothin'. Just lays there. Vet says he don't know if something's wrong with her or ..."

"Or if she's just broke inside."

"My daddy and the vet said horses don't feel things like that. Grief and stuff."

I walked to the horse and leaned in next to her. She whinnied and snorted and laid back at my touch. I placed my hands on her broad barrel and closed my eyes and I imagined: *Hen is riding Girly-Girl through the field, galloping fast and sure. The wind blows through her mane. Through the horse's eyes: she flies through wheat fields and past trees. She gets to a fence and soars over it, taking her into the sky.*

I felt the now familiar euphoric burn in my palms as it spread through my fingers like tentacles of light. Then I felt my hands curl and withdraw and I opened my eyes as the mare got to her feet. She whinnied and shook her mane. Henry stared at me. The horse. Me. His mouth gaped and he forgot to exhale.

I looked Henry in the eye. "Don't tell nobody."

CHAPTER NINE

That night I could still smell the horses on my skin. I washed pots and pans and plates and silver, almost mechanically, as my father and sister finished their meals. My mind was elsewhere. The chicken fried steak had been overcooked, the mashed potatoes had been lumpy and the boiled carrots had been reduced to an orange mush.

"Well, that really hit the spot," said my father, patting his stomach, obviously lying through his teeth. I looked at him, shocked, and an impish grin crept across his lips. I burst into laughter and he burst right back.

"My tummy aches," said Lily. And we laughed even harder. "Supper was really good, but I'm full as a tick." She joined in the roar of our bond.

My father scooted his chair out and braced himself on the table. He tried to conceal the stab of pain that always happened when he stood too fast, as if he'd forgotten for a just that moment. And then he flipped, just like that. His manner was an unpredictable pendulum. "I'm going on up. Been a long day," he said, sourly. He headed upstairs, pulling himself along with the banister. "Get your sister some of that pink stuff in the medicine chest," he called out. And then the soft click of his bedroom door.

I remembered the time I stood outside my father's room, spying through a crack in the door. He'd removed his shoes and coveralls down to his baggy boxer shorts and T-shirt, stained yellow at the collar and under the arms. I watched him switch on the dim lamp on his nightstand and slide into his side of the bed. He'd stared at a framed photo of himself and my mother; the picture I'd snuck in to look at when I feared she was disappearing from my memory, and he kissed his finger and placed it on her lips. "Night, babe. I'm sorry," he said, sadly, lovingly. And then he turned off the lamp and settled next to the vacant place.

It was something I knew I should not have seen, the absolute emptiness of him. And I suspected that this was a ritual he performed every night, and it altered the way I felt about him, having glimpsed at the burden of his humanness, of being undone, and it created a space, a pause, when I was angry with him or disappointed in him, that always seemed to give him another chance.

I tucked Lily into her bed with Joyce at her side. I'd found a bottle of Pepto Bismol in the medicine chest and started to pour a tablespoon.

"I hate that stuff. I want you to rub my belly instead," said Lily. She smushed a pillow into the perfect angle for her head and pulled my hand to her stomach under the covers. "Tell me about the night I was born."

"Aw, come on, Bug, I gotta finish cleanin' up the kitchen."

"Please," she begged.

I sighed, relenting, then began, low and menacing, "Well, it was a dark and stormy night..."

"Stop it! For reals."

I lightly rubbed her soft belly in a circle. "You've heard this story a million times."

"Tell me again."

I stuffed a pink hippopotamus between my back and the iron headboard and settled myself. "Okay. Let's see, we were all having dinner at the kitchen table, Daddy and Mama and me. And it was raining outside and Daddy left the oven door open 'cause it was so cold. And then Mama says, 'It's time.' And Daddy gets up to get dessert."

"He thinks it's time for dessert!" laughed Lily, her cheeks pinking up.

"But Mama says, 'No, I mean it's *time.*' And Daddy jumps up and he keeps saying 'It's time! It's time!' like a crazy man. And he's laughin' and flippin' out all at once. And Mama's just sittin' there waitin' for him to calm down. And Daddy gets her suitcase and they run outside and they start the car and drive off. And a minute later I hear the car come back in the drive and Daddy runs in and picks me up under his arm like a sack of potatoes and carries me out the door."

"'Cause they forgot you!"

"They forgot me! All they was thinkin' about was you. And Daddy's racing to the hospital by way of Saw Creek Road, and it's really coming down by now like cats and dogs. And Mama's laughing at Daddy but she's tryin' to breathe big and slow and she says, 'We got time, George, I ain't gonna have the baby in the car!' And Daddy slows down some, but you could tell he just wanted to get to the hospital." Lily gazed at me with eyes so wide and glossy that one might think she didn't know what was coming next. "So we was driving down Saw Creek Road, and a deer stepped out onto the middle of the road and Daddy swerved to keep from hittin' it…"

"And then there was the accident," said Lily, softly.

"And then there was the accident. And Mama and Daddy was hurt really really bad."

"And you too."

"Yeah, but I didn't know it yet. I didn't feel it yet with all that was goin' on. So, I got out of the car and looked everywhere for help but it was real dark, and finally I found a house up the road a piece and a man called the ambulance and they came and took us all to the hospital."

"And Daddy's leg was hurt real bad. And that's why he don't walk so good," said Lily.

"Yes."

"And that's what happened to your hands."

"Yup. Snapped my wrists clean through."

"And Mama was broken all over."

"Yes, all over."

"And the doctor said they had to do an operation and they didn't know if Mama and me could both stay alive."

"That's right," I said, resting my hand on her tummy.

"And all Mama kept sayin' was `Save my baby.' And that was me."

"That was you."

"And they had to decide," said Lily. "But Mama told `em to save me."

"Yes, all she cared about was makin' sure you was okay."

Lily paused and I paused with her. "And then Mama went to heaven."

"Yes," I said. "But she knew it was okay to go."

"Yes, it was okay."

I stroked my sweet sister's hair. "And besides, she ain't really gone. She's here with us. She helps us. All we have to do is ask."

Lily nodded and hugged Joyce to her chest, and she pondered. "Why don't Daddy let Mama help him?"

"I don't reckon I know. Maybe he don't ask. Maybe he will someday." I pulled the covers up under her chin and kissed her on the forehead. "Now you need to go to sleep. It's gettin' late."

I turned off the overhead light leaving the room in the glow of the Cinderella table lamp. And then I folded myself next to Lily and I sang.

Sleep my child and peace attend thee,
All through the night
Guardian angels God will send thee,
All through the night

Soft, the drowsy hours are creeping,
Hill and dale in slumber sleeping
I, my loved ones' watch am keeping,
All through the night.

Lily began to nod off. "My tummy's better," she said, and her voice fell into a soft purr. "You always make it better."

I closed the door and paused outside it. Then I crept to my father's bedroom door and listened for silence and then peeked in to see him sleeping, mouth open in a permanent yawn. I nervously approached the bed, nearly tripping over his tossed coveralls and work boots. In the black plastic ashtray on the nightstand, the last of a burning cigarette clung to a cylinder of delicate ash suspended against all laws of physics. I stubbed it out and the gray smoke wafted into the soft light of the lamp that had likewise been ignored. I switched it off and moved closer to the bed. Then I reached to touch my father's left leg, the bad one, careful not to wake him. I closed my eyes and I imagined: *My father trotting down the stairs with a brisk even pace. The limp is gone. He is smiling. "Good morning monkeys!" Lily runs to his arms and he lifts her, kissing her on the forehead. Lily is twirled round and round, finally being tossed on the sofa and she screams with delight. Then from my daddy's eyes: He is walking with me in the sunshine, steady and even, and tousles my hair and pulls me in close.*

I felt it work. Even more so than I had before, and it was exhilarating. I wanted it. And I was glad to feel my hands coil and cramp to proclaim completion. My father shifted in his sleep and sighed. The lines in his forehead softened and he seemed almost childlike. And then I sneaked out of the room, a slight limp in my step. I would not sleep.

CHAPTER TEN

The next morning I was up too early and found things to do. I scrubbed a stain on the living room carpet, reorganized a kitchen cabinet, tightened a loose screw on the screen door. Lily skipped downstairs and colored at the kitchen table—a purple giraffe with fried eggs for eyes. I made breakfast, hoping the smell of bacon would rouse my father, and I removed the spitting skillet just in time to avoid a grease fire. Lily took a too-big gulp of orange juice, ballooned her cheeks to swish it, and spit it back into her glass in a stream. "Stop it," I admonished. "I just cleaned that table."

"I'm a fountain," she said, as if her explanation was an obvious, unarguable fact, and I was an idiot for not realizing it.

Suddenly, I heard the creak of the stairs and my father's familiar unsteady rhythm. He appeared in the doorway and paused there. He'd not yet showered and dressed, and his faded, striped boxers hung on his narrow hips. "Mornin'," he said, softly, the gristle of his voice oddly missing. I struggled to gage whatever was sitting behind his questioning eyes. Something had changed, I knew that. But I couldn't tell what. Apparently, not his leg. I thought maybe it didn't work if I wanted it so badly for someone I actually loved.

I pulled a cup from the cabinet and began to pour my father's coffee. "I'll get that," he insisted, as he walked toward me. I studied him out of the corner of my eye as I busied myself unfolding and refolding a tea towel. He found footing at the counter and carefully poured coffee from the percolator. I could feel him holding his breath as I held mine. Then he lifted the cup with one hand and carried it to the kitchen table, circumspect, his eyes glued to the surface of the liquid. Not a swish. Not a ripple. He set it gingerly on the table and started to sit, then changed his mind and began to walk around the table. Just around, slowly, and around.

Lily laughed. "What are you doin', Daddy? Are you playin' a game? Can I play?"

"I'm walking," he said. Just that. I'm *walking*. So much in a word. So much behind, beyond a word. Lily rose and began following him, grinning wide. My father seemed confused, his eyes worried and scrunched, nearly scowling. He stopped and lifted the knee of his bad leg, so that his thigh was parallel to the floor, and he held it there, lowered it, then lifted it again. Lily mimicked the move. He shifted his weight and lifted the other knee. Lily followed suit. He resumed circling the table, finding an even rhythm as he went along, more agile and faster with each lap. His eyes wandered and his mouth gaped then buckled, and he shook his head in small jerks, as if waking himself from a dream. Lily aped each move.

"Okay, my turn, Daddy!" she cheered.

"Okay, your turn," he said, unsure.

"You too, Theo. Play with us! It's called Copycat!"

I joined them. It was Simon Says without the orders, like the episode of *I Love Lucy* with Harpo Marx, mirroring each other. Lily leaned to the side and so did my father and I. Then the other side. She hopped. We hopped.

I saw the moment it struck my sister that my father had changed. He saw it in her too, and in me. Tears swam in my eyes and I pushed them back, laughing through them. All of us, it seemed, were afraid to say it out loud, to acknowledge the wonder, as if we might curse it and send him to the floor like so many other times when he'd pushed himself for normal. My father smiled and shrugged as the tempo of our game increased: a swift, Chaplin-esque duck walk around the kitchen, jumping jacks, waving arms, silly faces, finally culminating in lifting our knees and hitting them like Austrian slap dancers.

I was lightheaded and giddy and I wondered if this was what it felt like to be drunk. Lily and I followed my father into the living room and he trotted up and down the stairs with his hands in the air then scooped up my giggling sister, twirling round and round with her arms extended like a beautiful spinning blade, just like he used to do with me. He switched on the radio and "Jumpin' Jack Flash" was playing. He turned up the volume to a joyous blare and the three of us danced, screaming and shouting and celebrating. "A goddam miracle, that's what it is," shouted my father. "Get dressed, we're going out!"

We sat, stopped, at the single traffic light at the center of town. There was no traffic in any direction. No one crossing the street. Dalton was dead. "Goddamn Dewey Logan!" my father yelled, still smiling ear to ear, and Lily and I echoed with irreverence, "Goddamn Dewey Logan!" We both knew nothing could get us in trouble, not that day, and the three of us bounced on the worn leather front seat in anticipation, squished together like a Dalton sandwich, waiting. Goddamn Dewey Logan.

The light had been installed in 1963 with much celebration as a symbol of metropolitan progress. There had been a ribbon cutting. Dewey Logan, who'd reigned as mayor for twelve straight terms, had grown too old for the job but was bestowed the honor of "custodian of the traffic light" as a consolation. In addition to maintenance, Dewey's responsibilities included timing the light so that pedestrians could comfortably cross the street before it changed. Dewey tested it bi-monthly when he would walk across the street with a stopwatch. As he grew older and more stooped, the time had incrementally increased to a groan-inducing duration, but no one in Dalton wanted to insult Dewey, so it was understood that the extra forty or so seconds would be tolerated.

"Just go Daddy!" screamed Lily. "Aunty Li does it all the time. There ain't nobody coming."

It made no sense to stay, still my father refused to go. But when the light changed from red to yellow, he revved the motor like we were at the starting line of a drag race. My father held his arm over Lily's chest and when the light switched to green, he shifted into drive and we screamed with joy.

The Riverview Roller Rink did not have a view of the river, or of anything else for that matter. It was a windowless, never-used airplane hangar left over from the war, so the people of Dalton had voted to convert it to a skating rink in lieu of tearing it down. High on the north wall just under the arched ceiling was an electric sign that lit up at the manager's discretion: All Skate, Waltz, Foxtrot, Ladies Choice, Reverse, Couples, Robbers, Rhumba. We skated through them all.

Lily was unsure, but my father held her hand and patiently helped her gain balance, shuffling more than skating, but making headway nonetheless. I raced round and round on my own, daring to try the leg-cross-over turn at the curves of the rink. And then my father handed Lily off to me. And he sailed.

The Hokey Pokey blasted through the speakers and all the skaters quickly formed an enormous circle. We put our left skates in and our left skates out and our left skates in and we shook them all about. When Lily attempted to turn herself around, her skates rolled out from beneath her, but my father's strong hand refused to let her fall. She looked up at him and said, "Daddy, this is the best day of my whole entire life!"

Session 6

She gathers courage. "I've been thinking a lot about when I started to gain weight." She waits for a response, but I decide to let the moment sit. She goes on. "I mean obviously there's a correlation."

"How so?"

"I remember that she started feeding me. My mother. More and more. My father would give me little gifts and my mother would feed me. Big breakfasts with pancakes and whipped cream. I would always come home from school for lunch, it was only a few blocks away, and there would be enormous sandwiches and cookies and chocolate milk. She put cupcakes in my book bag. And there were sweet snacks after school and desserts after dinner."

"What do you think that was about?"

"I was trying to figure out when it started. It was in high school, sophomore year."

"What do you think that was about?" I ask again.

Her shoulders lift in a nearly undetectable shrug. "Some kind of reward, maybe."

"Reward?"

"No, I don't mean reward. I think the gifts from my daddy were rewards. The things I kept in the box. I think with her it was, maybe some sort of, I don't know—empathy? As cold as she was, it might have been some way to give me something good. To make up for something she knew was bad."

"So you think she knew."

"Yes." Sorrow threatens but she deflects it. "By the time I was in high school anyway. Or maybe that's when she finally admitted it to herself." She turns her liquid eyes on me. "I think she always knew."

"That's a painful thing to realize. What are you feeling?"

"Angry. Sad. Angry."

"That she didn't do something about it?

"Yes."

"And do you have any idea why she didn't do something about it?"

"The truth is Daddy and I would've both denied it and I think she knew that. I would have protected him. And our family would've fallen apart."

"Why do you think she didn't take you out of the situation? Gotten you some help?"

She anxiously twirls the fraudulent wedding ring. "He would've fought for me and I would've chosen to stay with him. I hated her."

"Do you think you hated her *because* she didn't do something about it?"

"Maybe. Subconsciously. I don't know. I certainly didn't get that at the time. She was the enemy."

"It's so complicated, I know. So confusing as a child and perhaps even more now. Are there any other reasons you think she kept quiet? That she didn't protect you?"

"I think maybe she thought she *was* protecting me," she smirks. "In her mousy lame-ass way."

"How so?"

She closes her eyes and sits quietly. "Because she knew she was the one who would be out of the picture and she needed to stay. With me." She falls into anger. "I'm not forgiving her."

"I wouldn't ask you to."

She throws her head back and laughs unexpectedly. "It's so stupid. It's so backward."

"What?"

"Her weakness. She was the staunch one. She was the one in charge of everything. But she was so weak. I mean it was the mid-nineties, not the mid-fifties. And her answer was to keep quiet and feed me?"

"So, you started to gain the weight. Go on."

"Big time. And Daddy seemed to like it. He told me I was beautiful, which was what I wanted to hear because I knew I wasn't. He would encourage me to eat more too, always asking if I wanted seconds and thirds. One time we ate an entire chocolate cake with our hands! We laughed and laughed. It was decadent... and disgusting."

"What do you think might have been the reason he did that?"

She pauses. She ponders. "I don't know. It was embarrassing. Everyone in high school was dating. Daddy had chased off Rick after the time I snuck out. My bad boy." She gazes at the floor, then to the arm of the sofa and plucks a stray thread from it and rolls it in her fingers.

"Do you think it's possible that he fed you to make you less attractive to boys?"

"Maybe."

"And what about your mother?"

"... To make me less attractive ... to him."

She sniffles and I pick up the box of Kleenex I always keep next to the sofa and offer it, careful not to touch her. She takes one but doesn't use it. There is no need. No tears. Just a kind of disbelief.

My years in my work have taught me that it is the task of the human brain to assemble all the information of our lives into some sort of comprehensive narrative. That's what memory is, a fine-tuned linear account that we construct about our past to form our identity, to make sense of what got us here. But what happens when that storyline becomes fractured? What happens when a life can't be rendered into the definitive story we'd created in the first place?

I speak softly. "That's a very lonely and scary feeling, not being protected by our guardians. It's the most basic need we all have—to be sheltered when we're young. By the ones we're supposed to trust to take care of us."

She seems puzzled, her thoughts a twisted perplexity. "I mean I guess there was something," she says in a hush. "Some instinct, deep down, that I knew it wasn't... right, but also I truly believed this was what girls did with their fathers. He told me so. And I believed him. I needed to believe him. I believed no one could love me as much as he could. He told me so. And if he didn't love me, who would? Certainly not my mother!" she bursts. "How stupid is that?"

"You were a child."

Her eyes well again but she switches gears, gaining in rambling speed. "I should have known. I should have figured it out. Jesus, I mean I knew about child abuse, it wasn't like I lived in a cave. There were cases in the news. I remember some girl had been locked in a basement for years. And I didn't put any of it together. That was about sexual *abuse*. Forcing children to have sex. That wasn't what it was like for me. I never had a single bruise. I was never threatened. My father didn't force anything. Ever!" She is treading water in an ocean of anguish.

"There are many ways to force someone to do something," I say, attempting to maintain a smooth but firm tone.

"Especially a child. It's not just physical. It's psychological. It's manipulation. And at its worst, it's under the pretext of love."

Her shoulders fall. "It's so funny, isn't it," she says. "What you said, about parents taking care of their children. When I think about how all I wanted was to take care of my daddy... I wanted to protect him. From her. We were a team, me and him. He was the good one, my mother was the bad one."

"Do you think it's possible that you had to make *somebody* bad? Make someone responsible for all that was happening? Because your father, this man, the one who said he loved you so much, more than anyone ever could, could not possibly be the bad one. If he was bad, then who was left? So your mother had to be the bad one—the one who didn't show she loved you. For children, understanding the gray area is nearly impossible. It's black and white, good and bad, heroes and villains."

Her mouth moves open and shut as if waiting for words to come. "I think I believed if I could make his pain go away and heal him, then he would stop. I always thought it was something temporary. That he would be fixed and he would be happy and then I would be happy." She grows somber. "This is so fucked up."

"No shit."

CHAPTER ELEVEN

Henry and I walked along Saw Creek Road, me with my swift gait and Henry with his springy step. The heavy air did not diminish our stride.

"It's like he's another person," I said, alive with excitement. "I kind of remember him this way but Lily for sure ain't never seen him like this. I don't know, I'm startin' to believe these things are really happening and stickin.' And it's a good thing."

"Can you do it the other way?" Henry asked. "Like put a curse on somebody? I got a list. Toby White is at the top of it."

"I don't know. Want me to try it on you?" I exaggerated my hands into talons like a wizard casting a hex.

"You could really cash in on that," Henry said, and punted a cow chip from the side of the road. "Prob'ly even more than the gettin' better part."

"You know you still can't tell nobody, right?"

"Who am I gonna tell?"

I stopped dead in the road and stared at Henry gravely. "I need you to swear."

"I ain't gonna tell!"

"Swear!" I demanded.

Henry's arms danced like he was shaking mason jars of flour and water to make a paste. "I swear! What do you think I'm gonna do, take out a full page in the *Dalton Courier?*"

I pulled Frank's jackknife from my jeans and snapped it open.

Henry nervously laughed and stuttered, "Whoa. Back off, Jack."

I raised my hand and cut a shallow *X* into my palm, wincing. *Shit!* I'd read about the custom in a book about Native American rituals from the school library, but I didn't know it would hurt this badly. Blood trickled and dripped to the ground and the hot dust soaked it up, leaving a rose-colored stain. I handed the knife to Henry. We stood, looking at each other for an uncertain moment, then he lifted his hand and cut an *X* into it, clenching his teeth, but never leaving my gaze. We pushed our palms together and pressed them tightly, sealing our covenant. Then Henry pulled a white hanky from his pocket and ripped it in half, and we crudely bandaged our hands. We walked, soundless and steady.

I kicked at the earth and a puff of it rose and fell on my shoes. "I'm glad you moved here."

"Me too," said Henry.

When we reached the driveway leading to Frank's trailer, I pointed. "This is where I wanted to bring you."

Henry was flabbergasted, as if we'd come upon a mythical and forbidden land. "What? Shit! This is that man's place, ain't it?" He stepped back. "I heard about him from my mama soon as we moved here. She said to stay away no matter what, but I didn't know if it was really true."

"He's real."

"She said he murdered a soldier in the Korean War. In his own troop! Shot him dead, crazy as a horn beetle.

Shoulda rotted in prison, that's what my mama said. Would just as soon shoot you as look at you."

Frank came out of the screen door and it slammed with a clatter.

Henry screamed, "Run!" and he flew off.

"Hey, Frank!" I called out.

"Mornin', Theo!" Frank called back.

Henry halted, stunned. This was a jaw-dropper. He edged back to me with meticulous caution.

"This is the guy I was tellin' you about," I said, "who told me about my hands."

"What?" muttered Henry. "You're pullin' my leg. You didn't say nothin' about..."

"He ain't so bad. Unless you stand in his driveway. Then he'll kill you." I pushed Henry into the driveway and he shrieked like a five-year-old girl whose Barbie had just fallen over a banister. I laughed. Frank laughed. And then Henry laughed.

"It's hotter than a three-dollar pistol," Frank shouted. "You boys wanna come in for a pop?"

I leaned in to Henry and whispered, "It's prob'ly poisoned."

We went inside with Henry nearly needing to be pulled. The scene overwhelmed him: the worn furniture, the dirty dishes, generally crappy. When he saw the gun mounted on the wall, he swallowed hard.

"Frank–Hen. Hen–Frank."

Frank reached out a hand but pulled back when he saw the bandages. "What happened to your hands, boys? Rub `em raw? You know you could go blind if you do that too much," he burst with a laugh. Frank fetched us icy Cokes and Henry gulped his like a carbonated waterfall. "First time in a trailer?" asked Frank with a smile, sending the bottle cap of his Coors flying.

Henry froze, parched even still. Half-formed words died in his throat. "I got in the back of one once with one of our horses."

Frank laughed. "Well, I been called an ass before but never a horse. Course, I have been called a horse's ass." He slapped Henry on the back and he nearly spit up his Coke.

Henry searched the room, holding his bottle in front of him. "Do you have a coaster?"

"You think you're gonna ruin my fancy furniture?" chuckled Frank.

"I'm sorry."

"Don't be sorry, Hen," I said. "Frank's all right."

Frank took a swig of his Coors. "I'm guessin' your family's got some casheesh. Rich enough to buy a new boat when the other one gets wet, am I right?"

"My daddy does okay, I guess."

"Thing about a mobile home is it's mobile. That was the idea anyway—always ready for a quick getaway," he snickered. "But I ain't been mobile for a long time. Kinda ironical. Shit, I ain't even been into town on foot for goin' on twenty years. 'Course I was *unavailable* for ten of that." Henry glanced to me to confirm he'd heard what he thought he'd heard.

"Good thing is I always know you're gonna be home," I laughed.

"Unless I got some social engagement at the country club," Frank said earnestly.

The fizz of the pop whispered through the silence.

"He's joking, Hen!" I said, knocking him with my shoulder.

Frank went on. "I ain't got a pot to piss in or a window to throw it out of and I like it that way."

"I wanted you guys to meet," I said.

Henry swallowed the last of his Coke with the shadow of a grin. The danger was exhilarating. "It's good to meet you, sir."

"Good to be met," said Frank, and he winked at me.

Chapter Twelve

Pappy Ray's Same Day Auto Repair was painted in loud red capital letters over a white background near the top of the brick building. A grayish awning bearing the address, 311 Dalton Blvd., hung over the glass door entrance.

My father pulled onto the blacktop along the side of the building. "Here we are," he said, springing from the truck. As we headed to the entrance, the punch of a motor set in motion the raising of the enormous roll-top windows in a grand investiture like castle doors at the end of a drawbridge, and I was taken by its majesty. There might have been trumpets. But it only revealed Grady Sikes.

"Mornin' Grady," hollered my father.

"Mornin' George," he hollered back, less than enthusiastic. He searched for a something lodged between his two front teeth with his diligent tongue and made a sucking sound. I guessed Grady was about fifty, but then he'd looked about fifty for as long as I could remember, except for his hair, full and black, combed up in a shiny pompadour which was at odds with his craggy-lined face, speckled with broken capillaries. His skin looked like he'd barely survived a violent sandstorm. Grady had the same permanent black under his fingernails as my father, and wore the same blue coveralls with the same grease spots dotting it like a faded leopard. His embroidered name tag was sewn to his breast pocket bursting with pens and air pressure gauges. I'd met Grady several times, and Boyd and Ray too. I didn't like him much.

"Mornin', Theo."

"Mornin'," I answered.

"Theo's come to see what his old man does," said my father, with satisfaction.

"Ain't really no place for kids."

"Aw, Ray won't mind."

"Ray ain't here. And Boyd ain't neither. I don't want to be responsible if a socket wrench hits him upside the head." Grady located whatever was in his teeth, plucked it from his tongue and flicked it to punctuate the mandate.

I realized that, though I'd been to my father's workplace more than a dozen times, I'd never actually been inside the garage, and I was captivated by the world beyond the roll-top glass doors: a pea green Chevy hoisted in midair on a hydraulic lift as if levitating like a magician's trick; fire-engine red rolling tool boxes; tires unevenly stacked in a corner; an ancient metal desk, gray paint flaking off, strewn with papers, orders, invoices, cans of WD-40; jugs of anti-freeze, oil; wrenches and gadgets and odd-shaped tools hung like exhibits on a pegboard, ordered from small to large. *And my dad knows about all this stuff*, I thought.

"Son! Come on over here and take a look," said my father, snapping me from my reverie and causing me to trip over a dishpan full of kitty litter meant to absorb oil spills. "This," he said, gesturing to a shining gunmetal blue station wagon, "is a 1967 Mercedes Benz 230." I stepped forward and touched its fintails. "Belongs to Melva White, lives up on the hill, more money than Carter's got pills." I'd never met or even seen Melva White but I knew who she was—Toby's mother, and for a moment I wished I could scratch its length with a crowbar.

Grady wiped his hands on a soiled rag. "I'm gonna get to some paperwork," he said, before slamming the office door.

"Sorry about that," my father whispered to me. "He can be an asshole."

I laughed, nervously. "That's okay. Are you sure it's okay if…"

"I can do whatever I damn well please, Theo. He ain't got no authority over me." My father opened the hood of the Mercedes and pointed to the various parts inside. "This is the piston, this is the rack, the voltage regulator, the choke assist, the fan, the fuel injector." He went on and on, as if he was a surgeon—heart, liver, pancreas, lungs. "Pull up that stool and watch and we can talk."

Talk. Talk? I rolled a mechanic's seat to the front bumper of the car.

"This Mrs. White brings her car in every few weeks like it was an infant gettin' regular checkups," he said, scratching his chin as if deciding which organ to remove. "Can you hand me a Phillips screwdriver? Top drawer in that tool box." I rummaged around, hoping to deliver the correct size. "Course, she don't need to do that at all, but if she wants to spend her money I ain't gonna argue!" He leaned over the grill and buried himself in the guts of the car. "You know your mama didn't much care about money and things." My father rarely, if ever, spoke of my mother so I sat quietly, secretly begging for any morsel he offered. "One time, long time ago, you was just a baby, me and your mama went up to the White house. Ha! The White House. Might as well have been! And there was this party celebratin' the new addition to the library and they decided they needed a real Dalton to cut the cake and be in some pictures for the

Courier." He nodded his head in the direction of the wall. "Socket wrench is on that board. Bring me that case of bits right over there." I did. "Thanks, son."

Thanks, son?

"And that house was full of people I seen once in a while around town or at the shop, but me and your mama didn't know any of `em by name. They was nice enough, I guess, but I felt like I was the help, you know, like I shoulda been passin' around a tray of little sandwiches or somethin'. And I said to your mama, `All this fancy coulda been our life you know, if my granddaddy hadn'ta give away our money.' And you know what she said to me?"

"Tell me," I said, my eyes locked, my breath caught.

"She took my face in her sweet hands and she said to me, she said, `Georgie'—do you remember she called me Georgie?"

"I don't think so."

"She said, `Georgie, I wouldn't want this if it was handed to me. We don't never need none of this. These ain't our people.' She said, 'Too much pressure to have this kind of money, everybody tryin' to show off and everybody always wantin' something. Too much to keep up with. I'm just fine with what we got.' Now don't that take the cake? Hand me that torque wrench." I froze. "It's that one looks like a head on top of a stick." I found it. "You're a mighty fine helper, son."

"Thank you, Daddy." I wasn't sure what was happening.

"Now," he said, "we gotta clean the carburetor." I peered under the hood. "A carburetor gets dirty from one of two things. It's either runnin' lean, which means there's too much air and not enough fuel, or it's runnin' rich, which means there's too much fuel and not enough air." He laughed. "Course Melva White's carburetor tends to run rich. That means a lot of black smoke goin' every which way. You breathe it in it'll make you sick." He walked to the corner of the garage and rolled two creepers back to the car. "You wanna learn how to clean a carburetor?"

"Sure, I guess." I was afraid I wouldn't be very good at it.

"You'd never know it from lookin' at her, so little and all dainty-like, but your mama could clean a carburetor. Damn straight. She could change a tire, she could change the oil. And you're gonna learn—just like your mama, just your daddy."

For the next hour my father led me, step by step, letting me do all the work as he explained how to remove the air filter cover, locate the fuel bowl vent, add carburetor cleaner into the fuel vent, reinstall the air cleaner cover *in case there's a backfire*, set the choke, and finally run the engine, throttle up and down. He was patient and kind, and he seemed to know exactly when my hands prevented me from doing a necessary task—leaning in to tighten a screw, supporting the filter when I dislodged it, laughing comfortably when I messed up and praising me when I did something well.

There was not even the slightest similarity to the father I had grown to know. To re-know. Now there was someone new, someone to re-know once more. And I might have been angry at the time lost, but instead, I dared myself to be happy in the time that was.

SESSION 7

She sits high and straight, her guise of confidence betrayed by an index finger moving haphazardly on her knee as if spelling out what she's going to say. "I used to make up stories. I mean way back to when I was little."

"How little?"

"Elementary school."

"What kind of stories?"

"Stories about myself. When I was in fourth grade I told the kids at school that my family were descendants of Ponce de León and that I was part Spanish. I don't know if you're up on your history, Doc."

"The Fountain of Youth guy."

"Yes. And he was the founder of Florida. Which means *flower.*"

"How did you come to choose that story?"

"We were studying our state history and when we got to Ponce de León, I raised my hand and said, `I'm related to him.' I didn't plan it. I wasn't even a hundred percent sure I knew how to pronounce his name since I'd never said it."

"What did your teacher do?"

"I can't remember her name. She was really tall and school-marmy. Cat-eye glasses, the bun, the whole thing. Anyway, she was thrilled. She totally bought it and my classmates were super impressed." The corners of her mouth pull downward and she lets her posture melt. "After my sister died there had been this kind of—distance from the other kids. Like they didn't know what to say so they didn't say anything." She touches the gold locket instinctively. "And then when they found out I was related to the founder of our state it gave me some sort of—title, and that helped turn things around."

"Turn things around?"

"Make me, I don't know, visible again."

"How do you mean?"

"You know how kids are. They pull back if there's something different about you. When they don't know how to deal with something. Like wearing super thick glasses or having some kind of deformity."

She glances to my hands. I know that kind of different. "Yes."

"Unless it's a special kind of different." I know that kind of different too. "Like, well, being related to Ponce de León … Miss Eberdeen."

"What?"

"That was her name. Miss Eberdeen. So anyway, when we had to write our reports, of course I chose Ponce de León. And Miss Eberdeen had me read it to the class."

"How did it go?"

"I was a big hit. I got more applause than the other kids. And nobody else wrote about Ponce de León because they knew it was my territory," she laughs. "But after I finished, Miss Eberdeen said that the part about the Fountain of Youth was a myth. And I looked her in the eye and I said, `But Miss Eberdeen, I'm actually sixty-four years old.' And she totally lost it, like hysterical, and the class busted up, and they called me Poncey for the rest of the year." I can hear the smile in her voice. "And it really changed my life. I was a bit of a celebrity for a while. And they forgot about my sister dying. So I started making up more stories. I mean, it had worked once, right? So I said that I was born in Spain, but my parents moved to Florida when I was a year old. And that my name had actually been Flower but my parents changed it when we moved to the United States because they wanted to keep a low profile. And I told them our family had jewels from the 1500s and they were locked up in an ancient, secret wooden box and when I turned eighteen I was going to inherit them. And they bought all of it. I mean even as I'm saying this it sounds so ridiculous. But you know, Doc, people believe anything if you do it with conviction."

"How did that make you feel?"

"Special. Popular."

"Even though you knew it wasn't true?"

She falls still. "I think I started to believe it was true. I mean I knew it wasn't, but you know, when you tell a lie often enough it becomes true."

"It makes perfect sense that you needed to create some sort of fantasy life that was better and brighter than the one you had. It was a coping mechanism." *I think of Lily. And how she would create her own world in her drawings. Take something ordinary or even painful and turn it into something beautiful.* "And the need to be accepted because you were special, rather than rejected because you were different, falls in line with that as well. The mind is an amazingly resourceful survivalist."

"And the box," she says.

"Yes?"

"The ancient wooden box full of jewels…" She pauses, considering her words.

"Go on."

"… was my fantasy of turning the box of rewards from my father into something exquisite."

"Yes. Good."

"Turning something messed up into something deal-able, even beautiful." She becomes ruminative, searching for what is next. "I think that's why I started writing poetry. When I was a junior in high school I won a contest," she tells me with a slight hint of self-regard. "It was this tri-state thing and my English teacher, Mr. McDonald, told me I should enter. He said I showed real promise in creative writing. And I never thought in a million years I would win, so I said yes. And then I did. And it was terrifying."

"How so?"

"Because they told me I was going to read it in front of the whole school at an assembly."

"Sure, but weren't you proud of having won?"

"Yes, but the poem was really… personal."

"Do you remember it?"

"No."

"Do you remember what was so personal about it?"

"It wasn't confessional or literal, but it was, I guess, confessional to me. It felt like I was sharing too much."

"Did you do it? Read the poem?"

"Yes. It was the first time I'd read anything I'd written out loud since the Ponce de León report, which was a lie of course, and then this—this deepest kind of truth in the poem.

"How did that go?"

"Not like I thought it would," she recalls, a smile playing on her lips. "I was really overweight by then and I was sure somebody was going to yell out something horrible. *Orca!* or *Lard-Ass!* or something like that. The kind of things they would call out in the parking lot or whisper when they passed me in the halls. But they didn't. And I remember when I finished, it got really quiet. And then they applauded. Not like crazy applause, but really respectful."

When she is at peace, I find myself lost in the elegance of her face, the heart shape of her mouth, her soft eyes and the diminutive lines that trail from them. "So it was a good thing."

"Yes. I felt like there was something special about me that was different. Good different. And then the other sort of artsy kids kind of embraced me. I'd been in the popular group for a long time. Ponce de León went a long way! Ha! Jesus. But when I started to get heavy things changed. And, slowly I was, what's the word? ... dismissed. Nothing overt. Just dismissed. Which is worse I think."

"Yes."

"So I didn't really have a hang-out group anymore. And the poetry thing was kind of an entrée to new friends. There was this one girl in particular, Carrie Crapster. Seriously. Her name was Crapster. I mean if you've got a name like that you don't have a prayer. She could have been a beauty queen and it wouldn't have made any difference."

"And she befriended you."

"We were best friends. We'd gone to school together since kindergarten but we never really knew each other until then. And it was like *where have you been all my life?*"

"Tell me about her. About your friendship."

"She was super smart." Her eyes alight as she chatters, as close to contentment as I've seen her. "She was funny. Pretty, in a makeover kind of way, you know, like if somebody cut her hair and gave her different glasses and put her in cool clothes. We were both totally in love with Jon Secada and Mariah Carey and Joey Lawrence." Her smile is redolent of a precious time. "And she was the first kid I invited over to my house in a long time. We'd do our homework and listen to music. She played the flute and she was into classical music, and we'd sit on the floor in front of the speakers and listen to some sonata or concerto. It was really lovely."

"It sounds like she was a very good friend."

"She was." Her smile evaporates. "This one time she was over at my house and Daddy came into my bedroom and asked if we'd like to have hot fudge sundaes. And we were like *Sure! Who doesn't want a hot fudge sundae?* And he gave me ten bucks and told me to go to the corner market and get some ice cream and whatever else I wanted. And so Carrie and I started out and Daddy said, `Carrie, why don't you stay here? She can go by herself.' And it was really awkward. I mean, what kid wants to hang out with somebody's parents? And I said, `It's okay, we'll be right back.' And Daddy said, `Go on. I like to get to know your friends.' And I looked at Carrie and she just shrugged her shoulders like *whatever,* but I got really insistent."

"Because … ?"

"Because I didn't want to leave her with him. I was— afraid to leave her with him. And I guess, maybe, I don't know, jealous? And Daddy got mad. No, not mad. He never showed that. Just strong. And he told me to go and he just shut me down."

"So you went to the market."

"I *ran* to the market. I rushed into the store and picked up the first flavor of ice cream I saw and I threw the whole ten dollars on the counter and I didn't wait for change and I ran home. And I remember getting in the front door and yelling out `I'm back!' as loud as I could. And then trying to steady my breath as I went up the stairs to make it seem casual. And when I got to my bedroom they were sitting in the same positions I'd left them in." Her brow crinkles. "It's so strange."

"What's that?"

"For me to act on something instinctively when I wasn't really in touch with why. I don't think I thought *I better hurry because my father might be molesting my friend.* I just knew I had to get back. And there they were just talking. Same spots. Except..."

"Except?"

"When Daddy left the room Carrie was really quiet. And I asked her if anything was wrong. And she said no, but I could tell there was something. And finally, she said, `You're not from Spain.' And I didn't even know what she was talking about. And she said, 'When I was talking with your dad, I brought up the thing about you being from Spain and how you moved here when you were little and that you were related to Ponce de León.' And I hadn't thought about that in so long, but she remembered. She'd always thought it was something pretty cool."

"And that changed things?"

"Not at first. I told her that kids, you know, make up shit all the time and it was just something I said to get attention. And of course I wouldn't say that now. And she seemed to understand. But..." She drifts away.

"Go on."

"A couple of weeks later we had a sleepover at her house and her parents were away for the weekend. So it was just Carrie and me, and we got into her folk's liquor cabinet and we drank. And we promised each other we'd be best friends forever and I'd never felt closer to anyone my age like that ever. And we were playing this game where we had to tell each other secrets we'd never told anyone. And I was really drunk by then and I told her I'd been pregnant once, when I was fourteen. Nothing about my father. Just that. Just a way to get in, you know, open the door. But she didn't believe me. She said I was always making up things. Spain. Ponce de León. She said she didn't believe I'd had sex when I was fourteen and who was the father if I did? And I said I couldn't tell and she called me a liar. And I knew I couldn't tell her anything else. My secret was safe with me."

The room is quiet. The rumble of a truck comes and goes outside. "I don't think she told anybody. She just shifted. She was never mean to me, but we stopped hanging out. I guess if she thought I was lying she didn't want to be friends. And if she thought I was telling the truth she didn't want to be friends. I was stupid for saying it." She waves a hand, tossing off regret.

"You wanted to tell someone. You *needed* to tell someone. And it makes sense that you wanted to tell your best friend. It wasn't stupid at all. It was human."

"Can you imagine what she would have done if I'd told her more? It would have been the end of everything."

"She might have helped you. The end of everything could have been a good thing."

"What if, what if, what if."

"You did the best you could do." I can't tell if she's heard me. She is somewhere else.

"She was...humane," she whispers, almost to herself. "I think of her from time to time. More since I've started here with you. I still think of her as a friend, isn't that funny? Maybe someday, someday I'll find out where she lives and what's going on in her life and I'll tell her what happened. And how sorry I was that I told her the truth. And maybe even how sorry I am that I didn't tell her the whole truth."

CHAPTER THIRTEEN

I checked the address against a slip of paper I'd been given by Kevin Brown, Mr. Elijah's son. It was one of the nicer neighborhoods in Dalton, not one that I frequented. The freshly cut grass was a striking green, no water spared there, and a stone path, hemmed with moss, led to a brick two-story house covered in ivy that seemed like an extension of the lawn, wrapping the house like a blanket. A small rose garden burst in a riot of color on either side of the porch steps. A white door was centered with a brass lion's head knocker and I rapped it too loudly. Then I pulled my shoulders back to correct my posture and waited.

A man of fifty or so answered, wearing a grayish cardigan over a blue button-down shirt and a pair of khakis with a braided leather belt—the kind that are sold together. His teeth were brown at the seams. He wore thick glasses that magnified his eyes owlishly and he squinted at me, shading them from the sun.

"Mr. Beckman?" I asked, and the man pulled me inside, craning his neck to scan the neighborhood as if he was harboring a fugitive.

"Thanks for coming," he said, showing me in. "You know Yolanda Curtis?"

"No sir." I studied the fancy wood paneling and the plush beige shag rug.

"Yolanda's been my maid since before you were born. She said you've been doing some sort of voodoo over in Colored Town."

"No sir," I said, as politely as I could muster. "It ain't voodoo. I ain't exactly sure what it is."

Mr. Beckman led me past the foyer and into the living room. I could taste the stench of cabbage cooking in the next room. "I don't much care what you call it. I've got a condition in my eyes. Called *onchocerciasis*. That's a big fancy word for going blind. Deterioration of the retina. Do you know what a retina is, son?"

"Not really, sir, I ain't no doctor."

"Well, it doesn't make any difference. It's been getting worse for some time. They tell me I got it years ago in Venezuela when I was on sabbatical and never knew. Bitten by a black fly. A damn fly! No cure. My retina is ..."

"Pardon me, sir," I said respectfully. "I don't mean to interrupt, but I don't much need to know the details. Just have a seat and close your eyes, sir."

"Well, alrighty then." Mr. Beckman pulled up a chair from the kitchen table and sat tall with his penny loafers set neatly in front of him.

I placed my hands over the man's eyes and I felt the tremble in my throat, moving down to my gut like a necktie, then up and out through my arms to the hot prickle in my palms and through my fingers, swelling and lengthening. The process was getting quicker, more efficient. And I imagined: *Mr. Beckman is sitting atop a hill, at peace. He is reading. From his eyes: he looks up to a beautiful view, bathed in a golden and pink sky. Breathtaking.* My fingers retracted and the deed was done.

"You can open your eyes now," I said, and the man squinted and blinked. He took off his thick glasses. He blinked again.

"Stand over there, boy," he said, pointing to the stove. I did as I was told. "Hold up some fingers. Don't tell me how many."

I put my hand in the air with three fingers up.

"Three!" said Mr. Beckman. "Do it again."

I held up four fingers.

"Four!" he yelled. "Do it again."

I held up two fingers, then five, then raised my other hand and went through all possible combinations. Mr. Beckman stood and looked at himself in a wall mirror. "I can see. A little bit blurry but I can see. It's real."

I had come to believe it was real as well. Slowly, with each time, I believed a little more. And each time my hands withdrew, their task complete, I grew sad, craving their wholeness. The man turned to me, weeping. "It's like magic, boy. I don't know what you did and I don't know how you did it. But thank you. Thank you. What Yolanda said about you is true." He pulled his wallet from his khaki pocket. "How's two hundred?"

"No, thank you, sir."

"I can go to five."

"No, thank you, sir."

"Well, alrighty then. Yolanda said you wouldn't take money. Follow me."

Mr. Beckman led me down a hallway covered with fancy university degrees and family photos that dated back half a century. We came to a set of double doors. I stopped to get my bearings, my vision slightly blurred. He opened the doors and gestured for me to enter, and when my vision cleared I saw them.

Some stood together by the mantle and others sat on the sofa, and others, still, were huddled at the bay window. Conversations fell to a hush and all eyes were on me as I counted them in my head:...eleven, twelve, thirteen, fourteen. Fourteen. Waiting to be healed. Among them was Scooter Watson, no longer in uniform, which made him appear smaller and more broken than he'd seemed in church. Behind his eyes was a crushing torment forged by a past that could not be undone, and I wanted to feel his pain so that he would not be so lonely with it, and take it away. I would begin with him.

Session 8

"I went through my mother's things," she says as she falls into the couch and begins digging through her bag. "I have several boxes in my garage. Stuff I packed up when my mother went to the home a few years ago. I never looked at what I packed, I just packed."

"What did you find?" I'm expecting her to pull something relevant from her purse but it turns out to be Reese's Peanut Butter Cups. "I'm not sure," she says, and she tears the package with her teeth.

"How do you mean?"

"Evidence, I guess."

"Evidence of what?"

"Evidence that my mother was ... I don't know—a human being," she snickers, imitating a smile.

"How so?"

She slides the cups into her hand and leans forward to offer one, and I decline. "I found pictures and letters. Things I never knew."

"Such as?"

She nibbles around the circumference of the candy like a ritual. "Such as, my mother had two older sisters. At least I think they were her sisters. I never even knew she had siblings. There were photos of her with her family when she was a baby—mother, father, three kids. And then when she was about, I'd say three, suddenly there aren't any more photos of the whole family. Just her and her mother—my grandmother, who I barely knew. She died when I was four."

"What do you think happened?"

"Well, there were papers." She uses her teeth to delicately remove the thin layer of chocolate on the top and bottom of the candy, leaving the peanut butter center. "I felt like a sleuth digging through some mystery of my own past. Papers with my grandmother's name as the only parent. And nothing about the sisters. Or my grandfather. My mother never talked about her father, he was non-existent. I thought he'd died when she was a kid, but I think he left them. I think he took the two older girls and just split." She plunks the final piece of candy into her mouth. "The best part," she says, and lets it sit on her tongue like a lozenge while she repackages the remaining cup and returns it to her purse.

"What gives you the impression he left?"

"I found a letter from him from several years later, asking about my mother. Maybe when he left, taking on a toddler was too much for him, so he left her behind, who knows?" She sucks a spot of chocolate from her thumb.

"Okay, so your mother grew up an only child, raised by her single mother, abandoned by her father and sisters. What do you do with that?"

"I guess I feel sorry for her." Something flashes beneath the surface of her hardened expression, but she quickly recovers. "But I don't want to. I don't want to pardon her."

"Fair enough. What else did you find?" I keep my face neutral, and when she catches my eye, give her a benign smile.

"I think they were really poor. The pictures say as much. I knew she didn't go to college or anything like that, but it looked pretty meager, the house, the clothes."

"And she never talked about her childhood?"

"She never talked about anything. I found out she worked at a toll booth. There were check stubs from nineteen seventy-two and seventy-three, so she was in her early twenties. All I could think of was her sitting in that toll booth with all the fumes and the exhaust day after day. What a horrible job. Can you imagine? And all those people going somewhere and her just sitting there, suffocating, going nowhere."

"How do you feel about that?"

She ignores the question. "And then I found all these poems from my daddy. Really beautiful. I mean kind of corny, but sweet. *You are the sweetest rose* kind of thing."

"Were you surprised?"

"Yes. I mean I'd always figured they must have loved each other at some point. And there were all these pictures of them together, laughing, his arms around her. And she was dressed really stylishly in, like, halter tops and floppy hats. And smoking. I didn't know my mother had ever smoked."

I wish I could go through my own mother's things, and I lament the secrets I will never know. "It sounds like a very different person from the mother you knew."

"Night and day. I remember some of that, her being happy, when I was really little." Her eyes dance around the room. "But definitely not through most of my childhood. Certainly not after my sister died."

"Has this changed how you feel about her in any way?"

She considers a moment of tenderness but shakes it off. "It makes me detest her even more. Why didn't I get the mother who was laughing and smoking in cool clothes? I don't want to feel sorry for her. I don't want to stop hating her."

"Can you do both? Are hate and compassion mutually exclusive?"

"They are for now."

"Completely understandable."

"And I don't want you to try to make me feel better about her." Her jaw works side to side, teeth grinding.

"I'm not. I wouldn't do that."

"It feels like you are. I hate her and I don't want to give that up. Not now, maybe not ever."

I nod to let her know I understand. "Anything else?"

She begins to rattle, amp up. "Why was my sister more important? If that was the turning point, when my sister died, why didn't my mother take care of me even more? I had a loss too. She was my sister, not just her daughter! I mean if her own father took her sisters and left her, and she knew what that was like, then how could she not be there for me? It's like she abandoned me without leaving. Like the idea of a family..." She stops at a bolted door.

"Go on."

Her shoulders fold forward. "It's like the *idea* of a family was the thing she was holding onto. Maybe the family she didn't have growing up, the man she didn't have. And she wasn't going to give that up. It's like what we appeared to be was more important than the reality, no matter what condition it was in."

"Good."

"I have a question, Doc." Her back stiffens and her chin raises in a challenge. "When you say *good* after I've come to some sort of conclusion, it gives me the feeling you know everything and you're just waiting for me to come to it on my own. If that's true then just fucking tell me and get it over with." She arches an eyebrow and her expression locks as straight as a poker player's.

"I don't know everything. I don't know anything. So I don't know what you're going to find. But when you do find it and land on it, then we both know, and I say *good*."

"Try to find another word. It sounds pretentious and superior and … omniscient."

"I'll work on that." *I will.*

"One more thing. I found an empty bottle of Valium. Well, not empty. There was one pill. I don't know why she kept it. It expired in like 1995."

"What do you make of that?"

"Obviously she was anxious or depressed or something. Surprise! She didn't drink so I guess it was her way of … dulling things." She sweeps her hand in the air as if to clear smoke. "It doesn't matter. I'm not here to psychoanalyze my mother. And certainly not to feel sorry for her."

"Why do you think you went through her things?"

"To find out about me not her. If she was doping herself up to deal, it only makes her worse. More selfish. I'm the one who needed the fucking Valium!"

CHAPTER FOURTEEN

Henry pushed the service button for the third time. The staticky voice buzzed through the speaker. "What can I do for you?"

He gave me a wink. Henry always seemed to be winking, as if the world was a private joke between us. "I'd like a cherry limeade please."

"Order one for me too," I said.

Henry shushed me. "Next time."

The voice crackled, "Coming right up."

We sat on our bikes balancing flimsy, overfilled cardboard boxes on the handlebars and our laps at Sonic Drive-In, an Oklahoma staple, which served burgers and fries and shakes and earlier in the year had introduced Pickle-O's— sliced dill pickles battered and deep fried—all delivered by *Service with the Speed of Sound.*

It was unusual for bicycles to park in the diagonal spots meant for cars, but it was Henry's idea. He knew we'd be served by roller-skating carhops wearing short, pleated skirts and cleavage-bearing tops tied in a knot above their exposed midriffs.

"You can't keep orderin' like this," I warned.

"Sure I can! The more we order, the more trips they make. Last time my nose nearly rubbed her titties."

A dyed-blonde, ponytailed teenager rolled from the swinging *out* door and up to us. "One cherry limeade," she said, and offered it on a tray that separated her from Henry. She'd learned to keep her distance by the third delivery. Her cheeks were a constellation of acne covered by heavy pancake makeup a shade too dark, which ended at her jawbone like a mask. But Henry and I weren't looking at her face as she turned and skated away.

"So what do you want next?" said Henry with his finger on the button. "That cherry limeade? If not, I'll ask for extra ketchup."

"What I want is for you to stop pushing the damn button." The challenge of my hands made this entire episode a juggling act.

Henry stuffed his mouth with too much of a burger. "Okay, we'll take a break, but I'm for sure gonna want a shake. Then I might drop my straw and need another one." Henry's mouth was circled in ketchup and I decided not to tell him, hoping it would give the carhop an avenging laugh. "My mama would have a coronary if she knew we'd rode our bikes across the highway," he garbled, his mouth newly stuffed with fried pickles. "She wants me to wrap my knees in ace bandages and stuff `em with toilet paper just to walk down the street."

I shifted on my seat and my fries flew to the pavement. "Shit."

Henry pushed the button and an exasperated, distorted voice said, "May I help you?"

"We need another order of fries. Had a bit of a spill."

The speaker hissed. "You know you're welcome to sit at the tables in the courtyard. It might be easier to eat."

"No thanks. We like it here."

"Suit yourself," she exhaled. "Anything else?"

"That's it—for now." Henry offered me a Pickle-O but I declined. "Hey, does it bother you when I talk about my mom? I mean, you know..."

"No, not one bit. That's the way it is."

"Do you miss her?"

I contemplated while he chewed. "Yeah. I mean there's lots I don't remember. Lily makes me remember, but my mama's been gone a long time, half my life. I think—I think mostly I miss what I imagine it'd be like if she was here now."

Henry slurped his pop and the carhop rolled up with the order of fries. "Here you go," she said, practically throwing them at Henry, but then she snickered when she saw the ring of ketchup and skated off.

I started to speak but Henry raised his hand to shush me. "Hold it," he said. "I don't want you to distract me from the view." The girl rolled into the *in* door, the hem of her short skirt swishing back and forth under her rump cheeks. Henry turned to me. "I think she likes me." He chomped savagely on a handful of fries before handing them over to me. "I wanna see you do it again."

"Do what?"

"You know. The thing you do. Let's pick somebody."

"It ain't a magic trick," I said. "And besides, people come to me, I don't go to them. It don't work that way. Folks have to want it."

"How come?" asked Henry.

"I don't know. Like that lady who sits in front of Judson's with her back all messed up."

"Vinita?"

"That ain't her real name. Anyway, I tried it on her and she's still there."

"What about your daddy? It worked on him and he didn't know it," said Henry.

"That was different. He wanted it bad. He was sleepin' and I think it's all he ever dreams about. I reckon he was dreamin' about it when I touched him."

"You did that," said Henry, pointedly. "You. Did that."

"I might have set his leg right but I didn't have nothin' to do with what's happened to him since. He's like a new man."

Henry pushed the button one last time to close his running tab but made sure to give her a twenty so she'd have to go back in again to get change.

We waited at the curb for a stream of trucks to pass and quickly rode across the highway and into town with such decisive intention that an observer would swear we had a destination in mind, but the destination was the ride itself. Henry's bike was superior to mine in all ways—a new Coppertone Schwinn Panther with whitewall tires and even a headlight, though his mother would never approve of him riding after dusk. I zipped and sped and coasted on my yard-sale Schwinn, still a Schwinn but barely, and stood to take the shock out of the occasional pothole. Henry would be damned if he didn't go pedal-to-pedal and he raced to keep up.

When we reached the Dalton Post Office, we hopped the curb and skidded to a stop, tearing the turf. I let my bike fall to the ground and lay back on the yellow grass and stretched my legs and arms like a snow angel in the wrong season. Henry plopped the kickstand down and fell to his butt, trying to conceal his short-windedness.

"Hey Theo!" It was Missy Johnson. I sat up like a shot at the sound of her voice, then caught myself and rested back on my elbows awkwardly.

"Hey Missy," I said, my voice as high as a girl's, then cleared my throat and switched to the lower octave. "What's shakin'?" *What a stupid thing to say.*

"Mailing stuff for Monica." She always referred to her mother as Monica when not in her presence. "See you later at the house." Missy sashayed to her mother's Mercury and tossed a wink to me before she disappeared into the driver's seat. I trembled.

"You know her?" said Henry, having pitched forward on his knees to a near topple.

"Sure. Missy Johnson. Lives down the street from me."

"What does she mean she'll see you at the house?"

"Her mom watches my sister during the day." I let the moment settle, then—"I seen her naked in the shower."

"No shit!"

"Yes shit."

"Like totally naked?"

"No, she usually showers with her clothes on. What a stupid-ass question."

"What did she look like?"

"Naked. Ain't you ever seen a naked girl before?" I basked in my vast experience.

"Course I have."

"Who?"

Henry paused, then stammered, "My daddy's *Playboys.* And my mama."

"A— that don't count, and B— that's perverted." But I knew I wouldn't mind seeing Henry's mother naked at all. I'd pictured it even. And my cheeks blossomed into a guilty crimson at the thought.

Missy pulled away with the rev of the motor and the gas-brake-gas-brake-gas-brake staccato of a new driver. Her arm shot out from the window for a last wave. Henry sat in awe and I was in no hurry to break the spell.

"Let's go," he finally said, rising to his feet and mounting his bike.

"Where to?"

"To my house to look at my daddy's *Playboys*."

"Oh, come on, Hen! We seen 'em a hundred times."

"Then let's go to your house. Where does your daddy hide his?"

"Nowhere. He ain't got no *Playboys*."

"All dads got *Playboys*. You just gotta know where to look. Under his mattress or in his nightstand or in the garage. They're somewhere for sure. Just like behind my daddy's tool rack."

"I don't know…"

"Well, I do. And the thing is, once you find 'em, they can't move 'em if they know you found 'em, 'cause they don't want to talk about it. Perfect situation."

"…Well, he don't let me go down in the basement."

"Bingo! Let's go. Your daddy's at work, right? Prob'ly got a whole collection. Miss July here we come!" Henry stood on the pedals for a faster launch and I followed. This time it was me who could barely keep up. Incentive was everything.

Mr. Dewey Logan came creeping down the walkway from the post office hunched and bent. I could tell from his burdened step that the downtown stoplight would soon be timed even slower. "Look out!" I yelled, but it was too late. Henry barreled into Dewey, throwing them both to the ground. People on the lawn ran to Dewey but I ran harder, beating the other Samaritans. "Mr. Logan, are you okay?" I lifted him to his feet, bracing his back, pressing, steadying him. I felt my palms open without my consent. I imagined nothing. It was as if they were independent of my arms, my body, my thoughts.

When I released him, the old man resumed his stoop; it was what he knew. But then he stretched a little higher, and his chest inflated and his mouth dropped.

"Are you okay?" I asked.

"I'm okay. I'm better'n okay," he said, confused and elated at once. "Thank you, Theo, I'm fine." He grew taller and it surprised him. "Better'n fine. You tell your Daddy I said *hey*." And Dewey Logan strolled off with an ease that just might shorten the timing of the traffic light and move all of Dalton just a little bit faster.

Henry knew what happened. He pulled himself up and brushed the dirt from his clothes. We walked our bikes to the street and Henry opened his mouth to speak but changed his mind.

"Put everything back exactly like it was," I warned. The basement was dank and sour. Bottoms of cardboard boxes were water stained in squiggly dark lines from when the hard rains had seeped in two springs ago. A single light bulb hung from a splintery header and the cord snaked between nails to an exposed outlet. The light hid behind things, sneaking around edges and through crevices, and magnified shadows marked the cement walls like puzzle pieces. We might have been anthropologists in the bowels of an Egyptian tomb.

Henry shuffled through the drawers of the workbench: manuals of ancient appliances, yellowed receipts, inkless pens, keys with no locks and locks with no keys—the clutter that no one throws out and an excellent hiding place for the treasure we sought.

I flipped through books of my father's stamp collection: 50 State Flag, Susan B. Anthony, George Eastman, Oklahoma Statehood, and a hundred others. Nothing after 1962. I dusted off the paper labels peeling at the edges on canning jars lining narrow wooden shelves. It was my mother's hand—a round, bowed cursive that tilted to the right like it was heading somewhere: Strawberry Preserves 6-4-61. Sweet Pickles 8-2-61. Peaches 4-7-60. Blackberry Jam 11-4-59. All long expired of course.

Henry pushed a rickety drawer shut and wiped his blackened hands on his shirt. "You ain't helpin'. There ain't no magazines in a jar of pickles."

I carefully opened an unsealed box. It was my mother's wedding dress, wrapped in tissue paper, that I'd seen my father holding the day I'd found him on the floor. I pushed it to the side and dug blindly below to find a soft tickling fabric which turned out to be a pink cashmere sweater that I wanted to remember but couldn't. I held it to my cheek and took in the smell. Musty, nothing. Suddenly, I felt intrusive, as if rummaging through a stranger's property. I folded the sweater and placed it beneath the wedding dress, careful to wrap the tissue paper around it just so.

Henry ran his fingers behind the workbench. "Aha!" he yelled, grasping a dusty manila envelope and raising it in the air like a trophy. He flipped it open and pulled out the contents—a *Popular Mechanics* magazine from 1959 with a cover illustration of a man in an overcoat pushing a helicopter into his garage. A clipping fell out. Then another. And another. I picked them up as quickly as they wafted to the floor: travel articles for Miami Beach, San Diego, even one featuring the paradise of Acapulco. TWA brochures and scraps of notes in my father's choppy scrawl with airfares and schedules and hotels. Surprise vacations never taken.

"Damn it!" said Henry.

I carefully collected the clippings and placed them back in the magazine, into the envelope, and gently behind the workbench where they belonged. "Let's get out of here."

"No way! We're on a mission." Henry canvassed the room and targeted a small trunk on a reachable shelf that was just about the perfect size for the goods. "Dads can be crafty. Gotta look in places where magazines can fit but they don't show. I reckon we're about to hit a goldmine."

He pushed the brass buttons on the front of the case and the latches snapped open. I stood over him, more and more sure that my father would notice the smallest thing out of place and there would be hell to pay. Henry recklessly pulled out papers and more papers, practically tossing them to the side while I stacked them, trying to keep up. Beneath the pages were several dozen photographs with the dates printed on the scalloped borders—black and whites of my mother and Aunty Li as girls, and the grandparents I never knew. Christmases and birthdays. A formal sweetheart dance—my mother with the boy who would become my father, standing hand in hand with their eyes sparkling in that somewhere place between first love and first lovers. I stared at it, microscopically, trying to memorize every nuance of her face: her delicate nose, the arch of her brow, the shape of her wistful smile which quirked up on one side. I wished I could see the color of her eyes in the black and white photo. I couldn't remember and it frightened me. Her image had been fading in my mind more and more and I wanted to cement it before it was gone forever. I pocketed the photo, but then a wave of panic struck me and I put it back.

Beneath the pictures were folded letters bundled and tied in soft pink silk ribbons. Henry pulled at a bow. "Don't touch those," I said, and I seized them and held them to my chest. It was my mother's trunk, her keepsakes and most private memories, and they were not to be raked through in some sort of careless frenzy in Henry's presence, or anyone's—but I knew I would be back. "There ain't no dirty magazines in there. I wanna go."

"Wait a minute." Henry had emptied the trunk of its contents and found a small black ribbon connected to the bottom of the box. He pulled at it, lifting a panel from a false bottom. It was filled with pages of yellowed and brown speckled parchment, handwritten in the same style as the print I'd once seen on the banner of the *New York Times*—all fancy and proper.

Last Will and Testament
On this 2ⁿᵈ day of March, in the year 1918, I, Jebediah G.
Dalton, being of sound mind and body...

It was the document that had damned my father and his father before him, leaving the vast Dalton fortune to the maintenance of his various philanthropic endeavors which were listed in full: the orphan's home, the widow's colony, the hospital, the library, the sanitarium, the school for the deaf. *Seven million dollars!* The will went on to bequeath the house on Garfield Street and its contents to his wife, Dolly, along with a stipend of five-thousand dollars for each of his three children to be used explicitly for higher educational purposes.

I had never mourned the loss of what could have been in the way my father had. Perhaps it was because I was two generations away from the immediate impact and that I'd never even remotely touched the bounty of my would-be life but for the out of place antiques which filled our house. But as I held the brittle pages in my hands, I felt for the first time the coldness of a man who must have believed he would leave a more lasting footprint in brick and mortar than in flesh and blood.

I wondered why the final heartless wishes of my great grandfather were hidden among the sentimental belongings of my mother. Perhaps to keep the record but shield it from my father? I straightened the pages and placed them in the bottom of the trunk, but just as I was about to level the secret panel into position, I saw the smallest corner of a page peeking through the edge of yet another thin panel. I was afraid to pull at it, should it tear.

"Get me a screwdriver," I demanded.

Henry snatched the tool from the workbench and I carefully pried up the black velveteen plank to find another document of the same size, the same frangible parchment, with the same lettering and the same date. I read it aloud:

"*Addendum. I bequeath the sum of two million dollars and the plot of land known as Dalton Ridge to Mrs. Hazel Mae White, (currently residing at 407 Washington Street) with the provision that she never remarry and that she bestow all monies, properties and other assets to her adopted son, Charles J. White, when he reaches eighteen years of age. After said estate is relinquished to Master White, Mrs. White shall be provided the allowance in the amount of five-thousand dollars per month for the length of her life. Should Mrs. White expire before her adopted son's eighteenth birthday, all elements of the estate mentioned herein shall be placed into a trust in the name of Charles J. White, allocated at the discretion of Jacob Shay, Esq. until such time as Master White is of age.*"

I knew that my great-grandfather had died a week after Armistice Day, only eight months after this will had been signed. I knew of Dalton Ridge and the mansion that sat on the only hill in all of Dalton—the place from which to look down on everyone else. And though I'd never heard tell of anything about a Mrs. Hazel Mae White or her adopted son,

Charles, I knew who lived in the mansion sitting on top of that hill now.

"Shit. I'm related to Toby White."

"What the hell are you talking about?" Henry was beginning to grow bored with the relics of the Daltons and was ready to give up his search.

"Don't you get it? Jebediah didn't leave any money to my family because he was leavin' the money to his other family. His secret family. This Mrs. Hazel Mae White. Washington Street is in the Widow's Colony so she was a widow. Her husband was prob'ly killed in the war."

"How the hell do you think that makes you related to Toby?"

"Listen, it says the money goes to the adopted son. Why would a single widow adopt a son? I'm thinkin' this kid, this Charles, was my great-granddaddy's son."

"I'm thinkin' you're jumpin' to a lot of conclusions," said Henry, wiping his filthy hands on his pants.

"Come on, do the math. It says she can't remarry or she don't get no money. And all the money goes to the kid."

Henry froze. "And Toby *White* lives in that big old house on Dalton Ridge."

"Exactly!"

And good ol' Jeb was makin' sure they was taken care of."

"Two million bucks worth."

This was getting exciting. Henry began pacing. "Okay, let's say you're right. How come your daddy ain't never said nothin'?"

"I betcha two million bucks my daddy don't know. My mama knew and that's why it's hid."

"Somebody in your daddy's family had to know. I mean it's a legal will. Jeb's wife had to know."

"Even if she did, what was she gonna say?—`My husband's been havin' an affair with one of his widows and he's leavin' his money to his bastard son?' I mean he was the founder of the town. I bet she had to keep her mouth shut instead of fightin' for the money and makin' a big scandal."

I wished that my mother was with me right then. Not in a sad or even tender way. I wanted to know everything she knew, the gossip, the hearsay, the backstabbing, the betrayal and all the dirty laundry that tied it together. "I bet my mama prob'ly found this stuff in some old pile of papers and hid it away where my daddy wouldn't never see it."

"Why would she keep it if she didn't want him to see it?"

"I don't know. How come they got a drawer full of keys that don't fit nothin' but they don't throw `em away `cause someday they might open somethin'? She prob'ly hadn't decided what to do. It ain't like she knew she was gonna die so young."

"You gonna tell him? You gonna tell your daddy?"

"Are you nuts?" I laughed. "He might go up there to the White mansion and tell `em what's his and burn the place down if he don't get it…"

"I'd like to see that, actually. I'd like to see that asshole's face when his house is goin' up in flames."

"My daddy told me about him and my mama goin' up to the White mansion just this one time for a fancy party—and how she told him she didn't like it at all."

"She was tellin' him that because she knew."

"I think so. They was standin' right in the middle of what shoulda been my daddy's and she wanted him to know that she didn't care one iota about such things. And she didn't want him to keep wishin' for somethin' he wouldn't have and she didn't need."

I wondered if Aunty Li knew. I wondered if Toby knew. Not likely.

"So wait a minute," burst Henry. "If you're right, and Toby White's grandfather was your great grandfather's kid ... that makes him your, what, half-asshole twice removed? Ha! I think your almost-half-brother got the bad half and you got the good half. Cain and Abel!"

Slam!

"Shit!"

"Shhh!"

My eyes followed my father's steady gait above us as it made its way from the front door and across the creaking floorboards. The thwack of a kitchen cabinet and the shriek of chair legs scuffing from under the table finally ended in silence.

"I thought you said your daddy was at work," whispered Henry.

"He's supposed to be."

"What are we gonna do?"

I tried to think fast but everything seemed slow. "We're gonna have to wait 'til he goes up to his room or somethin'." First things first. I carefully repacked my mother's trunk and lifted it back onto the shelf in the exact same position, dictated by its dusty outline. Then I clutched the dangling pull chain on the light bulb and switched us into darkness but for the border of light seeping around the doorframe at the top of the stairs. Henry pulled the chain again and the light bulb swung.

"I gotta pee," he whispered with too much urgency.

"What? Now? You're gonna have to hold it."

I jerked the chain back down and off again. Henry fumbled for it in the dark and snapped it back on.

"I can't. I gotta go. Emergency pee." Henry searched the room and stumbled toward a corner.

"No way!" I yelled in a whisper. "You ain't gonna take a piss in my basement!"

Henry dug through the trash bin next to the workbench and found an empty Dr. Pepper can, but it slipped from his fingers and clanked on the cement floor.

"Theo?!" called my father from upstairs.

I dove for the pull chain and stifled the light. Silence. Not even the sound of breathing. And then the unmistakable ratchet of unzipping pants. "Don't you dare!" I threatened. The machine gun clatter of liquid hitting metal was Henry's response. I feared the sound would give us away. It went on and on and on, the racket rising up and up in pitch as the can filled, rippling, surging, higher, brimming. "Ahhhhh," exhaled Henry. And zip.

"Fuck you, Henry Hardy."

There was no sound from above us. I'd last heard my father in the kitchen and it was a safe bet he was still there. Henry and I crept slowly up the stairs, allowing our weight to settle on each step to avoid creaking, until we reached the top. I opened the door a crack, then another, then peered out and around and motioned for Henry to follow me quickly to the front door, which I opened softly and shut with a slam. I let out an over-exaggerated laugh as I made my way to the kitchen with Henry in tow. "You're kidding! That's the funniest thing I ever heard!" My father was hunched over the kitchen table. "Hey, Daddy, whatcha doin' home so early? This is my friend, Henry."

Manners dictated that Henry shake hands, but the smell of canned urine might incite suspicion, so he parked himself casually in the doorway, crossing one foot over the other, holding the pee-filled Dr. Pepper can as if enjoying a refreshing drink. "Hey, Mr. Dalton, it's nice to ..."

"I thought I told you to stay outside in the day," growled my father, "instead of sittin' home foldin' clothes and dustin' and sweepin' like you was some housewife."

"Hen and I just came by to get a Popsicle. You okay?"

He raised his head up from the table. An empty glass sat between his hands next to a bottle of Wild Turkey. "Do I look okay to you, boy?"

"Your leg still good, Daddy?" I said with trepidation, afraid it hadn't stuck.

"Oh, my leg's still good all right. So good Ray's tellin' me he wants me to work overtime for six months to pay back what I owe him now that I ain't lame. I told him 'I don't owe you nothin'.' And he's tellin' me he's been keeping me on all these years 'cause he felt sorry for me, but I ain't been pulling my load." He poured himself a finger. Two fingers. "Said Grady and Boyd been bearin' the brunt of the work and it's time for payback." He threw the glass back and poured another. Henry slunk out of the kitchen.

"Well, don't overtime mean more money?" I said, desperately optimistic.

"You deaf, boy? He said it's a payback! Said if I'm gonna keep my job I gotta work extra hours for no extra pay, 'least I can do,' he tells me. And what am I gonna do, quit? I got you and your sister to raise. Wantin' me to buy this and that and wantin' to go here and there and I'm underwater as it is."

"We get along fine, Daddy."

"'George Dalton can't get ahead in the town his grandfather built,' he said, mockingly. "That's what they say, you know. This name's a curse, I tell you. Nothin' good happens for me here. And now it just got worse than it ever was. Go on boy, get out!"

I slipped out of the kitchen and into the living room where Henry was standing at the front door. "I'll see you later," he said. "I'm sorry."

CHAPTER FIFTEEN

When I arrived at Frank's trailer my cheeks were still wet. He was scrubbing spray-painted letters off the side of his trailer with a steel brush and a pail of soapy water. The remaining letters read:

SOLDIER KI

"Hey kiddo, how's your day?" said Frank as he leaned into the letter *I*.

"Same as yours."

"Aw, this ain't nothin'. Had my house burned down a few years back," he said with a rough chuckle. "I don't scare off easy." I couldn't picture Frank living anywhere but in his trailer. "Hey son, grab a brush and gimme a hand."

I joined in. "My daddy's leg gettin' healed don't seem to make no difference."

Frank wiped the sweat from his brow and removed his shirt. His skin was brown and smooth but for an angry pink scar pulled across his belly like a sunken snake. "People don't change overnight," he said. "Gotta give him a chance. Wanna tell me about it?"

"I can just tell he ain't really changed. I just know."

"I'm sorry, son. Tough stuff. The thing is, you did your part. What happens after that ain't none of your business. Action without the hitch, remember?" Frank filled the pail with fresh water from a pipe and spigot that shot up from the ground and threw in a handful of Borax. "It's a two-way street—they gotta want to be healed. And sometimes the part that really needs the healin' ain't got so much to do with what a person *thinks* needs healin'. You can't do nothin' about that. People gotta participate. That bird wanted to fly. It didn't just lay there in its misery. It flew."

"What about the baby?"

"The baby knew," said Frank. "Babies know everything."

"And Mr. Brown?"

"You give him the start. You took off the outside damage. What he does with the inside is up to him."

"So, my daddy didn't really want to be healed?"

Frank climbed on a step stool to get at the top of the K. His arrowhead necklace was glued to his chest with perspiration. "Men want things to be fixed," he said. "They want to tie it all up to make sense. Like the cars your daddy repairs. It's broke, you fix it, and that's that." Frank wiped his brow with the heel of his hand. "But we can't fix everything. We can't fix the past. Your Daddy can't fix his life or your life and I betcha he hates himself for it. Everything that's happened and even before he was born. And that hate can be stronger than the healin'." He reached out to me. "Hand me that bucket."

I lifted the pail and sat on the cinderblock step. "My daddy thinks he was responsible. He blames himself. He thinks he killed my mama. But it was an accident."

Frank climbed down and sat next to me. "Two people can have very similar things happen in their lives and one decides they're a victim and one gets more...what's the word? Sympathetic? Empathetic. Empathetic to folks—to the world. Folks get to choose."

"But things that happen make us who we are."

"No, son. Things that happen don't make us who we are unless we let `em." He leaned into me and his face grew soft. "Or, they can show us who we can be."

Frank stood and scrubbed at the remaining word, *SOLDIER.* I scrubbed at his side and then turned to face him. "I bet I can heal your scar."

"No thank you."

SESSION 9

Our last session had left me so very sad, sad but deter-mined, and I've thought about her constantly.

In the ten-minute break I have between clients, knowing she is next, my mind is consumed with the violence, both physical and emotional, that has befallen her. Her gentle soul smashed against the face of it. Some of us carry our scars on the outside, like me, but there are many more of us carrying our scars on the inside. Like me. And we look on, powerless, except to give whatever compassion we have to spare, even as we try to heal our own wounds.

But this is my expertise, the very reason I have a career, so why am I so jolted? Why am I still shocked that the peo-ple we know— our mothers and fathers, our neighbors and friends, our wives and husbands and lovers, all have the capacity for violence, both physical and emotional, as well as the capacity to be violated? I pass strangers on the street and I'm both suspicious and compassionate. Which are the violent and which are the violated?

I am more acutely aware than ever of how impotent I am to confront this disease of body and soul, especially when it is cloaked as love or God or righteousness. Can I save her from her scars? Can I even begin to tell where the scar tis-sue ends for the healing to begin? The healing. The bless-ing and curse of it.

But it's also the first time in so very long that I feel I'm doing something valuable and making a difference. More than spouting questions meant to lead to examination and revelation; more than the babble I pass off as sage advice hour after hour, day after day. Now, I feel an urgent desperation to do something I promised myself I would never let happen—to make a personal connection in order to find some sign of life inside of me that I can't even locate. To find the safe place I once knew with Frank and with Henry, or with Lily, when I dared to reveal myself fully.

I realize that I've become obsessed with this woman. Or rather, her issues. She has reinvigorated me. Or rather, her issues have reinvigorated me. *Right?* It weighs on my conscience that I feel good about myself at the expense of her tragedy.

I think of my father. Her father. How you can love a parent in spite of them. As I delve into my own history, I know that it doesn't compare to hers. But I know that everything is in relationship to our own experience.

I recall a patient early in my career whose parents had both survived Auschwitz. He was very successful, the CEO of a major corporation, at the top of his game. But he never felt a sense of any real achievement. His not having endured any crisis that could remotely compare to his parents' left him with such guilt that no matter what he did, no matter what he accomplished, it could never be enough. Though his parents never actually said those words to him, there was a tacit, pervasive attitude that his obstacles were nothing. Nothing, at least, that he shouldn't be able to shake off without much effort. How could they be anything but?

I told him that just because his life had not put him in the situation of surviving the worst kind of horror didn't mean he wouldn't have summoned the same strength as his parents, had he been in the same circumstance. But that was *not* his circumstance. And his issues were not trivial simply because they didn't overtly compare to others. There is always someone worse off. Always someone who has suffered more. And that doesn't reduce our own suffering to inconsequential. Otherwise there would be no depression, no suicide, and everyone not subjected to the most dire tragedies would be happy. It's what people do with their circumstances. That is up to them. Up to her. Up to me. *Physician heal thyself.*

That's what I tell myself, but I know it's bullshit. The truth is I don't know that I would have the same strength that she did in the same circumstances. I barely survived my own.

The inevitable knock at the door comes and I pull myself up to a position of some semblance of confidence. "Come in."

She enters my office in a flurry. She's wearing a festive blouse, green and red and purple, with a tiny bow at the V-neckline. She lifts her sunglasses to the top of her head to hold her hair back and is barely in the door when she says, "So, this guy tells his buddy, `I've been making a lot of Freudian slips lately.' And his buddy says, `Yeah? Like what?' And the guy says, `Well, last week I called American Airlines and asked for two pickets to Tittsburgh.' And the buddy says, 'I did something similar the other day. My wife and I were having dinner, and instead of saying, 'Honey, please pass the salt,' I said, 'You ruined my life, you evil bitch!'"

She waits for my laugh and I summon a chuckle and an eye roll, then she smooths her skirt beneath her and sits at the other end of the sofa away from her regular spot. It places her several feet further from me. "What's up, Doc?!"

"Oh, just making a few new ink blots and thinking about déjà vu. But then I realize I'd already thought about it." Anxiety lies behind my ambitious smile. "How are you? Besides being the bearer of old bad shrink jokes?"

"Fan-fucking-tastic! It's beautiful outside! It's crazy isn't it, Doc? It feels so good to feel—good! I think the last time I was here was a real breakthrough."

"Good." *Shit, I said the word.*

I went to a movie. I found an empty section and spread out with my sweater and my purse so that no one could sit next to me and I had popcorn and candy and a soda that was large enough to bathe a small child. For five bucks it *should* be large enough to be bathe a small child!"

"That's great." *Better.*

"I went to the farmer's market in my neighborhood. It's really wonderful, I'd never been. All the fresh vegetables and fruit, blueberries and strawberries. I got two bunches of lilies and an empanada and I sat on the grass in the sun and it was pretty glorious."

"Did you have any issues being near people?"

"Sure, I mean I was in a public place. But I was careful to stay clear. There were a couple of close calls but it was worth it."

"I'm happy for you. I hope you can take in how far you've come. These are not the words of the woman I met not so long ago." I am proud of her, and myself.

"Goat cheese! They have the most delicious goat cheese. Garlic and rosemary." Her thoughts flitter, her eyes alive as an electric current, but then a brief hiccup in her delivery that tells me not to quite trust her.

"Sounds like something I would love."

"I should have brought you some." She clasps and unclasps her hands as if slowly applauding herself. "I haven't felt this good in a really really long time. And I have you to thank for it. I feel really … clear. About everything."

"You've been making a lot of progress. I know it isn't easy."

"The truth is I've accepted what happened. And I know it wasn't my fault. I really do know that," she states assuredly, as if saying *I rest my case.*

I want to believe that this euphoric breakthrough is more than a manic episode. I've seen it happen this way before, but rarely. The path to freedom is more often paved with broken glass. But all I can do at this juncture is believe her. She has trusted me and I must trust her, and I feel – dare I say it? – satisfied with myself. *Well done, Dalton.* "You've made some very big steps. So what's going on? How's your head in all of this?"

For the next twenty minutes she talks about how she's seeing the world differently. How she's happy for the first time in years. Shopping in Silverlake, buying new shoes, simple joys. Then finally, "Enough about me, I want to talk about you." She leans forward and folds her arms on her lap.

"What?" I'm not sure where this is going.

"And you don't have to pay me a damn dime," she laughs.

I laugh with her. "Your session, not mine."

"Oh, come on, Doc. You know everything about me and I know nothing about you. How am I supposed to keep spilling my guts to a stranger?"

"What do you want to know?" I'm skating on thin ice. Everything in me knows better. But it had worked that time before—being honest about myself, so I decide to tell a little, just a little, thinking it might get her to the next level of her own honesty. This is a person who doesn't have friends, anyone, really, to talk to. Except me. *I will remain in control.*

"First question. And this is really personal, so get ready."

I already regret this decision. "Okay."

"How can you work in this trash heap?" She throws her arms in the air and bursts out laughing. "I mean what gives? You're supposed to have it together, Doc, or at least appear to. Jesus Christ, hire a freaking cleaning service already!"

I don't find it funny but I find her funny and I wonder how that can be. "It's a good question," I say, and settle into myself and sigh and I realize I sound just like her. "Well, it didn't happen all at once. I used to be more fastidious about things like that. But as I've gotten older I realize that maybe I don't give a rat's ass. About how I appear, about what people think of me." *I think of Frank and his disheveled trailer. And how he didn't give a shit what anyone thought.* "My work is my calling card, not how I decorate."

She peers at me, resolutely unimpressed. When she looks at me this way, it's as if she knows what I'm thinking. "There's a difference between interior design and flat out dump," she says.

Why am I explaining myself? I pull back. "Moving on. Let's get back to you."

"Not a chance. You promised."

I did indeed.

"Why didn't you ever marry?"

Really? "I came close a couple of times, but it didn't work out. If I'm being honest, I suppose I've had some intimacy issues myself." *What the fuck? Why am I doing this?! Who is the therapist and who is the patient?* I reel myself in and get back to business. "I'm only sharing this to let you know that I relate to you on a personal level and not just a clinical one."

"You're afraid to be touched? Like me?"

"No."

"You're afraid to touch other people. Your hands. You have issues with your hands."

"It's not like it sounds. It's complicated."

"I'd say you still have intimacy issues, Doc. You're a regular bundle of nerves, trying to be in control behind your iPad whatever that thing is, when it's clear you're not. I mean look at this place!"

I will restrain myself. I glance at the clock. "Our time is up for today."

"How convenient. Just when we were getting somewhere ..." She smiles slyly.

After she leaves I immediately regret what I've done. What a disaster. Rule number one: stay neutral. Be the safe place, share but don't get too personal. She is not my friend. She is *not* my friend. But I'm the only one she talks to about anything. I'm it! I thought she needed balance; a way to get her to the next place by offering something personal about myself. But she twisted it with her cool, offhanded superiority. Who does she think she is, diagnosing me?

I've always been able to step back and analyze the situations of my life—remove myself from myself. It's a tool that has made me a good therapist but has kept from me from myself as well, because I know deep down it's merely intellectual. The truth is I don't talk to anyone either, about anything. I contemplate when I began to isolate. When I stopped touching or allowing myself to be touched—not physically like her, but rather, compatibly, passionately, with anyone. I'm angry with this woman for cracking the door, and I'm angry with myself for allowing it. I am not her. We have nothing in common. She is not my friend. She is *not* my friend.

Chapter Sixteen

Late as usual, Aunty Li walked as fast as her lavender silver-buckled pumps could carry her. Lily trailed far behind and I stayed with her. Lily suddenly stopped and bent to the sidewalk. "Find a penny, pick it up. All the day you'll have good luck," she said, and attempted a wink that came out as a lopsided blink.

"Hurry up, Little Missy," hollered Aunty Li. "You are slower than molasses goin' uphill in January."

"I'm tryin' Aunty Li," said Lily, breathlessly. "My legs are shorter than yours."

"If excuses were gooses…"

Lily and I mouthed the rest of her familiar argot, *"we'd all have a happy Thanksgiving."*

"What's the rush, Aunty Li?" I called out, dragging my sister to keep up. "We been late before. Pretty much every Sunday."

"Today is different!" she said, and kicked into a faster gear. "I reckon that's why there's no parking!"

Vinita sat on the sidewalk in front of Judson's Drugs, same as always. "Any change?" The only change was that she had acquired a ratty fox stole, the kind with the head that clasps to the tail, its dead, black eyes shining, and she stroked it as if it was her pet. Lily stopped and reached out to the woman, handing her the penny.

Aunty Li slapped Lily's wrist. "Don't touch!" She popped Lily on the bottom to scoot her along. "Word is somethin' big's gonna happen in church this mornin'," she quipped. "Darlene Riddle said Pastor Flynn was mad as a mule chewing on bumblebees but didn't tell her what for. My guess—he's gonna call out Deacon Baker for takin' a nip or five before the second morning service. Everybody knows, why you can smell it on his breath from the second pew. I told Clayton Doyle he better not light a cigarette around him or we all might be blown to smithereens." Her shoes tiptapped with fervent anticipation. "You watch, Theo, Pastor Flynn's gonna deliver a sermon from Galatians. It's one of my favorites." Aunty Li pointed her finger in the air. "Envy, drunkenness and orgies! `Those who do these things will not inherit the Kingdom of God.' And he's gonna stare down Deacon Baker the whole time. Make the hair crawl right off his head. He won't say it outright, but he'll shame him into repentance."

When we finally arrived at the church entrance, Aunty Li smoothed her dress, straightened her hat and steadied her breath. I took Lily's hand as we entered. The service had just begun, and the choir lifted their voices:

Blessed assurance, Jesus is mine!
Oh, what a foretaste of glory divine!
Heir of salvation, purchase of God,
Born of His Spirit, washed in His blood.

As we walked down the aisle to our second-row pew, Aunty Li sang out in her fullest voice and widest vibrato. If she couldn't sing professionally, she would sing for the Lord. I noticed that all eyes seemed to be on us. On me. There were whispers, nods, arched eyebrows. We took our seats just as the hymn ended, and I was, once again, in my surroundings, but not of them.

Pastor Flynn motioned for the choir to be seated. He stood behind the pulpit to face his congregation. "Welcome brethren and sistren. Please open your Bibles to Matthew 7:15... I'll wait..." He pinched the bridge of his nose as if he had a migraine. "'Beware of false prophets, which come to you in sheep's clothing, but inwardly they are ravening wolves.'" He gently closed his Bible and lowered his head, letting the silence linger. Then he swept the congregation with his unyielding eyes, the power of his gaze remarkable. "I'll get right down to it," he said with a long exhale. "It has come to my attention, to the attention of this church, and to the attention of God Himself, that we have such a false prophet amongst us. A wolf in sheep's clothing. The clothing of youth. Of innocence. Professing to heal the sick and the lame. Professing to be the hand of God."

I shifted in my seat. Pastor Flynn stepped out from behind the pulpit and paced the altar, head down, hands clasped behind his back. "Some of you good people have welcomed this boy into your homes. You have opened your souls to him. But this child is no prophet, he is no healer. And he is no longer innocent. For one who claims the gift of divine inspiration is surely using his gift for evil ends."

Pastor Flynn let the moment mount so that the only sound was the rustle of crinolines shifting in seats. I sat rigid, my shoulders stiff and even as a hanger, and I could feel cruel, hard stares piercing my back. The minister continued. "But this child is not completely to blame. He has turned against God at the hand of Satan in the form of flesh, a human being so cunning, so vile, that he draws life by preying on the naïve. If Satan disguises himself as an angel of light to deceive the people, it is not strange if his followers also disguise themselves as servants of righteousness!" He paused, running his fingers through his hair. "My brothers and sisters, there is no greater glory for Satan than claiming the soul of the young." He took a sip of water and cleared his throat. "This boy has been consorting with a murderer. The convicted murderer of an American war hero! And then straight out of prison, this man decides he's a pacifist, marching with the communist agitators. God was agitated! God was angry! But even the Lord's holy fire could not drive this evil from our midst." The preacher's rage curdled the air as he continued. "He remained, crouching like a leopard, waiting for the innocent to fall into his lair."

Aunty Li was riveted, palpitating with the thrill of the hunt, oblivious to the tension and the hiss of sibilant whispers surrounding us. I could feel contempt laying on my skin like a poison. I turned my head and saw for myself what I already knew to be true: I was the target of every eye. Panic rose from my stomach, up through my chest and neck, ending at the clench of my jaw.

Pastor Flynn lifted his Bible in the air, then slammed it on the pulpit and pointed, straight-armed. At me. Lily gasped and Aunty Li looked around to find the destination of his wrath and finally realized it was her own nephew. I stood and faced the preacher. A stillness infected the air as sure as a virus. Aunty Li gawked at me, befuddled, with unblinking eyes. But when I reached out to her, she knew enough not to take my hand. I made my way out of the pew, squeezing past people who pulled their legs tightly against the bench so as not to brush against me. "Theo!" called Lily, but I did not look back.

Pastor Flynn was not finished. "'And the devil that deceiveth them was cast into the lake of fire and brimstone, and shall be tormented day and night forever and ever.'"

I trod up the aisle slowly, precisely, my heart pounding, surrounded by gnashed teeth and sneers, determined not to let myself run. A little girl reached out to me as I passed, and her mother yanked her back. "Don't touch!"

"This church will not abide false prophets!" admonished Pastor Flynn.

"Amen!!" cried a voice from the back.

Pastor Flynn reveled in the drama. This, it seemed, was his greatest role. His Lear, his Vanya, his Willy Loman. But, unlike these tragic figures, he was determined to triumph over his co-player, Satan, or me, it seemed—making him deserved of the final bow at the curtain call.

I passed Mr. Beckman, the nearly blind man, who pretended not to see me. I passed so many of those who'd been at his house only days ago. Which one had betrayed me: the woman who'd been cured of palsy? The man who could now walk? The woman who'd recovered from emphysema? She looked at me with compassion and her eyes pleaded for my forgiveness, but she would not risk revealing herself. There was Scooter Watson. His face was softer, smoother, less burdened, and I knew that the scars he wore on the inside were softer too. He tried to stand but his mother gently pulled him back to his seat. "Shhh, now," I heard her whisper. I wished Mr. Elijah and Kevin Brown, and Mr. and Mrs. Lewis were there, but they would not have been welcome.

"This church will not abide sorcery!" bellowed Pastor Flynn. Then I heard him begin to whimper behind me, tragically, slowly at first, as if he was desperately attempting to contain the pain inflicted upon his pure soul, grieving for my lost one. Like compassion. Like pity. Like the father who says, "this hurts me more than it does you."

"Amen!!"

I felt strangled by scorn. Halfway up the aisle I reached the pew where Henry sat with his mother and I dared to flash my eyes to him for strength. And he stood. And he held his palm high to show me the scabby *X* of our covenant. To the gasping revulsion of the crowd, Henry made his way out of the pew and followed me, keeping his distance, keeping in my step.

Pastor Flynn's voice then rose to an angry cry, piercing the back of my neck, pulling the spotlight back to him, if only for a moment, and I was grateful for the distraction. "This church will not abide the wicked ways of the lost!"

"We will not! Amen!" The numbers were growing.

Toby White sat with his arm around his girlfriend. He lowered his eyelids to a piercing glare and let the cut of his lips curl into a smirk. Face after face was a glossary of silent speak, a few kind, more not. I passed Miss Monica, whose expression was stalwart, giving me courage, and Missy, who leaned forward as if to stand, but was glued to her pew against her will. "I'm sorry," she mouthed.

"We shall cast him out," Pastor Flynn wailed, "and with him the scourge that has blighted this church and the very name of God." He inhaled, sucking in all the air surrounding him and roared, "Demon, I condemn you!"

"Get out!" blared a congregant's voice, and the words were repeated in a dissonant noise.

Henry was my friend. And I could feel him walking solemnly behind me, the depth of his fidelity in full measure. There were only a few more pews to pass. I chanted in my mind and nearly aloud: *Keep going, Theo, you're almost there. Keep going, Theo, you're almost there. Keep going...*

When I reached the last pew, a woman on the aisle stood and grabbed my arm. At first I thought it was in reassurance, but her eyes were hard and cold as blue marbles, her hand like ice. She lifted her chin and spit in my face. I wiped my cheek with my shirtsleeve and opened the double doors leading to the glassed-in foyer. I would not succumb to the pull of my beating heart, begging me to run. I willed myself a solemn mask and a stealthy clip until I was far away and long out of view.

CHAPTER SEVENTEEN

I inhaled in jagged hiccups, not caring that my face was wet with tears and snot. "And he stared me down like I was some kind of devil!"

Frank laughed tenderly. "Most preachers I come across in my lifetime seem to know a lot more about the devil's business than they do about God's."

Anger and remorse pulsed through the current of my veins. "A lady spit in my face. She spit in my face!" I said, my voice breaking. "I can't do this no more. It's wrong."

"How is it wrong?" said Frank, evenly, sitting back in his Lay-Z-Boy, sipping his Coors.

"If this many people are angry, then it has to be wrong. And what he said about you!"

Frank leaned forward and placed a comforting hand on my shoulder. "Aw, I don't much care what he said about me. People been talkin' about me for years."

"But that's when it got me. Maybe this is wrong for me but they don't even know you. They said you contaminated me. They don't even know you!"

"But you do."

"I can't think," I said, more to myself than Frank. "I'm just so confused. I don't know what this thing is. I don't know what's me and what ain't. I don't know if it's God. I don't even know if there is a god."

"Sounds like you do. And you think you're it."

I pulled away, enraged. "What? No, I don't."

"Okay. So what do you believe?"

My mind was a-clutter. Too many thoughts too fast, too large. I shook my head, searching. "In somethin', I guess. But not the somethin' they talk about. Not somethin' angry. Not somethin' to be afraid of." I began to find my breath. "Somethin' big, but quiet."

"Somethin' bigger'n you?" Frank asked gently.

"Uh huh."

"Good," he said. "Because a gift is a thing that's given to you. And if it's just you all by yourself, it means you're responsible for what happens after. That's a lot of pressure, son. More than a person can handle. It means you can fail. Fail a person. Fail your daddy. Fail yourself. You know what I'm gettin' at?"

I wiped away my tears and settled. "I'm not sure."

Frank pulled at the arrowhead dangling from his neck and rubbed it with his forefinger and thumb as if polishing it. "Okay now. Think of it like you was the wire that goes from an outlet in the wall to a lamp. The electricity is in the wall. The light bulb is in the lamp. The wire connects the electricity in the wall to the bulb in the lamp and it lights up. The current flows. But the wire ain't the electricity." Frank waited until I raised my eyes to meet his. "You followin' me, boy?"

"So far."

"If the electric goes out, it ain't the wire's fault. If the light bulb is burned out, it ain't the wire's fault. The wire is just the connector. You are the connector. That's all. Action without the hitch, son. What happens after that ain't none of your business."

I finally released the muscles in my neck and shoulders. "If I'm the connector, if that's my *gift*, I wonder how long I've had it. How long I didn't know. And I keep thinking about all the things I could have done if I had. All the things I missed."

"Like Bobby Kennedy?" Frank laughed. "You think you should get on a bus and go around lookin' for people who need a healin'? Like that revival preacher?"

"I'm talkin' about—my mama," I said softly, tears pooling once again. "My whole life, I always wondered what would have been different if I'd run for help a little faster. If I'd found the house where the man called the ambulance a little sooner. Then maybe—maybe things would have been different. And then ever since this whole thing started, I been thinkin' maybe if I'd known about it—this *gift*—maybe I could have saved her. I was there. I was with her in the car when it happened. I was thrown right on top of her. And she said, "Help me, Theo," like she knew somethin' I didn't know. Like she knew all along that I could do this thing. She always told me I was special but I didn't know what she was talkin' about. But I think she did. And I didn't listen hard enough so I didn't do nothin' when I could have done somethin'."

Frank smiled. "How old was you when she died?"

"Six."

"Ain't your sister six? Think about it, boy. You think she could handle this? You wasn't ready."

"What if I ain't ready now?"

"You're ready now."

"What makes you so sure?" I looked into Frank's eyes, waiting.

"Because you're doin' it now."

I began pacing the tiny room, back and forth, my head spinning. "But what if I was ready then and I didn't know it?"

"What if. What if."

"But what if I could have saved her?!"

Frank paused. "Then she'd be alive."

The shrill squeal of tires and the angry crackling of gravel drew me to the window. "It's my daddy!" I watched as my father slammed the car door and stood by it, clinging to the roof.

"You in there, boy? Theo? You in there?"

Frank pulled me back from the window and opened the door and stood in its frame. "Mr. Dalton, my name's Frank Katori."

"I know who you are! Is my boy in there?"

I slid under Frank's arm to see my father. He was drunk as Cooter Brown. "I knew I'd find you here! Git in the car!" he commanded. I didn't move, I was afraid to move. "Git in the goddam car!"

Frank stepped outside pushing me behind him. "Wait a minute," he said. "Let's you and me talk about this. Man to man."

My father steadied himself and then stumbled closer. "I got nothin' to say to you. This is all your doin'. You poisoned my boy and God knows what else you done. You been diddlin' my son?"

I pushed my way through. "Daddy, no, he ain't done nothin' like that. He's my friend."

"Your *friend*?" My father headed for the trailer door. "It's all over town, what you done, Theo. What you been doin'. And this, this murderer put you up to it. Fillin' your head with some kind of bullshit magic. He killed a soldier, did he tell you that? Shot an American soldier dead." He hocked a wad of phlegm into his mouth and bulleted it at Frank's feet.

Frank held up his hand calmly. "Mr. Dalton, I know you're mighty upset. Theo has a gift. A special kind of gift. Something you should be proud of."

"Don't say his name like you know him. And don't you fuckin' tell me what I should be proud of! I lost my job! You hear that, boy? I lost my fuckin' job because of you! Ray calls me up, says he was at church. Told me how they drove you out. Says he can't have me on no more `cause it ain't good for business." He slowed his breath and seemed to calm, and there was an eerie sort of stillness. "I ain't had a handout my whole life. I been holdin' on by my fingertips to get whatever little bit we got. I worked for it, that's one thing nobody can take from me. Take everything else, but not that. Until now."

Frank walked slowly to my father and offered his hand. "Mr. Dalton, let's sit down and ..."

Suddenly, my father heaved himself against Frank, throwing misguided drunken punches, clobbering with little result. Frank stood, anchored as a stone, holding him off with one hand and holding me back with the other.

"Daddy, stop!" I broke away and dashed behind my father and pulled at him, ripping his shirt, pleading. He whirled around and shouted, "Git away from me, boy," and smacked me hard across the face with the back of his ringed hand and sent me to the ground.

My father froze, panting with the rhythm of a motor. I sat hunched over in the gravel holding my cheek. My jaw was sliced from the top of my ear to the corner of my mouth. Blood ran between my fingers and down my neck. My father rushed to me but I stopped him with my hand in the air, never looking up.

"I'm sorry, son. I'm so sorry," he sobbed. "I didn't mean it."

He leaned down to take me in his arms but I pushed him away. "Don't you touch me," I declared in a slow, low timbre that surprised even me. I got to my feet and found my balance.

"Come on home, son," he begged, but I would not be driven by him.

My father was drenched in sweat and still trying to get hold of his breath. He wiped his hot red cheeks with his forearm and staggered to his car. He opened the door and then paused before getting in. Then he turned to me, locking eyes, in disappointment or admonishment or something in between. "Your mama would be ashamed," he said. And his words were like weapons aimed at the softest part of me.

SESSION 10

I find myself sneaking glimpses at the clock during my last session, barely present, in anticipation of her arrival. 1:50. 1:55. Stefani with an *f* pops in to ask if I need anything and I tell her to check into cleaning services. She seemed surprised and pleased. She's lasted longer than the others and I fear she'll make it through the summer.

My three o'clock has canceled and it occurs to me that I can offer a double session. It's the least I can do to get back on track. I went too far. I shared too much. I crossed the line and got too personal, making myself too vulnerable, not to mention my flagrant unprofessionalism. She was so happy and confident in our last session, even at my expense, but no one can maintain that kind of high through the process, and when the fall comes it can feel futile. The feeling that you can see the finish line —and then the devastation in realizing you are nowhere near it. Or if there even is one.

Stefani with an *f* shuts the door and moments later it opens again, and the woman enters and stands in the frame. I wait for her to sit, but she stands, rooted.

"Good morning... have a seat."

"I'd rather not." She is not callous, she is not cross. She has the look of unassailable confidence, bravery almost. But whatever it is, it's not good. She clears her throat. "You know the stories I told you I made up when I was little? About Spain and all that?

"Yes."

"Well, I'm pretty good at that kind of thing. I always have been. And the truth is—I've been lying to you the whole time. Most of the time, anyway." There is a slight drop in the room temperature. "Probably for the same reasons I did it when I was a kid. I'm bored. I want some attention. Blah blah blah. I mean it's what I do for a living. Put on voices, be someone else."

"Okay. Let's talk about it. Why don't you take a seat?" She doesn't.

"The sexual abuse, my horrible mother, my sicko father—all lies. My sister didn't die in a boating accident. We're not that close but she's very much alive." Her voice is low-pitched and resolute. "The part about drama class in college and Sergio, the gay boyfriend, is true. But we've stayed good friends. He lives in Portland and he's married to this great guy, Luke, and they have a kid and I'm the godmother."

"What's the child's name?"

"Ingrid," she says without missing a beat. "I don't know if you're trying to test me, but I'm not sure what that has to do with anything. The truth is, I was a pretty good actress in college but, you know, too fat to be an ingénue, too young to be a character actress. So I moved on from that. But I'm pretty good, right, Doc? And the Oscar goes to …" Her face falls into the absent look she has when recalling her past. She sighs the sigh. "It was horrible," she demonstrates. "It went on for years and years. My mother wasn't there for me. She let it go on and on and I hated her for it. But I loved my daddy." She whimpers softly. Then her face snaps back to nothing and the show is over. I don't know how to react. "And the haphephobia touch—pun intended. I mean how often does that come up? Pretty good, huh, Doc? So many conditions to choose from. You gotta give me that one."

"So you're telling me that all of it, all of what happened here was a sham? I have to be honest, I don't believe you."

"So you're *tellin'* me that all of it was a *sha-am*," she says, mocking me. "My mother does have Alzheimer's, that part is true. And she could be cold, that part is true. But she was also comforting and loving. I see her every week and I brush her hair and rub lotion on her hands."

"And your father?"

"He was a great dad. He had his moments, he could be pretty strict, but he always wanted the best for me."

"The Ferris wheel?"

"Lie."

"Thunderstorms?"

"Lie."

"Pregnancy?"

"One of my best."

"I'm asking you to take a seat. Please."

She does, but she sits at the edge of the sofa, unsettled, ready to go. I've had patients fabricate things before, but not with such detail. She is either lying now or she's psychopathic. "I feel foolish," I say. "I feel like you've wasted your time and mine."

"Last week when I told you how great I felt, it was my plan to just say goodbye then and not tell you the truth. Perfect exit. `Thank you, I'm all better. Crack open the champagne.'"

"Then why did you come back?"

"Because I didn't want you to think I was leaving prematurely. You know, before the *work* was done." She breathes relief, her speech being over, and waits for me to hate her. "You're a good guy. You're a good therapist. *Skilled* and *thorough* like the Yelp reviews said, but a lot more than that. You're a kind man. And I didn't want you to feel like you hadn't done your job. But frankly," she centers herself, "I've gotten bored with the whole thing."

"All right. Let's say I take you at your word and you've made all this up. You do realize that examining your desire to do that—to spend a lot of time and money for some kind of game is something that might merit seeing a therapist?"

"I've made up my mind." It's not a declaration so much as a logical conclusion.

"Okay, then. Well, we don't need to take the entire hour for this. I'm sure you have better things to do. I certainly do."

"Oh, come on, Doc, find the humor! It'll make a great story for your shrink friends at dinner parties."

I rise and open the door for her. As she passes I extend my hand. She looks at it then shifts her gaze to my eyes, smiles slyly, and takes it. She grips it firmly and shakes. I look for a sign, the smallest flinch. Nothing. Her face is like a blank sheet of paper.

"How about that, Doc? Did I pass the test?"

When she's gone I look at the clock and I'm left with so much, too much time. I am angry and confused, shocked at my own stupidity. The *purpose* I've convinced myself I had— my lofty aspirations to fix, to glue, to heal. I rewind through our sessions and try to find the truth and what kept me from seeing it. And it occurs to me that I was blind to that truth because she became my validation. I *needed* for her to be broken. I *needed* to fix her. I needed to heal her.

But even more so, she has set off something in me, bringing to the forefront a past I promised to face, but never expecting the brittle fragility of the reflection. And without her I realize I am afraid to confront myself with the same bravery I've asked her to.

I think of the way I fill my days with work, phone calls and emails, a walk around the park, the occasional weekend online-dating date, and the less occasional pointless sex that follows. Most nights I lie on my comfortable couch reading fiction about people with lives. I have little communication with so-called friends—therapist chums I share the building with, who complain about their wives and children and mistresses and trade therapy horror stories, though I never surrender my own. I've managed to hold them sacred, perhaps because my work has been the only place left that I have felt alive, of service, of value. But even that is waning. So I drink too much bourbon and watch reality-banality-TV, telling myself that I'm ever the observer of human behavior. What a crock of shit. I need to get a dog.

I'm left alone with myself. She has offended and humiliated me. Disparaged me. I am wounded. And I know it's childish and shallow, but I wish I could retaliate.

CHAPTER EIGHTEEN

It was dusk. Henry and I sat at McAffee Pond. He patted my wound with a wet handkerchief and I recoiled at the touch. "Ain't bad," said Henry. "More of a deep scratch. You ain't gonna scar." He observed me carefully and crinkled his eyes. "Hey, can't you just zap that cut away?"

"It don't work like that."

"That sucks."

I found a flat stone and skipped it across the pond one-two-three-four-five times. On another day the feat would have been remarkable.

Then Henry said, "I wish *I* could make it go away."

"Thanks. I wish I could make everything go away. I don't know what I'm supposed to do. I don't want to go home yet."

"You sure it's okay for me to stay over?" said Henry, washing out his handkerchief and wringing it dry.

"I want you to. If you're there, he won't... I just want you to."

"Maybe you should spend the night at my house. My mama wouldn't mind."

"Lily's stayin' over at Miss Monica's and I want to be there in case she comes home."

"...How about we go look at my dad's *Playboys*?" he asked, feigning enthusiasm.

"No."

Henry paused and thought. "Okay. Wanna egg Pastor Flynn's house?" A light burned in his eyes.

I laughed. "Yes, but no."

"Wanna pour sugar in his gas tank?"

"No."

A cow lowed in the distance. Henry sat for another moment, crooked his head and said, "I know! How about we steal a cow?"

"What?"

"Let's steal a cow!"

"Are you nuts?"

"Prob'ly."

"Why would we steal a cow?"

"Why not?"

"How?" I asked, not believing I was even entertaining the thought. "Where would we get a cow?"

"Where would we *not* get a cow?"

When the sun had set, the moon appeared with a mischievous smile. Henry and I crept through the field back of Saw Creek Road until we could see a barn in the distance. Not one of those newfangled barns made of corrugated metal that rattles like a railroad track when it rains, a good old-fashioned wooden barn painted the color a barn was supposed to be painted. I knew it belonged to Chubby McMorrow, whose family had run that plot of land for three generations. We dashed through the tall grass and then ducked below it, dashed and ducked, dashed and ducked, until we reached the barn. Light glowed from inside the house only a hundred feet away, close enough to hear the dialogue on the TV. *Bonanza.* Joe Cartwright had been taken hostage. It was inspiring.

We cautiously opened the slide bolt and rolled the heavy door open enough to creep in. There were several cows to choose from. "Which one do we steal?" I whispered.

"I don't know. I guess one cow's as good as another."

A bull snorted and stared at us with callous eyes. I carefully snuck past it to a cow and petted it on the nose. It moved toward me at my touch. "I like this one."

"Well, you've had the shittiest day ever so you get to pick the cow."

I grabbed a rope hanging on the wall and tied a slipknot. The cow groaned. "Shhh. Good cow, good cow," whispered Henry. I managed to snag the rope around the cow's neck and pulled. She wouldn't budge. Henry started to laugh, trying to contain himself.

"Shut up!" I said in a hush, barely able to keep from laughing myself. "You're gonna give us away."

"Front page of the *Dalton Courier*: Devil Child Steals Cow!"

"They'll burn me at the stake."

We finally got the cow to plod out of the barn, knowing one careless guffaw or yawning moo could foil our caper. Coonhounds yapped from their pens outside the McMorrow house. Henry slowly rolled the barn door closed and then followed me and the cow through the field, no longer able to duck and dash as the cow was incapable of both.

The moon became shrouded in clouds as if the stealing-a-cow-gods favored our crime. Henry said, "We have to name her."

"Agreed. Let's see, who do we know that should be a cow?"

"Or already is a cow." Henry bit the inside of his cheek in thought. "I know! Miss Patsy!" Both of us hated her and her Sunday school.

"Perfect," I said. "Didn't they sacrifice calves in the Bible days?"

The lights of the house glowed in the distance and we carried on through the pasture at a cow's pace. Henry asked, "Now what? What do we do with Miss Patsy?"

"I have an idea."

By two o'clock in the morning, we had walked some distance. There was one close call along the road when a Livingston Oil truck rattled by, but we crouched behind Miss Patsy knowing that a cow standing alongside a fence in a field was nothing unusual.

Once in town, we coerced Miss Patsy into the alley behind Judson's Drug Store and I poked my head around the brick corner to make sure the coast was clear. With a tug and a pat on the rump, we maneuvered the cow around the building to the sidewalk. "Shit!" said Henry, a bit too loudly. Vinita was sitting in her regular spot with a thin blanket pulled over her head like a flannel ghost.

"Don't pay her no mind," I said. "She's asleep. Come on." We kept moving.

"Where are we goin', anyway?"

"Almost there." I walked the cow as softly as a cow can walk to pass Vinita. Then Miss Patsy mooed—a deep, long, low, rumbling *moooo*—like sound in slow motion. "Shhh!!!" I begged.

Suddenly Vinita shifted and pulled the blanket from her head, revealing a dazed stare, her face lacking mobility. Henry and I and Miss Patsy all froze like the living nativity scene performed every year in the center of town. Vinita cocked her head inquisitively and then squinted to make sure she was seeing what she thought she was seeing. Satisfied, she pulled the cover back over her head and went back to sleep.

We crossed the street and I tugged Miss Patsy in the direction of the church.

"No way!" said Henry.

"Yes way!" I shot back.

The play yard to the side of the chapel was enclosed on three sides so it was the perfect place to sneak in a cow if one were inclined to do such a thing. "Stay here," I said.

"Where am I gonna go?" he shot back.

I padded around the corner of the building to the double doors at the entrance of the church and pulled. Locked. I ran back to Henry. "No good!" I said. "I thought churches was supposed to stay open all the time, in case somebody needed to pray."

"You nuts?" said Henry. "What if somebody decided to bring in a cow?"

Suddenly, I remembered the window in our Sunday school classroom that wouldn't ever quite close. It was above us. High above us. "You're about small enough to fit through it," I said. "I'll give you a boost and you can crawl in and open the door from the inside."

I laced my fingers and bent down for Henry to get his footing. I hoisted him as high as I could manage but the window was just out of reach. Henry jumped down with a thud. "What are we gonna do?"

My mind turned like a clock. "Okay, help me move Miss Patsy under the window."

"If you think I'm gonna stand on a cow you're crazy! I can barely sit on a horse."

"It'll be fine. Don't be a pussy."

Pussy could not be ignored. Henry wasn't about to back down now. I pulled at the rope and Miss Patsy moved into place. She was growing used to our touch and seemed more obliging. I laced my fingers again and boosted Henry to a sitting position on the cow. "Now be careful, Hen. Take your time. You can do this."

Using the wall for support, Henry gingerly placed one foot onto Miss Patsy's hindquarters, then the other, and slowly rose. His stability was unreliable at first, but he finally found his balance and stood straight. "Hey, I'm pretty good at this."

"Great," I said. "Maybe you can be a rodeo clown. I don't think they have a height requirement."

"Shut up!" Henry hoisted himself to the window and pushed it open as far as it would go, and managed to pull his body up and squeeze through it inch by inch. I watched his legs disappear and I held my breath. There was a loud thump followed by a clatter and a sharp "Jesus Christ!"

"Are you okay?" I said, wondering how I would get to him if he was injured. And what would I do with the cow? I'd have to call for help. We'd have to confess everything and be banished to a boy's home for juvenile delinquents somewhere in Arizona. The perilous ramifications swirled in my brain in a matter of two seconds, until I heard a hushed, "I'm okay."

I trekked around the church with Miss Patsy in tow. Henry was waiting inside. He opened the glass doors but Miss Patsy would go no further. Twenty-five hundred pounds of cow decided she'd gone far enough. Perhaps she was tired from the long walk or simply agnostic, but either way she was rigid and unmoving, solid as an anvil.

The streetlight glared on us as if we were suspects in a police interrogation. We were surely done for. Panicked, I handed the rope to Henry and got behind Miss Patsy, pushing with all my weight as Henry pulled. Then I pulled and Henry pushed. Then we both pulled, and at last, the cow slowly moved forward into the church foyer with a snort.

I ran to the heavy wooden doors leading to the sanctuary and opened them wide so that Henry could guide Miss Patsy without losing pace. Spotlights shone on the enormous plaster Jesus hanging on the cross above the altar. We coaxed the cow down the aisle and up the two steps to the altar, and I tied the rope to Pastor Flynn's pulpit. Miss Patsy seemed to be agreeable at last, peaceful even. We stood back and surveyed the spoils of our transgression: a cow standing on the altar in front of Christ on the cross. Spotlights backlit the scene, creating a tranquil halo surrounding Miss Patsy.

"Holy cow!" said Henry, unable to resist.

Suddenly, we heard footsteps. "Shit!" We scurried between pews and hunkered down low.

A door opened with a creak. "There's no one here," whispered a voice. It was Pastor Flynn. And then the click of heels and another voice, a woman. "Are you sure?" Henry and I traded surprise. It was the unmistakable stridency of Miss Patsy. The original one. And then she spoke the exquisite, glorious words we knew we would never, ever, in our wildest dreams, hear again: "Holy Mary Mother of God! Who put a cow in this church?!"

We remained crouched behind the pew until our legs grew numb. And when we were sure the coast was clear, we crawled up the aisle, me first and Henry following; the same path we'd taken that very morning to the jeers and spit of the congregation.

It was near on four o'clock in the morning when we headed out of downtown Dalton. "Do you think Pastor Flynn and Miss Patsy are doin' it?" asked Henry with a gleam in his eyes.

"Miss Patsy the Sunday school teacher or Miss Patsy the cow?" I cracked.

"Ain't no difference, far as I'm concerned."

"I think I'm gonna throw up either way."

Our snickers were interrupted by a siren wailing in the distance and we wondered if the police were on our tail. The day had taken an odd shape: A painful beginning and a horrible middle and a courageous ending that softened the blow. I didn't want this time to end because it meant another must begin.

It was too early for the sunrise, so at first I thought the soft amber glow on the horizon shone from the steel mill, though I didn't think it should be running at that hour. It grew brighter then dimmed, then bright again, as if controlled by a great dial. I quickened my pace as the sharp stench of burning wood and *rubber? sulfur?* came upon us. When we passed the grove of oaks at Lincoln and McKinley and rounded the corner onto Jackson Street, we could see that the idea of firemen rushing to the rescue was absurd. They could only attempt to protect the houses on either side of mine, spraying them with water like fountains centered by flames.

There would be nothing to save. The fire was savage, unapologetic. It had no regard for the Daltons of Dalton, no conscience, no mind. Its only purpose was to consume whatever it pleased. I stared, intoxicated, unable to move, as if watching a TV show rather than the evidence of my life surging up and up into nothing. I could feel the poisonous heat radiating on my face. There was no place for hope.

And yet, there was a kind of strange, aberrant tranquility in the commotion. Neighbors in summer pajamas and housecoats and slippers stood motionless across the street as the fire danced before them, showering their vision in strokes of color—reds, yellows, oranges—celebrating against the black canvas sky. It was all eerily dazzling; fire leaping, gathering speed like running water, and it sounded like the wind.

Lily! I was slapped into reality. *Oh my God.* "Lily!!!" I broke through the crowd and stumbled toward the blazing cyclone of my house, scouring the scene, calling for her. I spotted Miss Monica kneeling on the ground before I saw Lily burst from her arms and run to me through the smoke. "Lily! Are you okay?" I held her close, enveloping her body into mine.

"Theo, where you been? I was so scared! They said you wasn't inside but I couldn't find you nowhere!"

"Shhh. It's okay. I'm right here. I'm sorry I scared you."

"I was at Miss Monica's. Missy's the one first smelled the smoke and she called the fire trucks. I saw `em pull Daddy out."

"Is he all right? Where is he?"

"Over there with the ambulance men," she said. "They got him hooked up to a breathin' thing."

I scooped up my sister and ran to the ambulance, arriving just as a paramedic was shutting the back door. "Is my daddy in there?"

"It's okay, son," said the man. "He's taken in a lot of smoke, but he's gonna be all right. We're just gonna get him over to St. Francis. Tell your mama to meet us there."

"Yes. Right. Okay," I said. It wasn't worth explaining. Not having a mother at this particular moment seemed unnecessarily tragic. The ambulance pulled away and the wind shifted, raining down ash into my hair and eyes like great dirty flakes of snow. I couldn't run or scream or even look away. The flame seemed to die a bit as if it had lost its confidence, then roared back, more ferociously. In moments,

902 Jackson Street became the house of my past, and the oddest things flipped through my mind like flashcards: the kitchen table, my second grade spelling bee medal, Lily's cream-colored bedspread, my new brown corduroy pants I'd worn only once, the basement—the canned jams, the Jebediah will, my mother's pink sweater. Pillars of blackness plumed into the pre-dawn light and I wondered which smoke belonged to which thing. Which belonged to the photos of my mother? I wished I'd pocketed the picture I'd nearly stolen from the basement and kept it with me always. My memory of her was disappearing with the smoke.

It was as if the heat of the summer, the day, the church, the hate, had joined forces and concentrated themselves upon our house until it simply combusted, and I knew I was to blame. Whether the fire was by the hand of a God-fearing citizen, perhaps standing only feet away from me at that very moment, or by the wrath of the great arsonist God himself as a punishment, I was as guilty as if I had lit the match myself. The sour stench of sweat lingered in the air and I knew it was mine.

CHAPTER NINETEEN

It was the first time I'd been back to St. Francis since my mother had died. Since I'd been a patient there, broken and bandaged and stitched. My stomach felt sick. I told myself it had all happened a long time ago and in another wing, in some meager attempt to separate the present from the past. But the stinging antiseptic smell was the same; the black and white checkered floor tile was the same; the dull blue walls and the greenish glare of fluorescent light were just as I remembered, and the endless framed prints of St. Francis in his drab brown robe with doves and sheep lining the hallway, all conspicuously bolted to the walls. I wondered who would steal such a thing. I wished I'd said yes when Henry offered to come along.

I stood just outside my father's room and Lily sat in a hallway chair, shifting herself on the hard cushion. I peeked inside through the crack in the doorway. Aunty Li was staring out the window at a cypress tree tickling the glass with its fern-like leaves, and her back glared at my father, shoulders raised and tense like an irritated rooster. Sergeant Rance Bradley stood at bedside scribbling in a small spiral notebook. His brass badge was pinned to his ill-fitting, rumpled navy suit and his striped blue tie was stained with something yellow. *Mustard? Cheese?* I'd known Sergeant Rance since forever. He had the same flattop crew cut as almost every white man in Dalton, and he always smelled of Aqua Velva.

"Theo, where are we gonna live?" said Lily, balancing the only things she still owned on her lap—Joyce, her drawing pad, and her crayons.

"Hush up, I'm tryin' to listen!"

"Looks like the fire started upstairs." Sergeant Rance's voice was high and twangy and it didn't fit the muscle of him. "Do you remember anything?"

My father thought long and hard. "I remember hearing a crash like a window breakin', but I figured it was a raccoon going through a trash can, so I fell back asleep," he said, hoarse and faint.

Sergeant Rance jotted it all down. I strained to connect whatever muffled words I could make out. Something about arson. "Do you know anyone who might want to ..."

"No." My father hacked and gasped to catch his breath. "Well, maybe. I don't know if you heard anything about what happened in church."

"Yeah, I thought about that. Some folks around here been known to do worse."

"Rance, what am I gonna do?"

The sergeant closed his notebook and patted my father on the shoulder. "I'm calling this arson. Your insurance should cover everything. I'm just so sorry, George. It ain't right."

He promised he'd report when he knew something, then headed toward the door. I bowed away just in time, nodding as he left the room. "You take good care of your daddy." The door remained open and I ducked behind its frame to eavesdrop.

"Arson my foot!" spewed Aunty Li. "Sounds to me more like somebody falling asleep with a cigarette burning. You calling me at two o'clock in the morning all drunk and sloppy asking if I know where your son is. Crying on the phone telling me you struck your own boy. You're lucky you're not dead. And you're luckier Theo and Lily weren't home."

I wanted to lean in to peek but thought better of it.

"You don't know what you're talkin' about," my father said, weak but stern. "And I don't need you to tell me my business about my boy."

He coughed, then again, falling into a spasm of barks, but Aunty Li's voice rose above it and I hoped she wouldn't shut the door. "And you can bet that policeman could smell the stink of whiskey on you. The smell of smoke isn't *that* strong. I thought you were done with all that. You swore to me."

"I ain't had a drink in six years."

"I *know* when you last had a drink, George," she spit. "Shame on you. Shame on you!"

"Shhh! You want the whole goddam hospital to hear you?" he rasped. I looked to Lily. Either she couldn't hear or she was pretending not to. My father fought back. "You've never stopped blamin' me, Lorelei! Every time you look at me I can see it in your eyes," he wheezed. "I didn't *know* I was gonna have to drive Mary Elizabeth to the hospital." He was on a tirade. "We was having dinner like every other night. It was a Friday! I had a few drinks! Like every man on every Friday in this town!"

"I remember what you used to call a few drinks, George. And I'm not leaving these children, my sister's children, with you another minute. I'm taking them to my house for the summer 'til school starts. Give you time to get a job. And a place to live!"

My heart hammered in my chest like a cornered rabbit. I'd never known this about my father. About that night. And

I didn't know whether to blame him or feel sorry for him. Perhaps a bit of both. Or a lot. But I knew that what was happening now was my fault. If I hadn't been healing people or whatever I was doing then the church thing wouldn't have happened. Then my father wouldn't have lost his job. Then he wouldn't have been drunk. Then the house wouldn't have burned down. Then no one would be in this hospital, this place.

Or maybe it was Frank's fault like Pastor Flynn said. He'd been the one who told me about my hands in the first place. Or maybe it was Toby White's fault. If he hadn't chased me into that tree I wouldn't have ever met Frank and none of this would have happened. Yes, it was Toby's fault. And the entire White clan. The people who had taken everything from me and my family. It was their fault. I lost myself, snatching glances between the plastic louvered blinds banging softly against the window in the gust of the air vent.

"Here's what I know, George Dalton." Aunty Li leaned over him. "You better pull yourself together and figure out how you are gonna salvage this family, and quit sniveling and cursing the world for what you think should have been yours and be a man!" There was nothing my father could say. Aunty Li softened, bordering on empathy. "And Theo could use some time away from here. It'll do him good and maybe some of this talk will blow over." She touched my father unexpectedly, surprising both of them. Then back to business. "All right now. The doctor said they're gonna keep you overnight. Give you another one of those breathing treatments. I'll stay in town until they release you in the morning. I already set you up a room at the motel and paid the first week. Theo's gonna stay with his friend tonight and Lily will stay at the Johnson's and we'll leave tomorrow soon as you get settled in. That about does it."

"Thank you, Lorelei." It was nearly impossible for him to say the words, but he had no choice.

"You're welcome. Now you rest and I'm gonna run over to Solomon's and buy Theo and Lily a change of clothes and a toothbrush. They smell like chimney sweepers. I'll pick you up some coveralls too. Darnell's fixin' up the spare room for the kids."

Aunty Li flew out of the hospital room, squeezing my shoulder and pecking Lily on the cheek without slowing her stride. "Theo, if your friend's mama gets here, you wait and watch your sister until I get back."

"Yessum."

The sharp click-clack of her heels could be heard long after she'd turned the corner down the hallway.

I entered the room and softly shut the heavy door behind me until it clicked. My father had already fallen asleep and the soft, dusty purr of his snore was comforting. I walked to his bedside and placed my hands upon his chest. I closed my eyes and my fingers spread like a starfish, hot and sure. My father would be fine.

I bowed out of the room. "Come on, Bug, let's go down and get somethin' to eat." When I turned around I nearly fell back with shock. It was the woman who'd spit in my face at church, practically nose to nose. I flushed, remembering the horrible feelings from only yesterday, and stepped back inside to shut the door. I didn't want any more of whatever she'd come to spew.

The woman blocked the door with her foot. "Please," she said, and looked at me mildly. "Please don't shut me out." I relaxed the door but remained guarded, prepared to force it closed even if her foot was in the way. "Theo, I'm Melva White. I think you know my son, Toby." *What? Toby's mother?* Her words came in waves, strangling my breath, scrambling my brain. It was so much at once: the woman who shamed me; the mother of the boy who tormented me; the family who inherited what belonged to my father, my sister, to me. My head swam with something I couldn't define—some goulash of disbelief and antipathy, something both furious and sorrowful.

"I know you must not think very much of me and I don't blame you," she said, taking a moment to steady herself. "I am so, so very sorry for what I did to you at church. I am ashamed. And I am so, so very sorry for what you and your family have been through. It's just terrible. And I feel partly to blame."

"All right then," I said. "I have to take care of my daddy," and I pushed the door again.

"Wait. This is not easy for me." Her eyes swam with tears and she took a breath, trying desperately to remain unemotional and just present the facts. "My husband is here. Just down the hall. He had a stroke," she said deliberately, in a voice that I recognized as educated, not from Dalton. "He was complaining that he had a headache and felt dizzy, and then a little while later he started walking in circles around the kitchen like he didn't know where he was." The rhythm of her words accelerated like a hamster on a wheel. "I drove him to the hospital. And now he can't much move at all. His words are unintelligible." She began to weep. "They're saying he might have brain damage." She grabbed my hand. "Please, please help me. Help him. I know this is a horrible time for you, and I feel so very…inappropriate about asking you for anything, anything at all, but please, please come with me. I was wrong for what I did to you and I'm sorry. I beg you, please come."

A rope of hate gathered in my gut like a noose. I stared at her through half-mast eyes, blinking slowly as if I was about to fall asleep, and pulled my hand away. I inhaled the foulness of her agony and I relished in it. I could taste her sickness, her need and the urgency of it, begging for the very thing she had contemptuously ridiculed me for only yesterday. And the arrogance. And the hate. And the spit. Everything was her fault. And I was hungry for retribution. It would feel good to say no.

She babbled on, but I didn't hear a word. Suddenly I knew what it was like to be her. To be her son. To tease for the surge of power, the fix, at the expense of another. To be energized in the presence of terror. To know that victory is a foregone conclusion. To feed on fear like cicadas on the leaves of new spring willows.

But I would go.

I knew in that moment that I could not use my hands to boost myself at a cost to others, wielding power to determine who would and would not be deserving of restoration, of being whole—like the angry God from church that I didn't believe in. *We reserve the right to refuse service to anyone.* I knew I couldn't be that. And I knew that I would rather be myself with all that I didn't have, and my loss, and my deformity, than this woman with her money and her status and her spit. For even in the depth of her temporary humility and even humanity, I knew she was colorless inside. And I knew that when she became gratified she would not look back; she would return to her true self.

I am my true self when I am kind I thought. And the difference was vast.

I followed Mrs. White. "Lily, I'll just be a few minutes."

My sister shifted in her chair and flipped to a new page in her drawing pad. "A mountain I think," she said to no one, and she pulled a crayon from the pack and trailed it across the paper like a wriggling scarlet worm.

Mrs. White led me down the hallway to her husband's room. It smelled of disinfectant and tapioca. I could tell at first glance that the man was severely damaged. His body was tucked under white sheets and a pointlessly thin blue blanket with his arms resting at his sides on top. Plastic bags of clear liquids hung on spindly metal trees, and endless tubes, like strands of spaghetti, were attached to his wrists and arms and chest and nose. The right side of his face drooped like a wet painting left in the sun. He looked dead. This was more than I had ever been called to do.

"Harvey, I know you can hear me," said Mrs. White. "I brought someone to see you. I want you to do whatever this boy says."

I leaned in close to the man and whispered in his ear. "You don't have to do nothin', sir, except, if you can, just think about however you want to be. With your family. Whatever you want to do that makes you happy."

I laid my hands him. My muscles quivered and protracted and I felt them grow hot. And I imagined: *Him being wheeled out of the hospital by an attendant. A car pulls up and his wife, smiling, gets out as he stands up without assistance. He kisses Mrs. White and gets in the car. And then, through the man's eyes: he is playing golf with Toby. They are laughing.*

My hands recoiled. Upon opening my eyes, the man's face began to lift. His color tingled back. He moved his arms restlessly and turned his head and he spoke, slowly, delicately. "Melva?" he garbled. And she took her husband's face in her hands and kissed him.

I didn't want to wait for thanks. I hadn't agreed to help Melva White's husband out of any remote fondness, and what was there to say? *People talk too much,* I thought.

Before I could head for the door, the woman took my hand, her lower lip quivering. "Thank you, Theo. Please let me give you something," she said, as she opened her purse. "I heard about the fire and I'd like to help. I can write your daddy a check."

"Thank you, but no," I said, regretting the words *thank you* had come from my lips. I didn't want the crumbs of her fortune, and her pity churned in my stomach.

"Very well. I understand," she said, softly. "You are a gift, young man. And don't you let anybody tell you differently."

I turned to leave and saw Toby standing just inside the door. At first I was startled. His face was devoid of resentment and it made him nearly unrecognizable. I had never seen him calm, not moving, not red. His expression was fixed and his eyes were quiet. He had seen everything. I passed him without a word and grabbed the doorknob. I felt weak and my grip faltered. I focused and squeezed firmly but was still unsuccessful. Finally, Toby opened the door and let me out to the hallway.

I found Lily just outside, standing on her tippy toes, straining to spy between the slats of the window blinds. When she saw me, she came down on her heels, leaving a nose print and a spot of breath on the glass that shrunk into nothing.

"I saw what you did," she said. "Mama was right. You are special."

CHAPTER TWENTY

On our last afternoon, Henry and I went swimming at McAffee Pond. The late day sun sat like an apricot on the horizon and ash-colored clouds parked themselves as still as stones. Rain and Thunder were tethered to the ancient dogwood, and we stripped our clothes and climbed and jumped from an overhanging branch, diving, cannon-balling, belly flopping, competing for the biggest splash.

Until then, I'd never really noticed how truly small Henry was, skeletal really—his arms like rubber bands, the bump of each rib in his chest visible, his spine a trail of knuckles jutting down his back. He swam to the muddy bank and I followed. It smelled of bark and roots and wet leaves. "It sucks, that's all," he said, and sat on a rotting log. "Who am I gonna hang out with?" He stared at the ground and dipped his finger into the cool mud and drew shapes on a flat rock like a canvas. "I mean, who am I gonna talk to? Who's gonna call me short and push me in the dirt?"

"It ain't like I'm movin' to Alaska," I said, hopping on one foot, tilting my head and pounding it with the heel of my hand to get the water out of my ears. "It ain't even that far. Thirty miles. I'll take the bus sometimes. And it's just for the summer."

"I don't want to talk about it no more," he said, and he ran back into the water and dived deep.

When he surfaced, I was there. I circled behind him and took him gently by the shoulders. "Just relax. Let go, I got you," I said. "Now close your eyes."

"You ain't gonna kiss me are you?" We laughed. And then Henry stilled himself and lowered his voice. "You know, don't you?"

"I know. Why haven't you asked me?"

"I didn't want to be one of them."

I held my best friend and closed my eyes, and he gave himself to me, and we floated like logs on a drowsy river.

I knew Henry felt the strength and stretch of my hands and we both imagined and it was the same thing. "There," I said, releasing him. We faced each other, wafting, treading water.

"How will I know if it worked?" asked Henry.

"I guess someday you'll know."

"What do I do in the meantime?"

And I said, "Think bigger."

Henry rose up with a splash and dunked me down hard. And we wrestled and carried on in the silver spray until we grew hungry and surrendered to dusk. "Can I take Thunder out for a while?" I asked, my voice calm and even, as if this was any other day. "I got somethin' I need to do."

I sat on the tattered couch in Frank's trailer, pushing and tucking a piece of foam bulging from a ripped seam. I was tired of talking about the fire. Frank opened a Coors and the bottle cap flew to join the collection of other discarded bottle caps.

Thunder whinnied from outside and I knew I couldn't stay long or Henry's mother might find out I'd taken the horse. I wished Frank would turn off the TV but I didn't know what else there was to say. Although if I did, I knew it would be important. But then, nothing seemed that important to Frank. Or unimportant for that matter. Things just were what they were. "It's just for a couple of months," I finally said, more to convince myself than him. "I'll be back to visit. Just not every day."

Frank rocketed himself forward from his Lay-Z-Boy and switched the TV off. He leaned over and patted my leg. "I think it's a good idea. Give you some time away from your old man. Away from this town. Some time to breathe. Give these folks some time to breathe too." My eyes moistened and I didn't know if it was due to the last few days or the next few months or simply leaving Frank. All of it seemed too much to take in. He squeezed my cheeks in his rough hand, forcing a pucker, and shook his head with a laugh. "I ain't goin' nowhere. I'm always here."

"I know."

He lifted my chin. "And everything's gonna be all right, you wait and see."

"How can you know?" My eyes blurred with tears that pooled, teetering on my lower lashes, and I swiped them away with the back of my hand before they could fall.

"Because no matter what happens, it's gonna be all right if you want it to be. That's the way it works."

I reached up to his cheek to the scar where a beard would not grow. He grabbed my wrist firmly. "Don't!"

"I can make it go away."

"No, you can't." he said, sternly.

"How come?"

"It takes two, remember?" He softened his grip. "I don't want it to go away. Some things ain't meant to be healed."

"You told me things don't make us who we are."

"They don't, Theo. But it reminds me of who I was."

SESSION 11

I'm running out of things to do during the hour I still have not filled. Our sessions come to me like waves on rocks. A part of me has accepted she's gone. That she's a liar. A part of me wouldn't take her back if she begged, and a part of me wants her to come back just so I can tell her what I think of her. But I can't get rid of the remaining other part. Not yet.

I told Stefani with an *f* not to find a cleaning service, that I would do it myself. No one can really do it but me anyway—the paperwork, organizing piles of crap, tossing out the endless trash. I have a fucking VCR, for Christ's sake. I've stacked, filed, vacuumed, dusted. I sit, I stand, I dig out lint-covered pens trapped in the seat of my chair and crumpled tissues stuffed between sofa cushions.

I call my sister but hang up before the first ring and text instead. She texts back that she and her husband and my youngest nephew are touring universities. She asks how I am and tell her I'm fine, and I offer a joke about joining a therapist basketball team. She's already feeling the throes of empty nest syndrome, even though it's a year away, and my iffy desire to share that I am mired in a past she has successfully put behind her doesn't seem so important at the moment.

I find myself crawling on the floor beneath my desk, gathering paperclips caught in the carpet. The effort is no easy task for these hands, but distraction is my inspiration.

I sit in my chair and try to meditate. I've never been good at it and I hate it. I find an app with chimes and gongs, and one with a woman's voice, soft and sweet. It reminds me of her fake voice, her phone sales voice, and her pathetic tragic childhood voice. I see now how phony it was. Like her.

I can't shake the betrayal and it's affected my ability with my other patients. I am less invested, less sure. In my mind, I play through my sessions with her again and again and the lies grow more obvious to me with each passing day. The boldness and audacity of them. The haphephobia. She was right about choosing that condition. Brilliant. A solid ten for that one. I close my eyes and listen to bullshit Buddha crap and the loneliness of the fucking gong. My cell phone rings and my breath rises as it has every time it has rung since she left three weeks ago.

"Hello?"

"Hi." Silence. *Sigh.* It is her sigh.

I keep my voice steady, even a bit disengaged. "How are you?"

"Not fine."

I say nothing.

Another sigh. "I was lying."

"You mentioned that."

"I was lying about the lying."

"Okay," I say tentatively. I don't know where this is going. I don't know where I want it to go. I hope she can't hear the apprehension in my voice.

"I can understand why you wouldn't want to see me again."

I take a moment to decide, but there is no decision to make. "I'll see you again."

"Next week?"

"Yes."

"Same time?"

"Same station." My feeble attempt at humor in a humorless situation.

"You're showing your age, Doc."

"Call my receptionist and confirm the appointment."

"I'll see you then."

I hang up first. She needs me. I know I've waited for her to call, but I realize I'm not sure how I feel about it now that she has. I wonder if it could be more than I can handle. More than is healthy for me.

My head swims with half-formed regrets to the time before I lost the feeling of *feeling*. She makes me want to hurt again. I think about the people in my life who've needed me. The people I didn't even know. And how I failed some of them. And the people I knew. And how I failed some of them too.

CHAPTER TWENTY-ONE

We drove through Manford and Locust Grove, then Sand Springs, across the Arkansas River, brown and shallow, through South Tulsa and past Oral Roberts University and the eternal flame of the Prayer Tower, then on to the outskirts of the city, from where I could see the proud, intrepid face and hard hat of The Golden Driller—a seventy-five foot cement statue of an oil worker.

I'd never quite noticed the vast landscape of petroleum refineries with spewing smokestacks before, and the countless oil wells, teetering back and forth like those toy glass birds that insatiably sip water from a cup.

Aunty Li kept one hand on the steering wheel, and the other clenched Pall Mall after Pall Mall the entire way, with the windows rolled up to keep the cool air inside. She seemed to have other things on her mind than the gossip which usually provided her oxygen, and I was grateful for the silence.

Uncle Darnell met us at their front porch. For living so close, Lily and I didn't see him all that often. He was tall and slender in his fashionable low-slung, fitted slacks. His gray-paneled cardigan was surely worn expressly for our welcome. His hair was the color of Hershey's syrup and he wore it slicked back, giving his receding hairline a distinctive "M" on his high forehead where droplets of sweat beaded from being overdressed for July. He had enormous hickory-colored eyes and full lips that swelled into a pout so that, even when smiling, there was a melancholy about him.

It had been two or three years since my sister and I had spent the night at the Unwin's, and I didn't remember much other than that my uncle seemed to only really laugh when he watched *Hollywood Squares,* and he would whistle its theme song along with the one from the Old Spice commercial when he thought no one was listening. He seemed forever apologetic and had the odd habit of asking a question, providing a possible answer, and then trailing off for alternatives.

"How was your drive here, comfortable or ...?"

"It was fine, Uncle Darnell," I replied.

"Well, it's good to have you." His eyes flitted as if he was searching for invisible luggage to carry into the house. "I mean it's not good that ... you know what I mean. Do you want to come on inside or ...?"

The house had been decorated and redecorated over the past few years and each time I'd visited there was something different. A new no-wax vinyl floor greeted us in the entryway. "It's so shiny!" said Lily, and she performed a tappity little dance step. "I love yellow!"

"It's harvest gold, honey," said Aunty Li, "and stop that jiggin', you're gonna scuff it."

The overwhelming motif of the living room was avocado green. The walls were avocado. There was an avocado colored shag rug, an avocado crushed-velvet sofa with orange throw pillows symmetrically placed at each corner, which also coordinated with the orange and avocado side chairs, footed by avocado ottomans. The only things not green or orange in the room were a long Danish cabinet that hugged the far wall, framed by two potted plastic palms, and a

Baldwin spinet nestled in the corner on the adjacent wall. I hoped Aunty Li wasn't going to sing.

Uncle Darnell led Lily and me down the hallway, which was wallpapered in a shamrock-hued fabric featuring vines and cherries. It occurred to me that I'd never seen cherries grow on vines. He showed us to the room we would share. It seemed to be the only place in the house not given a color scheme. The walls were white—the kind of white that looks white until something really white is held against it. There was a small bed on one wall, neatly made, and an army cot draped with an unfitted-fitted sheet on the opposite. A round braided rug centered the room and a pine dresser was wedged below a mirror hung too high for Lily to see herself. There were no pictures on the walls or little round dishes on the dresser for pocket knives or loose change, or anything that denoted a human presence.

Lily and I stared at the room. There was no sound but for the buzzing of an angry fly knocking haphazardly on the casement window—up and down, side to side. It seemed to want out as much as we did.

"I didn't have much notice to make it homey for, y'all" said Uncle Darnell. "Since you're gonna be here for the summer, we'll fix it up soon as y'all get settled." He dashed to the closet. "But I got you a few things." He swelled with anticipation. "I tried to think of things you'd enjoy. Lily, what kind of stuff do you like, dolls or ...?"

"I like my doll just fine, Uncle Darnell."

"Well, that's good, 'cause I got you a whole bunch of 'em." He pulled a bushel basket from the closet and presented it with satisfaction.

Lily spoke up. "But I already got..." I pinched her arm and fired a stare that could melt stone. "Ow!...That's so nice of you, Uncle Darnell."

"And what about you, Theo?" he asked, "What do you like, trains or...?

"Sure, I like trains," I said, gratefully. I hadn't played with a train since I was five years old.

"I'm glad." Darnell pulled a box from the closet labeled with a cheery picture of a wooden train and track set. "I got you some clothes to get you started. I wasn't sure about the size, y'all are growin' so fast. We can exchange 'em if need be." He looked at us for a long, uncomfortable moment, and I realized that my uncle had not stopped smiling since we'd arrived—a plastered-on grin incongruous with the worry in his eyes. I wondered if his cheeks hurt.

Suddenly a tiny woman appeared in the doorframe. Her skin was the color of coffee with just a touch of milk. She was chinless, like a turtle, and her hair was rolled on the sides and pulled back into a small bun held in place with innumerable crisscrossing bobby pins. She wore a simple blue sheath dress that could have been a hospital gown sewn up in the back. "I'm just gonna get the rest-a my stuff out the dresser," she said with an evident tone that could be defensible as innocent if called out. She opened a drawer and gathered a stack of similar dresses, blues, whites, greens.

"Sookie, this is our nephew, Theo, and our niece, Lily," said my uncle with a slight warning timbre in his voice that said *please be agreeable.*

"I won't be a minute... if I got that long."

"Well now," said Uncle Darnell, his voice suddenly a tone higher. "I'm gonna rustle up somethin' for lunch. I got some peanut butter and strawberry jam, canned it myself. Would you kids like that or...?"

"That'd be fine, Uncle Darnell," I said, and he nervously disappeared into the hallway.

Lily couldn't take her eyes off the woman. "Did my uncle just call you Sookie?"

"Yes, he did. Been my name all my life so I reckon that's what he should call me."

"That's a funny name," said Lily, with a giggle. "What are you doin' in my Aunty Li's house?"

"Lily!" I admonished. "Don't be rude."

"I didn't mean nothin'," said Lily, hiding behind me.

"I works for Miss Lorelei and Mister Darnell the last five months."

"Why ain't I see you?" said Lily. "My Auntie Li brings me here after church sometimes."

"Am I a contestant on *What's My Line?* I don't work on Sundays if you has to know."

"Hush now, Lily!" I squeezed her arm hard. "Don't mind her, Miss Sookie. Aunty Li says she's belligerent." I felt awkward, out of place, and out of line. Though it was never discussed in school, I'd seen enough news on television to know what was going on—everywhere but Dalton it seemed. The protests, the Civil Rights Act, the one about voting and the one about discrimination in housing just last year. I'd heard about the Ku Klux Klan and that Stanley Pruitt's daddy was one of them.

And of course there was Martin Luther King. My father had cried when it came on the news that the doctor had been shot, and I remembered because I'd never seen my father cry until that day. Not even after the accident. That was too sad to cry about. I thought of Elijah Brown and Vida Lewis and I wondered if Sookie came from whatever colored town there was in Bent Fork. "Miss Sookie, did we take your room?"

"I sleeps here a couple, three nights a week if you has to know."

"I'm sorry," I said. "We didn't know we was comin'."

Sookie opened and shut drawers with a force as if they were stuck, pulling out thick compression stockings, nude-colored if she'd been white, a nightgown. "They got me movin' into the storage room off the kitchen. Ain't even a bureau back there. They tells me you comin' just this mornin' and now I'm cookin' and cleanin' and doin' laundry for four instead of two for the same fifty-three dollars a week, and I ain't heard nothin' about no pay raise."

"Our house burnt down," said Lily. "And my daddy lost his job."

Sookie slowed, then stopped. "Miss Lorelei didn't say nothin' about no fire. I'm right sorry to hear that, little missy."

"We won't be no trouble," I said. "We'll help out and I'll do the laundry and I'm good at cooking and it's just for a couple of months and we'll be outta your hair."

Sookie set the stack of clothes down on the bed. "Don't you worry, Mister... Theo?"

"Yessum."

"I knows how it is when you lose your home. When I was just so big, about your size, missy, my house was burnt to the ground and I lost my papa and my big brother all on the same night."

"What happened?" asked Lily, edging out from behind me and closer to Sookie.

"Don't pry, Lily. It ain't none of your business," I said.

"Well, Miss Lily—nothin' for you to worry your pretty little head about. Nothin' for me to think about neither, but I do. More'n I wants to. Now you git outta here and git some sun before supper. `Cause tonight!—tonight I'm gonna make you my famous fried chicken. Folks been tryin' to drag the recipe outta me for years but it's goin' with me to the grave. When they remember old Sookie they gonna say, `She made the finest fried chicken in Muskogee County.' Now skedaddle!"

That night, long after supper when the sun had finally set, the smell of fried chicken and okra clung to the air like a dream. Lily squirmed on her cot, finally climbing into my bed, fixing herself to me like a burr, and burying her head under my pillow.

I lifted the pillow to peek inside. "What's the matter, Bug? You okay?"

"I'm a-scared."

"Oh, don't you worry. We're gonna have the best summer ever. It's gonna be an adventure. And you can color pictures of everything we do and when we get back home you can show Daddy your whole picture book."

Lily liked that idea and she shifted out from under the pillow. "A real adventure?"

"You bet! Nothin' like we ever had before."

CHAPTER TWENTY-TWO

I'd said no when Uncle Darnell asked if I would mind if our shared bedroom could be designed with Lily in mind—Joyce seemed to be taking the move a little hard—but his décor ideas had, perhaps, gone a bit too far. The theme was pink, and everything, the walls, the furniture, everything in the room was pink to the degree that when the morning light shone through the pink curtains, it was like being inside of a giant wad of Dubble Bubble chewing gum.

There were no kids on the block to hang out with and my only interaction with anyone was between three and five-thirty every weekday when Uncle Darnell taught half-hour piano lessons, mostly to children between five and ten years old. He was a good teacher and he mattered, patient and sensitive, softer with this one, more disciplined with another.

On Fridays, Miss Claudia Dietchak booked an entire hour with Uncle Darnell. Five o'clock sharp, her special time. Her age was a mystery to me. When she arrived for her lesson, I guessed she was in her eighties, but by the time she left I was sure she could be no more than sixty-five. She always greeted me by saying, "Good afternoon, Theo. What do you know for the good of your country?" She came alive in my uncle's presence—coquettish, kittenish, smitten. She dressed for the occasion, always black slacks and a black blouse covered by a cream-colored angora cardigan, even in the heat. Her hair was mountainous and dyed honey-blonde, likely styled with the kind of enormous curlers women sleep in, and her lips didn't quite cover her teeth. She wore little makeup but for false eyelashes, too long to be natural on anything other than a mare, and lipstick, too red to be natural on anything other than an apple.

The age spots on her hands gave her skin a coffee-stained look. She gazed at my uncle during scales, her knobby-knuckled arthritic fingers never missing a note, and he smiled sweetly and she smiled right back. Sometimes he would stand behind Miss Dietchak with his arms reaching around her and ask that she place her hands directly over his so that he could demonstrate the correct fingering of an exercise, and she would lean back into him as he played. Her head nodded the tempo in constant motion, even after she'd finished playing, as if agreeing with sentiments no one else could hear—perhaps the ones she wished to hear from my uncle.

One Friday, when Uncle Darnell had excused himself to refill their tea, I nearly asked Miss Dietchak if I could place my hands over hers and feel her play, thinking I could heal her arthritis, but decided against it. My gift or curse or whatever it was had caused enough trouble.

Aunty Li was away from the house most days from mid-morning until mid-afternoon for various errands to the Safeway or the TG&Y or church ladies' luncheons with finger sandwiches and gin rummy. On Saturday evenings, supper was delayed until six-thirty so that she could perform a concert of popular songs with Uncle Darnell accompanying her. She closed the drapes and lit tea candles for ambience and insisted Sookie make cream cheese-stuffed celery and meatballs with grape jelly, and serve them between acts, during which there was always a costume change. She'd given Lily and me a lesson in recital etiquette: sitting up straight, proper applause, and a standing ovation at the end, prompting Aunty Li to phony up bashful surprise and exit to the hallway, then return for an encore. *And you wear something nice and put on your new Sunday shoes and leave that ragamuffin doll in your bedroom.*

On Sunday mornings the lot of us attended First Church of Christ, where Aunty Li was welcomed as if she'd just come back from a missionary trip to Africa. Some had heard of my "troubles" in Dalton. And the house fire, and the arsonists, which rumor had magnified into nearly tales of a mob, gaining in numbers as they strode through town to Jackson Street bearing torches.

The congregation stole glances at me with suspicion and a kind of awe, and I decided they were no better than my own. I was sure I'd be asked to heal somebody before long—an asthmatic child, a gouted grandfather—in secret, like the whiskey they damned in church, but kept hidden in locked china cabinets behind the good silverware.

But everything wasn't bad.

Lily and Uncle Darnell bonded over pretend tea parties and gardening. They would carry on for hours and he spoke to Joyce as if she were the third in their party, just like Lily did. He taught Lily to play "Twinkle Twinkle Little Star" on the piano, but of course my hands would never have been able to articulate the keys. I easily accepted such things.

Every night, Sookie drew a hot bath and Lily gave it the toe-test before stepping in. She would pull her knees to her chin so that Sookie could sponge her back and scrub her scalp with baking soda and oatmeal flour. They would laugh in a way unto themselves, high and clear and frivolous, and

Sookie taught her songs like "Polly Wolly Doodle" and "Shoo Fly, Don't Bother Me."

Late at night when Lily had fallen asleep but I could not, Uncle Darnell and I would sit on the front porch rockers and read passages from "Franny and Zooey" aloud, transporting us from the soulful melodies of crickets to the clamorous streets of Manhattan. I sensed in my uncle a heartache that he'd never had a child of his own and I knew he would have made a good father.

Lily and I were oddly, unexpectedly, at home. But I still missed my daddy.

I missed his easy manner when he was playful, and even the crusty part of him that would tell me to go outside, be in the world, remind me to be a boy. And I missed the person he was before my mama died, when he smiled more often and his eyes were soft, and he taught me how to hold a bat and catch a fly ball, when my hands could properly grasp a bat and catch a fly ball. And I supposed I'd never allowed myself to miss that part of him until now.

On a Tuesday morning, Aunty Li spun out of the house on her way to Tulsa for a sale at Solomon's Department Store—*owned by Jews but a bargain is a bargain.*" I knew she'd be gone for the day and I was grateful. I'd just turned off the shower and pulled back the plastic curtain when Lily walked in, casually sucking on a lemon. No one understood her love for a ripe lemon or how she could eat one, peel and all, like an apple, and not even wince just a little. "Theo, have you seen Joyce?"

I quickly pulled the shower curtain to cover myself. "Lily, don't come in here without knocking! I mean it!"

"Oh, Theo," she said, "You're so dramatical. I've seen your thingy and I don't care about it a snitch. Have you seen Joyce?"

"No!" I yelled. "Now get out!"

She dashed from the room and I could see her run out to Uncle Darnell from the open window. He was on his hands and knees, planting and weeding, his face shaded by a straw sunhat, stained nearly out to the brim from summers of sweat. "Uncle Darnell, have you seen Joyce?" said my sister, as she wiped away the lemon juice running down her chin and sucked another mouthful. "She was sleepin' on my bed pillow and now she's gone."

Uncle Darnell mopped his forehead with the back of his gardening glove. "Well, I suspect she's in the area if you saw her there. Look around the cot and I bet you'll find her."

Lily ran back into the house and moments later she yelled frantically from our bedroom. "She ain't here!"

I wrapped myself in a towel and joined her. Her face was burning and her eyes were wide with terror. She'd ripped the sheets from her cot. "I looked all around and she ain't here!"

Uncle Darnell ran in. "We'll find her, darlin', let's take a look together."

I quickly dressed and we searched all the places Joyce might have been: under the cot, between my sheets, under my bed, behind the bureau, in every drawer, between everything folded.

Joyce wasn't in the closet or among my books or the boxed train set I'd never opened. She wasn't in the kitchen, not in any drawer or on any shelf, why should she be? Lily grew more and more distraught and her panic squeezed my brain. Joyce wasn't in the living room hiding behind an orange pillow or in the bathroom under a pooled towel. Lily ran to the porch and crawled beneath it to find nothing but an old leather men's shoe, withered and misshapen from the damp and the heat.

Just then, Sookie came up the walk carrying a sack of groceries in each arm. "Miss Sookie will know where she is!" cried Lily. "Sookie!!"

Sookie dropped the groceries and ran to her, fell to her knees, and held Lily by the shoulders. "What's wrong child?! What happened? Now you just slow down and tell Sookie everything."

Lily rounded her lips and breathed out in puffs like blowing out a candle. "Joyce is gone. I can't find her nowhere. I'll die if I don't find her," she cried. "I'll just die!"

Sookie pulled Lily into her soft bosom. "Oh, sweet baby doll, we gonna find her," she said, rocking Lily gently, and for a second I wondered if Sookie had children, and I thought that this was the closest thing Lily had known to what it felt like to be held by a mother. Aunty Li never held her that way. Sookie wiped away Lily's tears with her thumbs. "She prolly gone out on an adventure. I bet that's just what's happened. She done gone out to some place on a big adventure and she gonna come back and tell us all about it."

"You really think so?"

"I bet so. Now you and me, let's go on inside the house and see if she done come back."

For a whole week Lily and Sookie looked and looked for Joyce but never found her.

"You got all those dolls your uncle bought you," said Aunty Li, spooning Rice-a-Roni from skillet to plate at dinnertime. "Brand new dolls! What do you want with that dirty old thing, probably got diseases all over it?"

"Don't say that about Joyce! She wasn't just some old doll. She was my friend. I had her my whole life and she was my friend and she knew me at my old house and at my school and with Daddy and Miss Monica and Lillytwo."

"Heavens to Betsy, if you want another new doll, we'll just get you one," clipped Aunty Li. "Now wash up for dinner."

Lily turned and walked away to the bathroom, muttering, "And Joyce didn't like it here. Not one little bit."

"I heard that, young lady!" hollered Aunty Li. "You watch your sass!"

When Lily was gone I saw the corners of Aunty Li's mouth pull up into the faintest smile and I knew she was glad she'd thrown the doll away.

CHAPTER TWENTY-THREE

I awoke to the sound of voices from the living room—a man's sturdy laugh and Aunty Li's high-pitched cackle. I looked at the clock. Almost 8:30. I'd slept later than usual. But then, there was nothing to get up early for. The pink morning light peered through the windows, or maybe it was just the pastel hue from the pink curtains. Lily was sitting up in her bed and drawing, her tongue sticking out and nearly tickling the tip of her nose in concentration.

"Theo! Lily! Wake up! Get dressed and come on out here, we have a guest!" Aunty Li's voice sang from down the hall with a too-sweet tone that indicated the guest was someone to impress.

"Be out in a minute!" I said, as I rose from bed, my boxers tenting in front as they did every morning. I covered myself and quickly made my way to the bathroom where I could pee and hopefully be able to pull on my jeans without too much incident.

A few minutes later, Lily and I entered the living room, clearly underdressed, since Aunty Li was wearing a honeycomb-patterned dress as bright yellow as a sunflower and a mood to match. Uncle Darnell was sportily attired as well, and I could smell his Old Spice from across the room. The guest was a man who looked strangely familiar. He was bald and fat and shiny and his nose was a color I'd never seen before. Then I knew. He was even more bloated than I'd remembered from the tent revival, though he seemed to have purchased a new, better fitting suit in the interim. Aunty Li confirmed my recollection.

"Theo, Lily, this is Brother Jimmie Dale Oldman," she beamed.

"It's nice to meet you, sir," said Lily. "But you ain't my brother."

A nervous *ha!* jumped from Aunty Li's throat. "Darnell, take Lily out to the garden and prune somethin'."

"Sure thing," said Uncle Darnell. "Lily, what kind of flowers should we pick today, roses or … ?"

Brother Jimmie stepped forward and offered a firm handshake, visibly bracing himself, clearly having heard about my hands. "It's good to meet you, son. Word is out about the work you been doing and how hard it's been. It took some doin' but I found out where you were stayin' and I came right away." He placed a blubbery hand on the back of my neck and navigated me to the sofa. "People don't understand, but I do. Your aunt, here, she loves you. She knows about my work for the glory of the Lord, and when she told me her nephew was gonna be stayin' here for the summer, well, God spoke to me, son." Brother Jimmie pulled up an avocado ottoman and sat across from me. "God sent me a message that a great opportunity awaited this boy. You. And that everything that's happened has led up to this moment so that you can truly do God's will."

My stomach swirled and I shifted in my seat.

Aunty Li patted my thigh. "Just listen, honey."

Brother Jimmie spoke with a low, round resonance that suggested he could have been a radio announcer or a doctor. "I do a service, God's service, Theo. I run the God's Hand Ministry, maybe you heard of it."

"Maybe."

Brother Jimmie explained that afflicted people come from all over to be healed. "People in pain and people looking for a better life." He said they don't judge and they don't cast stones; they are joyful and they are grateful. He leaned in close. I sat back and he leaned in closer. "And I want you to join me and use the gift God gave you to help these people."

Sookie brought in a tray of drop biscuits and coffee as she'd been asked to do, and when she bent down to place it on the coffee table, she looked at Brother Jimmie hard and her eyes burned. He met her gaze and quickly looked away. "Mmm-hmm. Thought so," she muttered, and returned to the kitchen, standing just inside the doorframe so she could eavesdrop.

Aunty Li piped in. "And tell him the other part, Brother Jimmie."

"Well," said the preacher, "You could even make some money from this."

Aunty Li was quick to add, "Your daddy doesn't have a job, honey. He doesn't even have a house for you to live in. And in a way, you're the man of the family for a while. And if you can help your daddy in his time of need, making some money by doing what you been doing for free, well then, why not? It's an opportunity, Theo. A downright miracle."

I thought for a moment. "What kinda money are we talking about?"

"Ten percent!" Brother Jimmie smiled, his tumid cheeks nearly popping with delight at his own generosity. "Ten percent of all donations."

"And a little somethin' for me and your uncle for takin' care of you on the road," gleamed my aunt. I could tell she relished the phrase, *on the road*. Connie Francis at last.

"But ain't the donations for the sick and needy?" I questioned.

"We got overhead, son," Brother Jimmie explained. "And Jesus wants to help those who help others."

I went silent. Brother Jimmie and Aunty Li waited in anticipation. "I gotta think about it," I said.

"You just haven't woke up yet, dumplin'," said Aunty Li, patting my head as if I was a cocker spaniel. "Theo, honey, why don't you eat some breakfast? Eatin' always makes me happy."

Uncle Darnell and Lily returned with a fistful of pink roses to decorate Lily's bedside table, though they might disappear in the palette. "Look how beautiful!" exclaimed Lily.

My uncle went to the cabinet for a vase and said, "Brother Jimmie, would you like to stay for breakfast? Sookie could make some pancakes or…"

Sookie cleared her throat with a growl and I feared she might poison the preacher.

"It was real nice meetin' you, Mr. Oldman," I said, offering my bent hand. "But I promised I'd help Miss Claudia clear some brush outta her back yard. And I overslept and I'm already late."

Aunty Li grinned. "That's my boy! Always thinkin' of others. When will you be back?"

"Prob'ly after supper. Don't worry about anything for me."

I sped out the door and ran the twelve blocks to the main road, where I walked backwards, facing the traffic, and stuck my crooked thumb out with each passing car.

CHAPTER TWENTY-FOUR

Frank was listening.

"I mean it solves so many problems," I said. "I get to help my daddy and Lily. We don't know what the insurance is gonna be for the house and Lily and me can't stay at Aunty Li's forever. First of all, I'd prob'ly jump off a bridge. And I get to do just what we talked about, about gettin' a gift and using it without being responsible for it myself."

Frank shuffled a cigarette up from the pack and pulled it out with his lips, patient as an oak. He flipped open his Zippo and lit it, then sat back and exhaled a thoughtful stream of smoke.

My pace quickened as I spoke. "And I won't even know these people I'd be using my hands on so it ain't personal. I don't gotta know what happens after, ain't none of my business like you said. And my own people don't want me anyway."

Frank scratched his head. "Theo, you remember what you thought the night we went to this man's tent revival?"

"Yes, but..."

"How he was robbin' all those poor people? Givin' 'em false hope 'cause he was a fake? A bullshitter? Didn't have much to do with anything but givin' those folks a show and takin' their money." Frank took another long draw on his cigarette and squinted from the smoke as he exhaled.

I'd prepared for this argument. I'd thought the same thing before I saw the situation more clearly. "That's the best part. With me it won't be fake. I'll be actually helpin' people so they ain't gettin' shafted." My script was going according to plan. When I explained it all, I was sure Frank would see that it was the right thing to do.

Then Frank said, "Who exactly are you tryin' to convince here?"

"Huh?" This was turning into a harder sell than I'd predicted.

"You remember when you asked me if you was ready?" said Frank.

"Yeah."

"Well, you ain't. Not for this."

I was getting nudgy. I'd expected that Frank would naturally have some concerns, which I would shed light upon, and then he would not only understand, but also be enthusiastic about the next obvious step in my life. Surely he'd be happy that I was reaching more people. But this wasn't going well.

"You get tired. They suck somethin' out of you," he said. "A few people is one thing, crowds of folks is a whole 'nother. You take on people's pain and you don't know how to get rid of it yet. How to clean up your insides."

I chewed on my thumbnail. "I do just fine, thank you very much. You don't know what goes on inside me."

Frank stared at me, his eyes as black as a crow's. "You got a lot of work to do before you start going around thinking you're God's gift."

That was it. "I AM God's gift! That's the whole point!"

Frank stubbed out his cigarette and a plume of smoke disappeared into the tension. "Well, it sounds like you got it all figured out. And it don't much matter what I think. You do what you gotta do."

I shot up from the couch. "I'm doin' the best I can! I'm doin' what you taught me. Action without the hitch, the rest is none of my business." I shifted from side to side. "Did you think I was just gonna just keep sittin' around this shit-hole hanging out with you all the time? I'm takin' action. Which is more than you do. At least I'm doin' somethin' with my life!" I paced. "You're so wise. You give out your advice. You sit here in the middle of nowhere with a picture of your son who don't talk to you and who you don't even try to talk to. You ain't even been into town in a hundred years." I lowered my voice to a deliberate intensity. "You're the one got me into this. You're the one told me, 'If you say *no*, you know what's gonna happen.' Nothing! Well, I'm saying *yes* and you're the one that says *no*! You wear that stupid arrowhead around your neck to protect you. From what? What are you afraid of, Frank? That you might actually *do* something?" I headed for the door. "You're right, it don't matter what you think. Why should I care what some commie soldier-killer thinks? I don't need you no more!"

I stormed out, slamming the screen door behind me, nearly knocking it off its hinges. I marched down the road and the gravel crackled under my feet louder than usual. I walked backward in the direction of Bent Fork and when I saw a pickup, I put my thumb out. It pulled up next to me, churning a swarm of dust, and I opened the door and began to climb in. "Thank you. I'm headed to ..."

The man's eyes widened. "Hey, ain't you that boy that does the healin'?"

"NO!" I spat, and I slammed the door and kept walking.

Session 12

"You cleaned up the dump," she says, as soon as she enters the room.

"You inspired me. Or rather you shamed me." I force a smile to attempt normalcy, but it comes off as too chummy. "You wouldn't believe the stuff I found. Notes and lists. Files on patients I haven't seen in years. Three of them are dead!"

"It's hard to let go of the past." She grins.

I've missed her wisecracks. There is no discussion of what happened. She is here now. She pulls a folded sheet of paper from her purse and I'm afraid she's made another list. Her defensiveness seems to have evaporated. "I warn you, I'm not saying this is good," she says as she opens the page. She clears her throat and reads:

Hope is hoping.
When the night comes.
Hope is hoping.
When lightning flickers snapshots in the dark
as the rain drums.

I do not close my eyes.
I hope.

Hope is not praying.

No pennies in a well.
Hope is not wishing
on stars or ladybugs or candles to blow out,
or fortunes to tell.

I do not beseech.
I declare.
I dare to hope.

Hope is knowing
there is a way forward.
Not a perfect way but at least a way.

I have to rise from this empty place,
this full of empty space.

But until I find the what and how,
my hope will be enough for now.

"It's lovely," I say.

"It's the poem I wrote for the contest in high school. The one I read to the whole school."

"I'm glad you shared it with me. It's the most personal kind of truth. Very brave." I wait for her lead. When none comes, "So, what's on your mind? What would you like to talk about?"

She shifts, nestling further into the sofa. Her bosom rises and falls with her easy breath. "I'd like to just sit, if that's okay."

"All right."

For the better part of the hour there is silence, oddly, remarkably—comfortable, the ticking of the clock unregarded. Another defection from all my years in this room.

People want bang for their buck—the value of the session based on the number of words yelled or wet tissues shred. Breakthroughs and breakdowns. Silence for the sake of itself just doesn't come up. Silence is what follows a monumental moment or is the calm before the next soul-ravaging storm. But not this silence. And I give myself to it. And it's as close to what I think might be meditation as I've ever come. I certainly wouldn't have the discipline to do this on my own. Or with anyone else.

But there is a sadness in her solitude. I wish I could make it all go away for her, heal her battered soul, piece together what is left of her spirit.

"I look at the sky," she says, from nowhere, gazing out the window.

"I beg your pardon."

"When we first started, you asked me what I do for pleasure. I look at the sky. I sit by my window and I watch the clouds and the shapes and I make things up." She smiles. "Don't worry, Doc, I don't mean make up stuff like make up lies."

"I know."

"I see myself in different places in different times, even as different people. That sounds juvenile, doesn't it?"

"Not at all."

"And sometimes when the sky is cloudless, like this one, I just stare at the blue. The nothing of it. That's probably why I moved to Southern California. The blue. Rain doesn't happen here very often. Where I grew up the sky could be very beautiful but it could also be very angry. I didn't like it at all. We almost never have thunder in California."

Her despair is not easily masked on her innocent face. It is discernible in the sweep of her brow and the bow of her full lips. I ache to soothe her. But I know that all the reassurance in the world cannot dare to rival this simple thing: the hope to which she clings. I see in her eyes, behind the sorrow, that she will fight against the unyielding current that ever threatens to overtake her. The world may have stepped on her soul but she will not let it destroy her. That stalwart hope. It is that which makes her beautiful.

I realize that it's not just that I've become attached to her maladies. I have become attached to her. The person. The woman. The indefatigable spirit of the single blade of grass, pushing itself up and up from between the jagged cracks in the sidewalk, and into the sun.

Chapter Twenty-Five

Four weeks after having moved from my house that was no longer a house, I helped Uncle Darnell pack up the car. Aunty Li bustled about, back and forth, gleaming all the while, going over her final checklist. "Did you get the snacks off the counter?" she blustered to anyone.

"Yes, Lorelei," said my uncle.

"And the mail. Did you tell Mr. Brooks to hold it?"

"Yes, Lorelei."

"Did you put toilet paper in the trunk like I told you to?"

I spoke up. "We ain't goin' to live in the woods, Aunty Li. Should I have got a lantern and a bear trap?"

"Don't you get smart alecky with me, young man! You aren't too old to take a switch to."

"Did you pack one of those?" I muttered under my breath.

"Come on," said Uncle Darnell. "We gotta go if we're gonna meet up by supper. Do you want to plan on stoppin' for lunch or … ?"

Lily watched the commotion like a tennis match. Sookie emerged from the house and headed in her direction. She was carrying a small pink blanket all wrapped up on itself. When she reached Lily, Sookie got down on her knees and she whispered kindly, "I know you scared, baby. I know you ain't sure what's ahead of you and I know what that's like. But you gonna be just fine. I wisht I could come along with you, watch after you, but you got your uncle and your brother gonna take care of you real good. And somebody else is comin' along if you want."

Lily looked at her quizzically. "What are you talkin' about, Miss Sookie? Who?"

Sookie unwrapped the pink blanket and gently lifted a doll made of cloth, entirely hand sewn with tight careful stitches, arms and legs stuffed just so, buttons for eyes and a tiny red mouth embroidered in a smile. She wore a white dress with little hearts scattered in a circular pattern. Her wheat-colored hair was made of braided yarn and Sookie had even woven in yellow, sun-streaked strands. "I knows she ain't Joyce, cain't take the place of her no how. Cain't never replace somebody you love. But I was thinkin' she might come along with you where you goin'. She all alone and maybe you could keep her company."

"I'm gonna call her Sookietwo." Lily pulled the doll to her chest. Then she threw herself into Sookie's arms and held her tight and Sookie held her back. "I ain't givin' up huggin' on you," said Lily. "Even if you let go first."

Chapter Twenty-Six

It was my first night at the tent revival. Shoddy black makeshift curtains were draped over pipes constructed to create a backstage area, with a tiny portioned-off corner serving as a sort of dressing room for me. In it was a small worn wooden table, a cracked stand-up mirror, and two cane-backed chairs with tattered straw seats that threatened to collapse at any time. I squirmed in a white Dacron suit Aunty Li had bought at Solomon's, and I pulled at the collar of my button-down shirt. Lily admired her pink poofy dress in the mirror as Uncle Darnell fluffed her curls.

The timing for this venture was perfect for my uncle since school was out for the summer, when he and Aunty Li would sporadically travel all over a thirty-mile radius of Tulsa County to churches and Rotary Clubs as a musical act. Aunty Li referred to their performances as "being on tour," and nothing had pleased her more. Now, at last, she really was.

The quiet of my dressing area was shattered by Aunty Li's burst through the curtain, wearing a blinding carnival-colored dress, as frantic as she seemed to be. "There's three hundred and eighty-seven people out there! I counted every single one of them myself. Twice the size of Brother Jimmie's regular crowd, don't say I said so." She checked her figure in the fractured mirror and shifted her breasts to a superior position. "They have heard about you, young man!

And I see some folks from Dalton. Pfft. Hypocrites. But a donation's a donation. Anything to help those in need."

Brother Jimmie barged in with the throaty bark of a dog. "Are you ready, Theodore? I'm calling you Theodore from now on, sounds more noble. And guess what, son? We got ourselves a spotlight! I want the people to know just how special you are!" Brother Jimmie squatted down to Lily, straining the seat of his green polyester pants. "And you!" he said to her. "I'm gonna call you Sister Sister!" He noticed the pile of envelopes on the table. "Theodore, I see you ain't even looked at the prayer cards. We made some notes on the outside, name and ailment, just in case God's message gets a little fuzzy."

"I won't be needin' those."

Brother Jimmie opened his mouth to speak, then paused, then said, "Well, of course you don't, what am I thinkin'?" He was clearly skeptical, fidgety, as he adjusted my lapels and proclaimed, "Hallelujah, this is gonna be a glorious night!" The organ music began from out front and Brother Jimmie scrambled away.

The buzzing hum of the people grew louder. *How can I feel so scared and so excited at the same time?* I thought. Then I knew it was because I wanted to do it. Yes, it was the way people looked at me when they'd been restored. But even more than that, I longed to feel the freedom from my drawn, clenched hands. Feel the muscles in my fingers expand, pull, my palms flat and open as if I was restored too, if only for moments.

"Okay, darlin', it's time," said Aunty Li.

Lily seemed preoccupied with the incongruence of her patent leather shoes against the sawdust floor as she scuffled them to make little piles like ant hills. "Can I take Sookietwo?" she said, picking up the doll.

"You most certainly may not! Now, when Brother Jimmie announces Theo, that's when you walk out and sprinkle the rose petals, you got the petals ready? ... I am talkin' to you, Missy!"

"What?"

"Don't worry, Lorelei," said Uncle Darnell calmly, as he yanked Lily's dress down taut. "I got `em in a basket with a ribbon on it. Looks real nice." I realized Uncle Darnell had not spoken a word until now.

"Okay, I'm ready, Aunty Li," said Lily. "I'm feelin' real special."

"`Course you are. This is so exciting! I'm as nervous as a prize turkey in November, Darnell, check my makeup."

He evened her out her rouge and powdered her with precision. A muffled Brother Jimmie could be heard from on the stage. "Welcome to the Hands of God Ministry, y'all! We are here to make miracles tonight! Who's ready to feel the hands of God?!"

The crowd applauded and shouted "Amen!"

"Okay, children, let's go," said Aunty Li. She lit a Pall Mall and tossed the flaming match to the floor, pushing me and Lily ahead of her. I turned to see Uncle Darnell stomp the smoldering sawdust left in Aunty Li's wake. We all bustled to the flimsy curtain hanging on the side of the platform where Brother Jimmie was revving the crowd.

"Brothers and sisters! I have been spreadin' the word and travelin' from town to town for nigh on twenty-five years." He paced, lowering his head gravely, and raised a hand high as all preachers do. And Brother Jimmie needed to do what all preachers do. "I have witnessed the power of God. And tonight, I have brought forth a gift. A new generation of faith. A new generation of healing. He's only twelve years old, hallelujah, but God has given him the command of a thousand. Are you ready to be healed? Give praise to God and welcome Theodore Dalton!"

The organ music swelled and the crowd applauded, percolating with anticipation. Aunty Li smoothed her dress and took a last draw on her cigarette before dropping it into an empty gin bottle left by the organist, Doretta Jane Barbour. I'd only known Doretta Jane for two days but I realized that she was drunk at any given hour. Word was she'd been with Brother Jimmie for a decade after she'd left the circus for a better life, or at least one with no animals. No one seemed to mind Doretta Jane's drinking as long as she could hit the organ keys and pedals at the same time.

Aunty Li pranced into the light, pumping the air above her as if receiving the holy spirit, leading the way for Lily, who entered with a sweet, nervous smile, sprinkling a path of artificial rose petals before her. *Step-touch. Step-touch.* The crowd let out a unison *ahhh. Ain't she sweet? Ain't she perty?*

I timidly entered onto the platform stage. I was blinded by the glare of the spotlight and raised my hand to shield my eyes. Tiny flecks of dust floated in the light and all I could see was the silhouette of the crowd. But I could feel their hope crawling on my skin.

Brother Jimmie's voice boomed. "You've all written down your ailments on your prayer cards. And God will tell this young man who needs healin'."

I walked to Brother Jimmie's side. "It don't work that way," I whispered.

Brother Jimmie was caught off guard. He leaned in to me with the broad smile and spoke through his teeth like a ventriloquist. "That's the way we do it, young man."

"It don't work that way." I walked to the edge of the platform and Brother Jimmie followed, pushing the microphone to my lips. I cleared my throat and spoke. "Y'all don't need to tell me what's wrong, just imagine yourselves healthy. Don't think about gettin' rid of your ailments, think about what it's like not to have `em."

The organ started up again with a jubilant gospel song and the people danced, shouting hallelujahs. I waved for the organ to stop and Doretta Jane sputtered out in an unfinished phrase. I pushed the microphone away. "Please, no music." Brother Jimmie took me aside.

"Boy, what are you doing?"

"Only thing I know how to, sir."

The preacher nervously considered his options and realized he couldn't call this shot. "Go on, boy. This better work."

I returned to the people and stood before them without moving. Waiting. Waiting. Slowly, the crowd stopped praising and stood solemnly. I stepped down from the platform and walked among them, laying on hands one by one. At first my hands opened and closed as I merely touched some and lingered with others, but as I imagined for them in a flurry of disparate visions that engulfed my mind's eye, my palms and fingers soon remained open, firm and hot, and I reveled in the sensation.

For many, the results were immediate and obvious. Others would find their recovery later. Or not. I couldn't know. For some, my healing was as imaginary as their ailments and I could tell the difference. But for most, there seemed to be a sense of having been stirred, deeply, authentically. And they smiled and they wept, in a sort of quiet awe and gratitude, and I was lifted by it. Lifted, yet weakened by it, as I struggled to shuffle off their afflictions as they passed them off to me. Brother Jimmie and Aunty Li stood to the side and Lily and Uncle Darnell watched from the curtained wings.

An hour later, I returned to the platform, bowed my head and said thank you. Aunty Li escorted me off the stage and to the cool of the dressing area, the noise behind me. I was floating but discombobulated. Oddly happy. Spent. My head hurt. My hands had become set and rigid, muscles twitching.

Brother Jimmie could be heard asking the people for their love gifts for the God's Hand Ministry. "God's humble servants will be waiting at the exit. Sorry, no checks."

Aunty Li kissed me all over until my face felt sticky. "You did it! They didn't know what hit 'em! Oh honey, I can see you're tuckered out. Makin' your debut and all can wear a person down and I speak from personal experience. I feel like a nap myself." She helped me to the army cot and poured water from a pitcher on the dressing table. Brother Jimmie rushed in like an eruption, bearing a goliath grin. "Boy, you are a blessing to all of us. This is gonna be big. Big!"

Session 13

It is a frigid color—less summer sky than the onset of winter—which looked warmer on the fan of color samples. Not exactly like I'd planned, but then nothing ever is. I've tried to scrape off the stubborn paint chips lodged at the cuticles of my fingernails to no avail. The smell of the room is both repulsive and inviting.

She enters and looks around, taking it in. "I like it."

"It was time."

"It's a pretty shade." She takes her seat and looks around the room once again. The blue. I wonder if she knows I did it for her.

She looks different. I can't pinpoint it. She's wearing the same kind of blousy blouse and wraparound skirt she always seems to wear as a uniform, but something has changed. There is an effortless elegance about her.

"I've always been happier outside than in," she says, pensively. The largeness of it. There was a time when you couldn't keep me indoors. It's ironic that my life has become so ... so small." She pulls her hair up with both hands and lets them sit there. I can tell this is one of those days when she is fully available. She's learning to give herself permission to find whatever memory or association she comes upon and enter it without my prompting.

"When I was seventeen my parents sent me to church camp on a ranch for the summer. Well, not my parents, my mother. She'd always gone to Trinity Episcopal and taken me every Sunday when I was little, but later she got really churchy and she started going on Wednesday nights as well and she dragged me along with her. She wanted to get some Jesus in me. Or maybe she just didn't want to leave me at home.

"The camp was up in the mountains. Apalachicola National Park. And they had softball and archery and swimming. All things I was either lousy at or just wouldn't do. But there was horseback riding and I really loved that. There was nothing competitive about it. I remember the first time I got on a horse I was actually afraid it wouldn't support me. I mean I was overweight but it was a ridiculous thought. I was kind of a natural if I say so myself." She smiles with a sense of pride. "I asked if I could work in the stables and I spent all my free time there, feeding them and grooming them. I would ride every day, every chance I got." She leans her elbow onto the arm of the sofa and sets her chin in the palm of her hand in a splendid, contemplative pose, like a painting.

"There was a horse I loved, Applejax. Like the cereal except spelled with an X. She had a kind of dignity about her. I remember the feeling of riding. The freedom. It was like we were one body. When she moved it felt as though it was my movement, as though she could read my mind. I could make the smallest gesture and she would respond. And when you're riding, all of a sudden, nothing else in the world matters. Your problems disappear. And when you canter, it's as if you're floating, weightless. You sink into the saddle and become a part of it." She closes her eyes wistfully. "I remember the feeling of my hair flying into my eyes, the green hills passing by, as if I was looking through a window.

It's like a dream, feeling the horse beneath you, clinging on." She opens her eyes but remains focused on the picture in her mind. "The thing I loved most is that you have a feeling of control, complete control over everything in your life, for once." She possesses a tranquility I've not seen in her.

"I have wonderful childhood memories of horses as well," I say. I regret interrupting her. My words have pulled her away and the muscles in her face become taut. Her eyes turn to me.

"Nighttime was a different story," she says. She bites the skin around her thumbnail and rips it off, chewing it as she speaks. "There were campfires. Bible stories and Jesus songs and lots of hand holding and swaying, all happy and huggy. And all the stuff about praying to God and that He would listen and protect you. He would always be there for you," she grimaces.

"And did you believe that was true?"

"What do you think?"

"I can certainly see why you wouldn't."

"I remember thinking that if I actually *did* believe, maybe all of it would go away. That my father would be healed. And maybe that's what was wrong with me. That I didn't know God."

"So you decided this was something that was your fault."

"Not so much for something I did as something I didn't do. I didn't have faith. Like the other girls. And like my mother. And that I might be punished for that." She snickers. "Ironic isn't it? That a person can not be sure if there's a god but be afraid they'll be punished by the god they're not sure they believe in."

"Did you want to be like the other girls?"

"I envied their complacency," she says. "And I despised them for it."

"What about your mother, and her faith?"

"I think it gave her something to hold onto after my sister died."

"And?"

"…And something to hold onto when it came to my father."

"And?"

"And me. My father and me. But it was pointless. It was blind faith."

"What do you mean?"

She gathers her thoughts. "That God will make everything okay if you just pray and wait. Like trusting something invisible without any obligation on your part to change anything or actually do anything. I knew I had to do something. That the hope I had, like in my poem, was just the thing to motivate me. But I didn't know what to do, so I did nothing."

"You were a child. But now, as an adult, here you are, doing something."

"I'm forty-two years old."

"You're here."

"I've spent most of my life avoiding it."

"You're here."

I wait. I'm ready to say it again. A dozen times. A hundred if necessary. She takes a deep breath and exhales slowly. "I'm here."

I'd promised myself I wouldn't do it again. But in the moment it seems right. "When I was a boy there were circumstances that forced me to grow up a lot sooner than I should have had to—my mother's death, my father's inability to fill the void, being a parent to my little sister, other…circumstances. I was sent away to my own version of a church camp for a summer, and faith and trust and miracles got all blurred and jumbled up."

"Miracles? What kind of miracles?"

The question throws me. "It doesn't matter."

"Look," she says. "I get that it's your job to keep your own stuff to yourself. Your politics, religion, I totally get it. And I promise it won't affect me one way or the other. But I'd really like to know—do you believe in miracles?"

I hesitate. "Yes, I do."

"Why?"

"Because I've seen them."

"You mean here? In therapy? Or like God miracles?"

"I don't know where they come from, but I've seen examples of miracles." *Don't go too far, Dalton.* "I just wanted you to know that I relate to some of your feelings."

"Were you abused?"

"Not sexually. I'm not comparing my story to yours at all, not remotely. I'm just saying I know what it feels like to be burdened and confused as a kid by adults who think they know better—dictating your life, even sacrificing part of your life for their own needs and their own selfishness. Children don't get a voice. They don't have the wherewithal to take care of themselves, physically or emotionally, so they're forced to rely on whatever adults are in their world who are supposed to know what's best for them."

"Even if they don't."

"Even if they don't. So the only thing we can do, as children, when it all gets too overwhelming, is to get out or distract ourselves or just shut down. Most can't just get out, so some kids find drugs, or cut themselves, or play endless video games to take them out."

"Or eat," she adds. "Or make up stories. Make up fantasy lies."

"Some kids act out negatively by breaking rules or even committing crimes—those are the lucky ones, at least they're in some sort of action, some sort of protest. And then there are those that just—desensitize, even dehumanize themselves."

"Just go through the motions. Like me."

"Yes."

"Or take their own lives."

"Or take their own lives."

"The ultimate get out."

"There is nothing scarier than feeling alone," I tell her. "Or having no sense of value. I was lucky. I had a sister I needed to take care of. Something bigger than me. Something bigger than all the other people I was supposed to take care of. That I was assigned to take care of—as a kid." *I think of my sister and her doll. I've always assumed that she needed Joyce and Sookietwo to comfort herself, but now it occurs to me that perhaps the dolls were the "something bigger" that she needed to take care of. For her sense of value.*

"Did your hands keep you on the outside? Like my weight? Like my—secrets?

"Certainly, in a lot of ways. But I had a friend. Two friends. A man who saw me for who I was. And a boy who accepted me for it."

"Which one gave you the necklace?"

I touch the arrowhead out of reflex. "The man."

"And the boy?"

"I haven't spoken to him in several years," I say. "I need to change that. I miss him." *And my sister,* I think. Too much small talk, not enough talk. She had been there, after all, the only one who knows everything.

"It's not that I didn't have friends," she says, "but there were so many things I couldn't say to anyone."

"Until now."

"You're my therapist."

"I'm also your friend."

The words fall from my lips with an ease I couldn't have imagined. She doesn't seem surprised, as if she was waiting for me to utter the something we both knew. And that was true.

She sighs her signature sigh and talks to the air. "Does it ever go away?" she asks.

"What?"

"All of it. The stuff that put me here. I feel…I feel as though my heart is missing something. Some fundamental piece that keeps it from working properly." Her grief is like an ocean. "And I don't know if I'll ever find it."

"You will, I promise. It's not missing, it's just waiting to be found." I lean in closer. "The brain doesn't understand the passage of time. It doesn't know how old our trauma is, or how old we are for that matter. We think when we grow up that all this is supposed to sort itself out, but it doesn't work that way. We are the same people we were, just with more mileage on the clock."

"How encouraging." She blinks away the mist of her eyes.

"It's where we put it and how we deal with it. It's understanding that we aren't born with our emotional issues. We acquire them. Through circumstances, obstacles, tragedies. And it's the understanding that if we acquired them, then they're not intrinsic to us. And while we can't make them go away, therapy is a way of understanding them. Diminishing them. So we are less—frozen by them—because we didn't ask for these things to happen, but they happened."

"Like your hands."

"That's a perfect example. I didn't ask for these. But I've learned to accept them without letting them run my life, stuck in what I can't do instead of being more in touch with what I can." *Could, won't, don't know anymore.* "And sometimes, if we look deeply into ourselves—we can even find the gift in the tragedy." *I can hear Frank in my head.* "We get to choose whether events inform us or define us. And that can be very hard when there's great conflict."

"So you're saying that I've let my tragedy define me."

"You are here for exactly the purpose of uncovering the source of your pain so you can accept it and place it where it belongs rather than being trapped in what you've grown to see yourself as."

Her introspection vanishes. "I think you know by now that I loathe self-pity. Whatever I've been through, I refuse to wallow in it."

"That's the fighter in you. But your personal history is not something you can just bounce back from."

"There have been many tragedies a lot greater than mine, Doc. People get cancer. My parents lost their daughter."

"Yes, but it's what we do with our tragedies. Once we accept them, we get to make choices. The cancer survivor can help people who have cancer. Parents who've lost a child can help someone else who's also lost a child. They can stand up for others. They can create from it, like your poetry. We can find resentment or we can find compassion. We can even discover our own gifts when we allow them to emerge. Gifts we didn't know we had."

"Is that why you became a therapist? To use your tragedies to help other people? Or to replace something else?"

"I don't know what you mean by that."

"Hey, Doc. Theo. I know you're very good at what you do." *I'm not as sure anymore.* "I'm proof. But I also get the feeling sometimes that you don't want to be doing this. That there's something else you want to be doing. That you should be doing."

"Please don't turn this around."

"Like, I don't know, building schools in Africa, making pottery, running a bookstore, whatever. Something else."

I attempt a chuckle to conceal the fact that I don't like where this is going. At all. "I love what I do," I say, a bit forced. "I have a successful practice and it's given me a good life. And I invest in my work, I think of it as my calling. I'm sorry if I ever gave you any impression that I don't want to be here. It's simply not true."

"I believe you. Or rather, I believe that you believe you. But you know the old saying: those who can't do, teach. It should be those who *don't* do. The art critic probably painted. The editor probably wrote. What's your gift, Doc? What are you replacing?"

"I think we need to step this back a bit." I am a jumble of brewing irritation.

"It's funny," she presses. "All this time all I've wanted from you is to tell me something, give me answers. But all you do is ask questions. And now you're finally imparting your great wisdom and frankly, it sounds like a pile of shit. What am I supposed to do? Write a poem? Volunteer at a child abuse center and then I'll be cured?" She grows hot. "I'll live a big fat happy life and I won't get nauseous or have palpitations when someone gets near me? It won't physically hurt if someone touches me? Give me a fucking break."

She stands and collects her things in a flurry and spins around, heading for the door. "See you next week!" she flares angrily, storming out, slamming the door behind her. I can hear her swift steps trail down the hallway. "And thanks for the blue walls!"

I imagine her driving away, cursing me, banging her fists on the steering wheel and crying the noisy tears she dares not show me. She will despise me for a day or two.

CHAPTER TWENTY-SEVEN

Summers had always been squeezed into the blink of an eye, flying by from the beginning of June through the end of August. The days of careless play had ended at dusk rather than with clocks, and the nights had hummed with katydids, scoring the spectacle of lightning bugs flittering in the dark. But the summer of `68 was eternal.

Pawhuska.

The size of the crowd had increased from town to town. A new banner hung prominently, if slightly askew, stretched between piping with rope. The hand-painted curlicue writing trumpeted "God's Hand Ministries" with an enormous hand reaching from above, a crude plagiary of Michelangelo's *The Creation of Adam*. Doretta Jane crescendoed on my introduction and cut off abruptly when I reached the center of the stage, then took a sip from her coffee cup brimming with gin.

I waited for the hush that always came when I didn't speak. I made my way through the crowd as each row took its turn spilling into the middle aisle for my touch, and then circled around to their rows of chairs like sheep into a pen. My hands swelled and expanded with the familiar prickling, almost virile energy. People were freed from their pain, disease, their burdens.

Halfway through the tent, a woman nervously made her way to me. I touched her shoulder and tried to imagine, and when I couldn't create a picture in my mind, I opened my eyes. The woman was tense and afraid, hostile even. I remembered what Frank said: not everyone truly wants to be healed. Some would rather cling to the identity of their sickness and wouldn't know who they were without it. And so I moved on to the next person.

Tahlequah.

Six towns later, *seven?*, the new-used chair and the new-used dressing table and the new-used stand-up mirror were among the many things acquired since the larger truck had been bought to transport the new-used bigger-better everything. But the amenities were a sorry thanks for the weariness that accumulated with each stop, each town, each ravenous crowd.

Lily sat in my dressing area, swallowed by the puff of her lilac organza dress, with her art pad in her lap, Sookietwo propped up at her side. She would draw until the crayon snapped or the paper tore, and then she would start again. She looked like a miniature bride, and Aunty Li told her she was *prettier than a glob of butter melting on a stack of wheat cakes*, but from the puckered expression on Lily's face, I knew she didn't think that sounded very pretty.

That night, Lily was drawing a picture of the new-used bright orange tent Brother Jimmie had purchased from the recently defunct Gerkin Family Circus after the Hands of God revivals attendance had increased so in number that he happily had no choice. When the thing was erected, Lily had laid on her back upon the sawdust in the center of the big top and studied the segments shaped like colossal orange slices, and now she was putting it on paper. The lines were rigid and regimented with none of her usual whimsy. "Hey Bug, why don't you draw me a picture of a flying elephant or a giant bumble bee?"

"I'm makin' this for Daddy for when we get back home," she said, pulling a brown Crayola from the new pack my uncle had bought her as a surprise.

I bent down and lifted her chin and met her soft eyes. "You doin' okay?"

"I'm doin' okay. Sookietwo is havin' a little trouble but I tell her everything's gonna be all right. Just takes some gettin' used to, that's all."

I wondered if you could get used to anything with enough time.

Enid.

August was more oppressive than July had been, and the torrid air smothered me like a wool blanket. The only movement was from the cardboard *Hands of God* fans that were passed out at the entrance of the vast tent. I'd walked among the needy for over two hours and was depleted. The amazement had dissipated. My gift had become a task, a duty; whatever joy that had once existed had melted into a kind of sorrow. While countless people had been cleansed of their infirmities, my own body consumed me and sometimes I felt as if it might devour me. I wondered if Frank had been right, and I remembered the things I'd said to him with shame.

I plodded to the wings of the platform stage, passing Brother Jimmie and Aunty Li, who were fired up in conversation with a man dressed in a seersucker suit, snakeskin cowboy boots, and a black Stetson. He chomped on the butt of an unlit cigar and I remembered the sugar cane Marjory Forrer had brought back from her vacation in Hawaii in the second grade, and I wondered what she was doing right then.

I got to my curtained room and stepped out of my toe-cramping white shoes and constricting white suit, and sat in a heap on the new-used tufted cane back chair. Uncle Darnell sat at my feet and massaged my hands with a concoction of camphor oil and lavender and mint, pushing deep with his thumbs, working his way up and out through each of my fingers. He smiled words of understanding. I closed my eyes and lay my head back on the chair and thought of Frank and Henry and McAffee Pond and my father and even Missy Johnson.

Brother Jimmie hurried in, his hot red cheeks blazing. "You know who that was?" he said, mopping his brow with his monogrammed handkerchief. "That was Oklahoma City! We're talkin' about ten days. Ten days! Must be a lotta sick and crippled folks in Oklahoma City!"

Aunty Li was quick on his tail. "Jimmie, you leave this boy alone. He needs to rest. Lily, honey, go on outside and give your brother some peace." Lily grabbed her crayons and art pad and Sookietwo and started out. "But you get out of that dress before you muss it!"

"Yessum."

When the preacher and Lily had gone, Aunty Li leaned down to me. "Theodore, darlin', I need one teensy-weensy favor if you've got the strength. I need you to help me. Help us. Your uncle is suffering from somethin' that I cannot even speak of," she said, hushed, as if she was planning a robbery. Uncle Darnell lowered his head. "He needs to be freed of the darkness inside him. We need your healing hands, baby."

I was empty, but nodded "okay," curious about my uncle's mysterious ailment, which I presumed had drawn Aunty Li to Brother Jimmie when I'd seen them in what seemed a year ago. Uncle Darnell started to rise, hesitant and unsure, and said, nervously, "What do you want me to do, sit or ... ?"

Aunt Li pushed him back to his knees before me. I placed my hands on my uncle's head and closed my eyes. Then I lowered myself to the floor to face him. I waited for my fingers to lengthen. I moved my hands slowly from his cheeks to his shoulders to his chest and then let them rest over my uncle's heart. I concentrated. I waited. And then I opened my eyes and smiled gently.

"Is he healed?" said Aunty Li, in a desperate, susceptible voice.

Uncle Darnell looked to me with hope in his sorrowful eyes.

"There ain't nothin' to heal," I said, and cupped my uncle's face in my hands. "Ain't nothin' wrong with you, Uncle D."

He hung his head. And then he began to weep, small at first, gusts of breath pulsing. And then he released an almost inhuman wail, like a wild animal—wrenching, aching, intestinal—and he lay his head in my lap. "Shhh. Shhh. It's okay," I said, stroking his hair. "Ain't nothin' wrong with you at all."

Aunty Li was bewildered. Her eyes darted as if she was following the flight of a mosquito. She left us alone, presumably to reconstruct herself, or to join Brother Jimmie for that glass of bourbon I'd heard him offer her.

Stillwater.

The flashing bulbs sounded like insects hitting a bug zapper and all I could see was flickering strobes and the dancing black spots that followed.

I stood in front of the new electric sign that blazed "Hand of God Ministries," properly dressed in my white suit for the *Stillwater Gazette*. My hair was parted on the side and slicked with Brylcreem, but Aunty Li still felt the need to repeatedly lick her fingers and paste down the stubborn cowlick at my crown. "Smile, honey, smile!" she said, grinning wide. Lily waited for her turn, primped and pretty.

"Now then," said the photographer. "Let's get a shot of the boy healing somebody."

"What?" I burst, my head shaking no no no. "I can't do it like that."

"I don't mean for real, young man," he said, and pointed to a woman, one of God's Servants, dressed in regular clothes. "Get on your knees in front of the boy and he can put his hands on your head."

"Aunty Li, I ain't comfortable doin' this. It ain't right."

"Honey," she said, taking me aside. "Just do what the man says. If he was takin' pictures at the revival it'd be just the same, only he ain't comin' to the revival and the light is better here." She prodded me forward. "Okay now, where should Theo stand?"

My mouth was pasty, like bubble gum chewed to a hard rubber after the taste is gone. I lay my hands on the kneeling woman and closed my eyes too tightly. My hands and fingers remained drawn and they ached at the betrayal.

Between Norman and Edmond.

Brother Jimmie had purchased an old school bus and painted it a bright green with *God's Hand Ministries* emblazoned on each side, like we were a high school football team en route to an out of town game. After each stint, when the sound gear and lighting instruments had been loaded into the truck, we would rumble through the dark from one town to the next, the entire crew in tow, to save on a night's motel bill. The weight of the day hung on me like a wet towel as we jostled and thumped along rural back roads, on and off stretches of turnpike that didn't require a bus toll. Lily and I always sat in the *way back*, as we called it, so we could spread out on the full bench. A scrunched up jacket served as my pillow and Lily lay beside the length of me, into the curve of me, and tucked her head under my chin with Sookietwo pulled under hers so that the three of us lay like nesting dolls. I stroked her arm up and down with the tickle of my fingertips. "Do you have any new pictures to show me?"

"I can't think of nothin' to draw."

"Oh, come on, Bug. You always draw interestin' stuff."

She nuzzled her body in closer. "I get out my paper and Crayolas but it's empty inside my head."

"Oh, you'll think of somethin'." I placed my hand over her chest—the protector.

"What do you suppose Daddy's doin' right now?" she murmured.

"Oh, I bet he's doin' somethin' he wished he was doin' with us."

"I bet he's takin' a swim at that motel. I bet that's just what he's doin.' Takin' a swim and wishin' we was swimmin' with him."

The rhythm of her breath slowed into slumber, and I took in the sweetness of her hair, like hay baked in the sun. Her heart beat softly into my palm and her tiny hand intuitively found mine as if assuring herself that I would not leave her, having entrusted me with the most delicate of things. I, too, wondered what my daddy was doing. Smoking, reading, maybe drinking. Something lonely. I gazed at the fleeting headlights whizzing past us, stinging my eyes against the pressing darkness, finally hypnotizing me to sleep.

Sometime later I was awakened by a moan. It was Lily's. I opened my eyes to see that her head had flopped forward, limp, as if her neck was broken, and it bounced with the rough of the road as we pulled into a rest stop. Her hair was worn fuzzy from the rub of my chest. She moaned again, and once more. I pulled her head back and felt her hot with fever. Everyone had gotten off the bus and there was no one to tell.

"You okay, Bug?"

She muttered something I couldn't make out. I sat up and lifted her to me, face to face, her arms burning in mine, and her chin fell into my collarbone, her breath hot against my neck. She started to shudder and I felt it quiver through me. "Theo," she cried, her mouth opening as if to speak again, and she emitted a hot, vile stew of vomit onto my cheeks, my neck, my chest. I unfurled my jacket and wiped her dripping mouth but there was little point as she heaved and heaved, bottomless, until it seemed nothing could be left in her, and then she heaved again, bile and spit and choke. She lay in my lap, pale as milk and lathered in sweat. She breathed little puffs, trying to find air, and raised her heavy eyelids only so far before they fell shut.

"Shhhh. It's okay, I got you."

I moved to pick her up but she stopped me with her words. "Don't leave me, Theo. Please don't leave me."

"I ain't gonna leave you. Let's go outside and get some air. It'll make you feel better."

"No, please. I don't want to move. I can't."

I settled back into the seat and cradled her, begging the fire of my hands to go through her in the hope of easing the assault on her tiny body. I turned my head to the window and in the dim light I saw a man, grizzle-bearded and baseball-capped, sitting high in a truck cab just next to us, staring back at me blankly, his arm jiggling a busy unseen hand at his waist. I was glad Lily couldn't ask what he was doing. Uncle Darnell boarded the bus. The stench grabbed him by the throat and he ran to us, finding Lily splayed in my arms. "What happened? Lily, honey, are you okay? Is she okay?" He pressed his palm to her head and met my confirming eyes.

"I think the worst is over," I said.

"I'll be right back," he declared, and scurried to his seat, grabbing something from his bag, then out of the bus to the rest stop washroom, returning moments later with two wet undershirts. He gently pulled the cloth across her face and wiped the sick and tears from it. He handed me the other and I folded it and placed it on her forehead, pushing back her hair, matted with sweat, letting it sit.

"You wanna throw up again, Bug?" I whispered.

"I think I'm all better now," she whispered back.

Just then Aunty Li and Brother Jimmie clomped up the rubber-matted stairs of the bus, him hee-hawing and she giggling in a skipping high pitch much too young for a woman of her age. She stopped three rows in at the wall of the stink. "What in tarnation happened in here? Did somebody die?"

Uncle Darnell held up his hand. "Hush, Lorelei! The baby's sick."

Brother Jimmie tucked himself into his seat and Aunty Li scuttled in our direction with a mix of concern and mild agitation. She leaned into each row along the way, opening every window as she got closer. When she at last saw Lily and the mess and the sour, she dropped her chin and cocked her head slightly, as if having stumbled upon a strange wounded animal in the wood. "Is she all right?"

"I think so," I said. "Must have been the chicken salad at that diner. I think she's empty now."

"I'm sure she is," she said, taking in the evidence. Aunty Li leaned into Lily, her nose squinching at the reek. "You're just a little car sick, aren't you dumplin'? Or I guess I should say bus sick." She stifled a congratulatory titter at her cleverness. "Baby doll, if you think you're gonna throw up again you just let me know up front and we'll pull over so you can do it *outside* the bus. Now you get some rest, honey, we have a big day tomorrow. Bless your little heart." She puckered her lips and kissed the air in Lily's direction, then turned and clicked back down the aisle to her seat across from Brother Jimmie.

Lily slept. Uncle Darnell lifted her from my lap and lay her across the long seat, placing Sookietwo in her arms. Then he took the wet cloth from my hand and slowly, methodically, began to clean me up, wiping my chin, my neck, the spatter on my arms. He pulled my soiled shirt up and over my head and balled it up and took it away, returning with a light sweater. It was large and soft on me. "You sleep now," he said. "I'll take care of Lily." His eyes were filled with a kindness. He was the fresh air we sought.

Everyone re-boarded the bus, the band last on, always last on—the sweet stench of skunk weed hanging over them like a cloud, overtaking the smell of vomit. An un-fresh air freshener. The bus coughed to life and we were off to somewhere once more.

Unable to sleep, I was resting my eyes when I peeked to see Brother Jimmie and Aunty Li stumbling toward me, bracing themselves on seatbacks for balance. I feigned sleep but Aunty Li jostled me, undeterred. "Wake up, honey. We got a surprise for you and we wanted to wait til everybody was out. You're gonna love this."

Brother Jimmie pulled a plastic suit bag from behind his back and unzipped it with grandeur. It was a new white suit with iridescent sequin lapels. I stared at it and couldn't find my voice.

"What's wrong, baby?" said Aunty Li. "You're gonna be so handsome."

I couldn't take my eyes off of the thing. It shimmered, reflecting headlights zooming past. "Thank you, but I don't want to wear suits no more. I think I'm just gonna put on jeans and a nice shirt."

"Jeans?" piped in Brother Jimmie. "You can't go out there in jeans! People don't come to see you lookin' like you just finished plowin' a field!"

"A suit makes me feel all strapped up." The gravity of my voice surprised me.

With the way the shadows hit just so, Brother Jimmie's cheeks puffed like sweaty plums, leaving black holes where his eyes should be. "This thing cost seventy-five dollars!"

"Hmm," I said. "I'll try to kick in a few extra healings to make up for it." I settled back into the seat and let my head fall against the coolness of the window. Brother Jimmie knew he was trumped and it delighted me.

Aunty Li leaned in and kissed me on the cheek. "Uncle Jimmie's just trying to make you look your best." I snapped my head up, speechless. *Uncle Jimmie?* Aunty Li became flustered. "Did I say uncle? Ha! Well, I guess it all feels like family to me. You go on back to sleep, sugar booger."

When they were gone, I found Uncle Darnell asleep at the other end of the seat, his head against the window, mouth open, his breath blowing little ghosts on the glass.

Lily scooted back to me and lay her head in my lap. Her face was cool and pink and I was relieved. Suddenly an unexpected sob caught in the back of my throat and I coughed to disguise it. It was a coward's sob. *This is how I stand up to them? By refusing to wear a suit? This is as strong as I am? I am as powerless as my baby sister. I am deplorable.*

As if she could hear my thoughts, Lily reached up and glided her tiny fingers across my cheek. I stroked her hair, still damp from the broken fever, and I said to her, "I know it's hard—not sleeping in your own bed in your own house. Motels and buses and no kids to play with. But at least it's you and me together. And before you know it, we'll be back in Dalton and everything will be back to normal, I promise."

Lily's voice was soft, barely a breath. "I think sometimes a promise can go for a really long time before it happens, even if you really mean it." And she snuggled into me and we pretended at contentment, waiting for sleep to find us.

Session 14

I am finding it more and more difficult to separate my own process from hers. I contemplate how I got to this place in my own life—the casualty of my own offenders; these cunning recollections I thought had been conquered, but are now consuming me. I want to turn them off. This, this *project* of writing down my own childhood story began with the intention of approaching it as I do all things—to precisely lay out the facts and face them so I can bury them once and for all. But coming to the statistics of a life doesn't make them benign upon their discovery. I know better, and yet, I thought I was being brave. How ridiculous that I've chosen a field built on the very concept of exploring all that is beneath the facts, yet I had no conscious intention of applying that depth of analysis to myself.

She has brought this on me.

The days since our last session have not been kind to her and I have fared no better. She is nervous, agitated, bubbling like boiling water about to spill over the lip of a pot.

"You don't look so hot," she blurts out.

I'm stunned, but not surprised, by her blunt assessment. Besides, she's right. "It's lovely to see you too."

"Rough night?"

"You could say that," I confess. "I haven't been sleeping so well. Bourbon makes it worse." I no longer protect myself.

"You've got to reel in the party, Doc. You're not as young as you used to be," she laughs.

"I was at home by myself."

"Oooh, even worse." She scrubs her scalp and her hair flies as she lets out an exasperated roar. "I AM SO TIRED OF THIS!" She deflates into the sofa.

"Of what?" I say, the answer being obvious.

"Of remembering. Of reliving. Of trying to put the pieces together. It's getting harder, not easier." She lets her head roll back and she expels a great gust of breath, more like the expulsion of the Heimlich maneuver than an exhale. "I wish I could just take something. Just dull it all a little bit."

"Like your mother did?"

The corners of her mouth curl and I think she's planning another clever zinger, but instead she emits a sound something like a grunt. "You mean like my mother did to *me*."

"I beg your pardon?"

She stills herself. "When I found that Valium bottle in her boxes of crap, something was right there in my mind trying to peek out but I couldn't pinpoint it. Then a couple of days ago it hit me. That one pill left in the bottle? I recognized it: blue with a V-shape cut out in the center. I knew it had looked familiar and I finally figured it out. It was the same kind of pill she gave to me for my *thyroid* condition. At the time I thought the Vs looked like little cutout hearts. It occurred to me that I never saw a bottle of pills with my name on it. They were her prescription, but they were for me. She gave me one every night at bedtime."

She lets the weight of her latest discovery land, almost manipulatively, as if she's waited for the drop, anticipating how I will respond. I watch her struggle, and try to resist the notion that I am making her whole, but the thought lingers, this feeling of purpose and self-congratulatory gratification I once knew before it went sour. Of course I know better, intellectually—I know that I don't have the power to do such a thing. But if it takes two, she is fully participating. I sense there is more to come. That the wrecking ball is held high and ready to swing.

"I haven't been completely honest with you," she says, with a tone that sounds more like control than confession.

It feels like a game, this toying thing she does, this trail of breadcrumbs to the latest disclosure. I pray she's not seeking a way out again, like she when she claimed it was all a lie.

"How so?" I say calmly, concealing alarm.

"My job. I'm not in phone sales."

"No?"

"Well, not technically. I mean I'm on the phone and it's sales of a sort."

"What do you do?"

"Phone sex." Her eyes are blank, her face a mask of nothing. She waits for my reaction, a shock, a flinch. She will not find it in me. "I'm one of those women who gets guys off on the phone. They call the number they got online or in some magazine and I get them off. I sound like I'm twenty-five. They want everybody to sound like they're twenty-five. Wanna hear?"

"That's not necessary."

She switches to the voice she'd demonstrated before—that high, soft, slightly breathy and ever efficient voice. "Hey Daddy, I'm touching myself thinking about that bulge in your pants. Take it out. Come on, take it out and stroke it. Is it out? Ooh, it's so big. Mmmm."

I keep my tone calm, unaffected. "You can stop now, I get the idea."

"I'm touching myself. I'm wet and I'm sliding my finger in and out. Come on, Daddy, put it in me." She moans but her face remains unaffected. "Oh, that's it. Give it to me! Give it to me, Daddy!" She snickers and her voice drops to normal. "And the thing is, I can do this while I'm cleaning or cooking or eating. And the voice switches back again. "Yes! Come on Daddy. Oh, it hurts so good. Oh! Oh! Faster!" She moans louder and louder.

"Stop. Please stop," I say insistently. "There are people right outside the door." *Shit!* "There could be a client in the waiting room."

"Fuck me, Daddy! She escalates into a cry of ecstasy and then sighs and shudders and finally settles and stares at me and our eyes lock. "Do you want one of your cigarettes, Doc? I really don't mind the smell."

CHAPTER TWENTY-EIGHT

B roken Arrow.
Brother Jimmie seemed to grow fatter with each stop and I predicted we had two or three more towns before he simply exploded.

This would be our new home for a whole week, the longest we'd set down anywhere, and the crowds had increased with each stop. The band had grown too, having added a trumpet and saxophone. Doretta Jane had been demoted to one of the octet, and that was okay by her. Less to play, more to drink. Aunty Li, on the other hand, had been promoted, singing hymns to the masses. It was the spotlight she craved.

I was in my new dressing room, now a small, furnished trailer, getting ready to go on. I studied myself in the mirror wearing my pressed jeans and blue button-down shirt. I was thinner, more drawn. Uncle Darnell entered for last minute details and dabbed a bit of concealer under my eyes to mask the gray circles. "Somebody's got a birthday comin' up," he said. "Thirteen years old! Practically a man. What do you want, Theo, a new pair of shoes or ... ?"

There was a scuffle outside the trailer and I heard a woman say, "He would want to see me! I am a friend." One of God's Servants was arguing to keep her out. "Theo!" the woman's voice called. I peeked out the door and saw Melva White. *What is she doing here?* "She's fine," I said, hesitantly. I was actually happy to see someone from my old life, even if she'd once spit in my face. "It's okay, Uncle D, I know her." He gave me a final once over and left us.

Mrs. White stepped into the trailer. "Hello, Theo. Thank you for letting me in." She glanced around the room, particularly impressed by the new dressing table and makeup mirror framed by numerous light bulbs. "I see you've become quite the celebrity. And well deserved." She smiled and took a breath. "I want to thank you for what you did for my husband, for all of us. I spoke in front of the church. I told them what you did for me and so many others, and the goodness of it. I'm sorry I ever doubted you. The whole town is sorry, Theo."

"How's Mr. White?" I asked.

"Well, dear, that's what I came here about. He had another stroke, and he passed away. He went on to meet his maker."

I felt my knees go weak and steadied myself. This was the first time I'd heard of anyone dying after a healing. "Oh," I said. "I'm—I'm so sorry. I'm just, I'm sorry."

She tilted her head and her eyes were kind. "It's okay, Theo. Really. I mean that. It's funny how it all worked out. He had the time he needed. He spent whole days with his boy, got to know him, which I suppose he'd never really had time to do, made time to do. They went fishing at Keystone Lake and Toby caught an enormous catfish and we had a fish fry. Mr. White and I got to talk about things we never talked about." She smiled with tenderness. "We went out to dinner. All you can eat. We ate it all. We went to the movies. We had the time we needed to make it okay." She gently took my hands. "And you gave us that. You're probably too young to understand, but Mr. White and me, see, we'd been—stuck for quite a spell, what with a child and too much work and too many worries and too little life. Mr. White—Harvey and I, we'd grown apart. It wasn't that we ever stopped loving each other. We'd just stopped...imagining." She squeezed my hands. "I wanted to thank you for giving that back to us. I wanted to tell you that."

"I gotta get ready." I squirmed and pulled away.

Brother Jimmie's amplified voice resonated to the trailer. Another introduction in another town promising more miracles that I was expected to perform. Miracles that apparently didn't always work.

"There's something else," she said.

"I really have to go."

"I won't be but a minute." Melva White cleared her throat and swallowed hard. "About seven years ago I got something in the mail, a copy of a will—written by your great grandfather. I don't know who sent it to me. There was a note attached that just said, `I thought you should have this.' No signature, no return address." I wanted her to leave and I wanted her to stay. "Everyone in town knows that your great grandfather left his family, your family, with nothing when he died. But what they don't know is that he left quite a fortune to my husband's grandfather when he was just a boy, a baby in fact, and his mother. I suspect I know why, and why your great grandfather didn't tell anyone."

I clasped my hands together to still the shaking. "You don't need to do this."

"I didn't tell Mr. White. I didn't tell anybody. My first inclination was that it was all legal and it's really nobody's business what happened half a century ago. But there was always a heaviness, like a stone in my belly. And I sat with it and it weighed on me, and I thought maybe I should tell my husband and I almost did, two years ago, but then the market took a downturn and we, my husband, lost quite a bit of money. Then Mr. White's health began to fail—it was all related to the money, I know it was."

I knew Brother Jimmie was moments from introducing me, but I couldn't tear myself away. "Things aren't always what they seem, Theo," she continued, pointedly. "It looks to everybody else like we live pretty large but you'd be surprised. Money can be a curse. So I held on to my secret." Melva White chuckled and rolled her eyes. "And I've been taking my car to your daddy's shop every three or four weeks, as if something so tiny could make something right that was wrong."

Brother Jimmie's voice thundered in the distance. "...for the sickly and the needy to be healed by the hand of God!"

"My names fixin' to get called and I got to be ready..."

"Just one more minute, please," she said. "The point is, I want to do something for you and your family. I can't turn back the clock but you all need a place to live. And we, I, have a property on Fillmore that we've rented out and now it's unoccupied. Nothing fancy, but it's nice and clean and furnished and it's a place for your family to stay for as long as you want, until you get a new house, or forever if you'd like." She leaned in to kiss me on the cheek, the same cheek she'd spit at, and I let her.

Brother Jimmie's voice echoed, "Please say an amen for Theodore Dalton, a gift from the Lord!" Cheers and hallelujahs erupted.

I regained detachment. "We don't need nothin' from you." I had failed her, her husband, and she'd hurt me once again by telling me as much, and I hated her all the more for her magnanimity. "I gotta go," I mumbled, flying from the trailer and racing to the wings as Brother Jimmie exited the stage.

"They're all yours," said the preacher, patting me on the back, and he moved to Aunty Li. "Hey little songbird," he said, giving her the once over. "You're lookin' mighty pretty tonight."

"Now you stop that, Jimmie Dale Oldman," she giggled. "You're gonna make me blush."

I walked onstage as the music crescendoed to a final chord and cut off. I lifted my hands and the crowd quieted, as if by magic, but I had grown used to it. I focused, trying to dismiss the thoughts colliding in my mind.

I walked down to the people and began laying my hands on them, but something was wrong. Off. My hands remained cold and drawn and crippled. I didn't know if it was the news of Mr. White's death or the confirmation my great-grandfather's narcissistic transgression, or just that I was so absolutely exhausted, or all of it. I was faltering. I could not imagine.

I surveyed the hungry faces of the crowd, unsure and unsteady, and my eyes rested on a man in the back, leaning against a post, unlike the rest. *Was it my father? Could it be?* The spotlight burned my eyes and I shut them tightly, so that I could then see more clearly. But when I opened them, the man was gone, and I knew that it couldn't have been him—that it was surely just my want of him that had created some sort of exquisite apparition.

I tried to muster strength but there was little left in me. I trudged back to the stage and faced the audience. "I'm sorry, but I can't help nobody tonight. Please come back another time." And I walked quietly away.

There was a confused stillness in the crowd. Then chatter, like the low rumble of a distant train. "I came all the way from Drumright!" yelled a man. *Boo!* Then more *boo*s. And still more. Brother Jimmie ran onto the stage with the microphone. "We just need a few minutes, folks. Please be patient. We'll be right back," he said, as if we were going to a commercial. Doretta Jane quickly put down her cup and the band started up again, with a rousing "Again I Say Rejoice," but the people did not.

Brother Jimmie caught up with me before I stepped into the trailer and grabbed me by the shoulder, whipping me around. "What in the hell do you think you're doin'?

"I can't do it tonight."

"Gettin' a little too big for your britches?" I had never seen him so hot. "This is our biggest crowd yet, goddammit, and you ain't gonna blow this after all I've done for you."

I felt vacant, blank, and I cast my eyes downward. I noticed that Brother Jimmie was wearing new shoes, two-toned, brown and blue. *Alligator,* I thought, and I smiled at the idea of Lily asking if there were blue alligators and then drawing one.

"Are you listening to me, boy?!" Brother Jimmie shook me and I didn't resist, joggled and limp. "You are going to go back out there to do the job you promised you'd do. The job you promised God you would do. Or He will smite you for abandoning Him!"

I met Brother Jimmie's blistering stare with no effort to conceal my contempt. "I never promised nothin'. I don't know your spiteful God. I didn't ask for this. And it ain't workin' tonight."

"They don't know that!" shot Brother Jimmie. "They don't know shit from Shinola! But they came for somethin' and you're gonna give it to them!"

I stepped up to the trailer but Brother Jimmie grabbed my arm and swung me around and delivered a swift smack to my cheek, hard enough to leave a fat red handprint. I looked fixedly at the preacher and then dropped my chin.

I had neither the will nor the energy to fight him. And I headed back to the tent. I could hear the anticipant buzz of the crowd but I could not feel it. All I knew was the heaviness of my body laden with their needs, like a thick rope pulling me down and down against my effort to straighten my legs.

I trod through the masses, touching them with my cold, buckled hands, never meeting a single one with my eyes for fear they might notice the emptiness. The memory of the revival I'd first witnessed spun in my mind, the disgust, the deception, and I knew I was no better.

SESSION 15

We sit knee deep in silence. Just silence for the entire session. Not the silence of serenity we gave ourselves to a few weeks ago; this one is thick and prickly. The clock hanging above the door ticks so loudly that I begin counting the seconds. As much as I want to initiate conversation, I maintain my cool and wait for her to speak, anticipating an explosion to bubble up and burst.

She adjusts her shoulders and rolls her head in a circle, slowly inhaling, exhaling, like she's in a yoga class. A decent effort, enough to fool the casual observer, but not me. I let my head drop to the side with a smile meant to encourage, but I know it gives away my anxiousness instead. The air is so brittle it could snap. It is a standoff—a blinking game, who will blink first? I look back at the clock, definite and insistent, marking the silence. She glances at it as well, then turns a cheeky arched eyebrow to me.

Our time is up.

She stands and gathers her purse, but rather than make the dramatic exit I expect, she just glares at me. "It went on after high school," she says defiantly. "For the first two years of college when I was still living at home. I told myself it was the last time every time, but I never said no. How messed up is that? I was a grown woman. He had no control over me."

"Of course he did."

"Please don't interrupt me, I've been trying to say this for a fucking hour."

"I'm sorry, go on."

"And it went on fairly regularly until I moved in with Sergio. Remember Sergio? My *boyfriend* who turned out to be gay? Yeah. Gee, that's a tough one to figure out, huh? Falling in love with a boy who was about as safe as you could get."

I sit back in my chair to assure her that I'm in no rush and she continues.

"There was no final moment. There was no confrontation, no discussion. When I moved out it was just over like it had never happened. I visited home less and less and I never spent the night. And then after college I moved here."

"And you got out."

"Three thousand miles out." She pauses for thought. "Then he got sick. It was all very fast. He was diagnosed with lung cancer in December and died in February." She glimpses at the clock. "I'm sorry. I should go."

"I have a few minutes before my next appointment. Go on."

She presses her middle finger against the bridge of her nose. "A couple of weeks before he died I went back home to say goodbye. My mother had moved him into my old room. He was skin and bones—that sallow, sunken death look and that awful rattle in the chest like you can't believe they're still hanging on. And he patted the bed, my bed, the bed that…" She melts into her past, then catches her breath. "And I sat down beside him. And he was so weak and more broken than ever. And he smiled at me so sweetly, I'll never forget that smile." Her voice becomes low and hollow. "And he took my hand and placed it under the covers and over his shriveled penis and held it there. That's what he wanted from me on his deathbed." She shakes her head as if not believing what she is saying—as if someone else is saying it. "That was his idea of comfort from me, like some sort of fucked up hug. And I didn't pull away." Her voice breaks. "I didn't pull away. It was worse than the sex." She lowers her head and then returns her eyes to mine. "It was the last time I intentionally touched anyone."

Desolation hangs in the air.

"I'm so sorry. I'm just so sorry." There is nothing more that I can, should say.

I think of my father's death. After he'd succumbed to the drink time and time again, without his permission, until cirrhosis finally took him at forty-nine years old. He had become a sweet drunk in his last years, drifting off nightly in his cracked-leather chair with the tv blaring, a short glass of melting ice next to an empty fifth of Wild Turkey on his side table. I remember the raging anger and the vast empathy I felt toward him for dying, and the confusion that the two emotions could coexist. I remember the emptiness of being an orphan and feeling silly about the thought because I was a grown man. I remember Lily and I sitting on each side of his bed in the final hours, and when he had taken my hand in his and placed it over his heart.

CHAPTER TWENTY-NINE

Chickashaw.

I woke with a start, tangled in sweat-soaked sheets, my breath stumbling. My fists were clenched and my heart raced against the sound of the ice machine clattering just outside my motel room door. Lily's bed was empty; she always woke before I did. I tried with all of myself to force the memory of my mother's face but it would not come.

It was my birthday.

I wanted to undream all I had dreamed: *I was in a tent the size of a football field, roaming through the seekers of restoration, cloying, needing me, sucking me into their sickness. I felt a presence behind me and I knew it was my mother but she could not, would not? help me. I turned to see her but her hair twirled with her exit into vapor. Suddenly, I heard a masculine cry coming from the entrance in the distance. I looked up to see my father desperately trying to force his way into the tent, but he was restrained by two of God's Servants.*

My father's arms were held tightly behind him as he struggled, and his chest bowed out like a ship's sail in a violent wind. "Theo! Theo!" he called. Brother Jimmie appeared in front of my father with Lily in his grasp, a hostage, and he smiled at me broad and aberrant like the dappled green rind of a watermelon slice. I knew I could do nothing to save either one of them. And then my mother's voice called out, "Run Theo! Run and get help!" But I couldn't find her in the hungry crowd because I couldn't remember what she looked like.

I was afraid that I would never remember my mother's face again.

I rose and splashed cold water on my face and stared at myself in the mirror.

Thirteen. The age my father had promised I could stop going to church if I wanted to. If only.

I knew I had changed. Fledgling hair was springing up on my body in new places. I was leaner, longer. It occurred to me that I could be growing into the same kind of handsome as my father. But those changes were nothing compared with the ones that could not be seen.

There was a knock. "Just a minute," I called out, and stepped into a wrinkled pair of jeans, hopping and tripping, and a sweatshirt that smelled of my older self. When I answered the door I found Lily holding a nameless, store-bought birthday cake with thirteen lit candles of varying length, and Brother Jimmie, Aunty Li and Uncle Darnell standing behind her, smiling as big as life. I thought of the watermelon grin in my dream.

Aunty Li wore a dress I'd not seen before. It was a striking green, black-trimmed, with lace at the collar and hem, and was an emphatically odd choice for seven o'clock in the morning at a motel in Chickashaw, Oklahoma. She began singing, "Happy birthday to you!" in her best and loudest soprano, prompting me to peek outside the door to make sure no one else was there who might be annoyed at this hour. The rest joined in. "Happy birthday, dear Theo! Happy birthday to you!" Aunty Li took the octave on the last note, then bowed her head slightly and pursed her lips as if expecting applause. The cake was small and round with blue frosting that peaked like ripples on a tiny pond and I thought of Henry.

They barged into my room and Lily laid the cake on the wood veneer desk. "Make a wish!" said Aunty Li, and I closed my eyes and I imagined. And then I blew out the candles and Aunty Li leaned in and kissed me on the cheek. "Theo, darlin', I wish I could have baked a cake for you myself, but they don't have ovens at the Highway Host Motel!"

Brother Jimmie handed me a small box wrapped in brown paper with a red ribbon on top—the kind that lick and stick. I opened it and lifted a tarnished pocket watch with a long brass chain and my eyes followed its sway, back and forth, while I tried to think of something to say.

"My daddy give this to me," Brother Jimmie pronounced proudly. "And now I'm passin' it on to you." He looked at me with raised eyebrows and his *ya know I love ya, kid* grin as if he expected to be believed. I didn't want to inherit anything from Brother Jimmie, and I knew that the watch had never belonged to his daddy, but rather was something old he already owned which had relieved him of the burden to shop. I'd be surprised if it worked.

Aunty Li was next. "I know this isn't much. But you know how money's a little tight. It's the thought that counts." She tugged at the hem of her new green dress. I opened the gift. It was a wool argyle sweater vest. "I know you don't like to wear a suit, but I thought this might dress you up just a teensy-weensy bit," she gleamed. "And it'll hide the sweat stains on balmy nights." Her logic was incomprehensible. "Fashion first, I always say!"

Uncle Darnell stepped forward with a single white rose and presented it to me.

"That isn't a gift, silly," snapped Aunty Li. "It'll be dead by this evenin'."

"But I'll remember it," I said, and I hugged my uncle resolutely.

Lily was last. She handed me a large white piece of butcher paper rolled into a cylinder with a sky blue ribbon tied around it in a bow. I carefully unfurled it and rested my eyes on a picture of our day at the roller rink with our father. She'd drawn all three of us holding hands and flying around the rink. There were strokes of multiple colors trailing us like a rainbow. I bent down to kiss her. "Thank you, Bug. I love it. And I'm gonna keep this for always and always."

Lily threw her arms around my neck. "You're welcome, Theo. For always and always is a very long time."

Aunty Li raised a knife in the air and brought it down on the cake.

CHAPTER THIRTY

L awton.
    I said nothing. I sat at the planked-pine folding table, which was gouged and pocked and carved with initials of people I would never know. The backstage of the tent wouldn't come alive with the buzz of the Holy Spirit for another two hours. Brother Jimmie faced me from across the table. He'd been yammering pointlessly and I knew it was the buttering up prelude to whatever he'd actually called me there for. And then it came.

"Listen, Theo, I know you and me ain't exactly close," he said, with the spurious sincerity that Lily and I had imitated in moments of naughtiness. I stifled a droll roll of the eyes but they drolly rolled in my mind. "You're thirteen now, pretty much a man, and you're old enough to understand some things." He laid his elbows on the table and tucked his fists under his lowest chin. "I wasn't always what you think I am now. I used to be like you. Never had the gift the way you got it, but I had some of it. And I believed in it just like you do."

I couldn't picture Brother Jimmie with the touch as a young man. I couldn't even picture him as a young man, for that matter. But I supposed that his boorish features and sweaty tomato cheeks had not always been that way, and when I considered his thick shoulders and sagging bosom, I could imagine his physique might have once been muscled before letting it go to flab.

"My daddy was a minister in Antlers," the preacher continued. "You ever been there?"

"No, but I expect I will be before long," I said, snidely.

"Had himself a Pentecostal church—First Apostolic—and I was all set to fill his shoes as minister when he got old. But then in the spring of `45 two tornadoes come to Antlers on the same night, and the whole damned town was just—gone. More than three hundred dead. And those tornadoes took the church and my daddy."

I'd never thought of Brother Jimmie as someone's son. I knew what it was like to lose a parent.

"Didn't even much make the news `cause FDR died the same day and that was all anybody cared about. It was like this—this thing happened and nobody noticed. So with the church gone and the town all turned upside down," he chuckled, "literally—I did what I grew up knowin' how to do: I pitched a tent where the church used to be and I held services. For months I held services every night of the week. And they came."

I sat forward, intrigued, but then sat back again so it wouldn't show.

"I was a beacon for the people. Their kin was dead and more than half their houses was gone and I had somethin' to give `em. It was the worst and the best thing that ever happened to me." Brother Jimmie tilted his head back and massaged the place on his neck between the base of his skull and his shoulders that swelled like a bratwurst on a grill. "And like I said, I had a little bit of the touch like you. Or I thought I did. The folks in Antlers thought I did. I knew how to preach the Good Word, strong and wholehearted, and people walked in with ailments and walked out without `em, that's the facts. And eventually, Antlers came back, and people started comin' from other towns until the congregation couldn't get no bigger. Not there. So I moved on. I ain't sayin' I wasn't ambitious. But I also had a mama and a little brother to take care of."

Brother Jimmie seemed almost emotional and paused to collect himself. "So I traveled. And I met my wife in Oologah and she left me in Picher." He snorted at his own misfortune. "I don't blame her much. Too many towns, too many women."

I found myself more engaged than I wanted to be and even felt the tiniest twinge of empathy for the man, and I hated myself for it. I would not be drawn in. Up until now, Brother Jimmie's every breath had been an angle and I didn't know why this tale should be any different—just another lie, like the fake healings and the pocket watch and everything that flowed from his mouth as acrid as vomit. "I don't know what this has to do with me," I said, coolly, and crossed my arms.

"Nothin' much, I guess. But I wanted to tell you I know a little bit about what it's like havin' people needin' you to help `em. To heal `em. And one day, after a year or two on the road, I knew for sure that whatever I mighta had in my hands wasn't really there. Probably never was to begin with, but I'd believed it so the people believed me. But I couldn't convince myself no more and I didn't know what I was gonna do. So, like when my daddy died, I just kept goin'. And I went town to town, pitching the tent and layin' hands on the people `cept now I knew it wasn't real. But here's the thing," he said, leaning in. "It didn't matter. The folks that came *wanted* to be healed so they *was* healed. The mind is a powerful thing, son."

"Don't call me son."

"I'm sorry. Didn't mean nothin' by it." Brother Jimmie reached down beside his chair and brought up a bottle of Ten High Kentucky Bourbon and a shot glass. "A lot can happen when folks want it to. They get all excited, their blood runs hot and a healing can happen if they make themselves think it can." He poured himself a shot. "And I learned the tricks. I learned how to put on a show: makin' it look like I could grow one leg to match the other'n, makin' it look like I was pulling cancer out of a body using chicken parts and a pan of blood, things I never thought I'd do to keep goin'."

I could taste the disgust in my mouth. "But it ain't supposed to be a show," I said. "And whatever you think works don't work as soon as they walk out the door."

"Well, after that," said Brother Jimmie, "it ain't none of my business."

"What?" I gasped in disbelief. "What did you say?"

"I said, what happens after ain't none of my business."

I shook my head. Frank's words could not have come from this sorry man's mouth.

"And I figured if people think they're better off when they leave then why not give `em that?" He threw back the drink and poured another.

"But it ain't the same," I declared. "Not at all. And it *is* your business. That's what makes it real. That I really do make a difference." I pulled myself back and willed my eyes dry. "And whatever you think you are or were, I ain't nothin' like you."

"Well, I guess that's what I'm gettin' to. You come along and I thought, `Well, hallelujah, this kid is the real deal.' And you are, son—I'm sorry—Theo. And what happened to you the other night when you thought you lost the power …"

"And you told me to fake it …"

"And you did."

"And I did…" I lowered my head because I didn't want to see the gluttonous victory in his eyes, or worse, any scrap of pity.

"Well, I just don't want you to lose faith in yourself or whatever you got faith in. You ain't nothin' like me. You ain't. And I don't want you to be."

"Well, I guess we agree on somethin'."

"And if there's a part of me that still believes anything I believed all those years ago, it's because of you."

I concentrated on a divot in the table and scratched into it with my thumbnail, then cleaned out the sawdust with my teeth. "I don't know what you want me to say. That you're a good man?"

"Maybe not a good man, but maybe a better one than you thought I was."

I didn't want to feel anything one way or the other. I didn't need a buddy, especially not this one. And I would never become him, never. Brother Jimmie replenished the glass, almost to the brim this time. Then he pushed it, rumbling across the table, to me.

"When I turned thirteen," said Brother Jimmie, "my daddy give me my first taste of whiskey and my first taste of a woman. A brothel down in Edmond, I reckon it's still there," he snickered.

I knocked my chair back and stood up. "I ain't goin' to no brothel!"

"Keep your shirt on, boy. I ain't takin' you to no brothel. Your aunt would slap me six ways to Sunday. But I reckon you're old enough to have a drink."

I sat. Brother Jimmie edged the glass closer with the tip of his finger. It was stained with water spots and the memory of a lipstick print and I wondered if it was my aunt's.

"Go on," said the preacher. "You do a man's work, you can have a man's drink."

I fitted my hand around the glass and lifted it slowly to my lips. My nose twitched at the spicy stench and it both repelled and invited me. I tipped it to my lips and let the liquid find my tongue. It was sweet and thick and sharp and grassy. It tickled the inside of my cheeks with a dull, pleasing tang and when it reached my throat it turned to nectar, leaving me numb and alive.

"Thank you, boy, for listenin' to me. You got somethin' special, somethin' real, and you got the world ahead of you. And you're makin' money hand over fist! Ten percent. Your daddy's gonna be proud."

I asked for another taste and Brother Jimmie poured.

CHAPTER THIRTY-ONE

Moore.

It was two weeks and three towns later and God's Hand ministries had graduated to a midsized amphitheater where community players had just finished a run of *The Music Man*. The day had pulsed in me like a flush vein. When the service was over, one of God's Servants met me in the wings with a frosty Coke and another took my arm to escort me to my dressing room.

It was typical that everyone stay until the last dollar had been collected from the exiting crowd so that we could return together on the bus to the motel, usually on the outskirts of town. It could take an hour, sometimes more. On this night, I changed into a pair of blue cotton shorts and a Fruit of the Loom t-shirt, then half-slept on the small brown couch not meant for sleeping. I dreamed that Lily drowned. *We were at sea in a small boat, only Lily and me, and she stepped into my outstretched arms, smiling, as the boat rocked and rocked, then tumbled her overboard. Lily! I pinned my feet under a splintered wooden seat and extended my body over the bow like a plank, and grasped her wrists once, twice, but she slipped away, sinking into the dark water. I heard my mother calling to me but, once again, the voice was faceless and I could not find her.*

I woke to hear my aunt yelling from the theater manager's office next door. She made no attempt to quiet her rage. "Don't you come anywhere near us, George Dalton," she spat. I walked to the door. *Is my father here?* "If you so much as show your face I'm gonna call child services and they will throw you in jail when I tell what I have to tell. And believe me there won't be a penny of insurance. Arson my ass."

I burst into the office and found her on the phone. "I want to speak to my daddy."

She slammed it down. "You will do no such thing!"

"I have a right to ..."

"Theo, your daddy is not ready to take care of you or your sister and you have to trust that I know what's best." She sweetened her voice and the words fell from her mouth in shards of patronization. "There will come a time, soon, I promise, where you can talk to your daddy, but for now he needs to get his life together. And until he can prove that to me, I don't want you to be dragged down by him. And your mama wouldn't have it any other way." She paused and placed her hand on my cheek. "Now you go on and rest. You're worn slap out. When we get back to the motel, we can get a pizza or something fun like ribs."

I returned to my dressing room and switched on the light and couldn't believe what I was seeing. Henry was sitting on the couch smiling ear to ear. His ankles were crossed on the coffee table and his arms were sprawled on either side of him as if he lived there. I hurried to embrace him but he socked me in the arm instead. I did not return the greeting.

"What are you doin' here?" I said. "Why didn't you tell me you was comin'? How did you get in here?"

"Slow down there, pal," laughed Henry. "Didn't you get my note?"

"What note?"

"The note I left for you with that creepy guy who stands outside your door."

"No."

"Well, go get it," he said insistently.

"Just tell me what it said."

"I want you to get the note."

"Just tell me what it said."

"Get the note!"

I sighed and opened the door and asked the God's Servant if he had a note. The guard told me he'd forgotten about it, and found the folded piece of paper in his robe pocket and handed it to me. I shut the door and read aloud: *Theo. I'm here. I took the bus. I told them I was your cousin. Henry.*

Henry shrugged and said, "I didn't want you to think I just dropped in unannounced."

And we laughed the same laugh we used to laugh and it felt good.

Henry helped himself to a pop from the ice chest. "You were kind of amazing out there. You're practically the Beatles. And you know what the Beatles do after a show? Let loose! Get wild! Let's do somethin' crazy!" His eyes were alive with complicated plans.

"Oh, man, I'm really tired," I said. "Can't we just talk?"

"Come on! Let's do something fun. Let's steal a cow. There's gotta be some cows around here."

"I can't steal a cow."

"Okay, then—let's sneak into an R-rated movie. I saw *Rosemary's Baby* is playin' at the drive-in on the other side of town."

I chuckled. "I can't, Hen."

"Okay, let's get one of your footmen to get us chili cheeseburgers and too much ice cream and we can puke all over the street," Henry begged. "Or beer! Let's get us some beers! We're thirteen for chrissakes! Kids in Europe have liquor for breakfast."

I smiled wearily. "Hen, I can't do that stuff no more."

"Wow. You're a barrel of laughs, a regular Red Skelton. I'm so glad I came."

"I'm sorry, really. I'm—I'm just so glad to see you, you don't know." I took a step back and gave him a once over. "Hey, I think you grew, you seem a little taller."

"I think you grew too," said Henry. "But you seem a little smaller."

I didn't know whether or not he was joking. There was a knock at the door and it swung open without invitation. It was Brother Jimmie. "That's my boy! They loved you. God is blessin' us all. You made a hundred bucks tonight!" he bragged. "You're raking it in now, son—Theo." He slapped me on the back and left the room.

"A hundred bucks?" asked Henry.

"I know. He gives me ten percent. I'm practically rich."

Henry paused, thinking. "There musta been six or seven hundred people out there. I saw them givin' ten, twenty bucks at the door when I came in and that was before they saw you do your thing. You're gettin' screwed, my brother."

"I don't care about the money. I just want to get outta here. Henry, I gotta get outta here."

Session 16

I got rid of my iPad contraption. She was right, it was a wall—to keep me in or to keep people out, it doesn't matter which. I feel naked without it and the feeling is distracting. I cross and uncross my legs. I fold my arms across my chest. I try to relax my body language so it doesn't scream out how uncomfortable I really am. Thankfully, she doesn't seem to notice.

"I want to apologize," she says, her voice delicate.

"For what?" As if I didn't know.

"I've been really horrible to you. I'm sorry. I think I've been testing you to see if you would stick around no matter what."

"Did I pass?"

"Yes," she offers, the corners of her mouth rising.

"I'm not going anywhere."

"I would have. I would have told me to fuck off and go wallow in my misery. I would have told me to …"

"Stop. Just stop."

She covers her face with her hands and speaks through them, faintly. "It was the friend thing."

"I'm not sure I follow."

"When you said you were my friend."

"I meant it."

I notice that she's no longer wearing the mock wedding ring. She takes her hands down and looks at me softly. Her eyes have lost their harshness and become rounder, more glossy, full in the moment. "I don't know what to do with that."

"I'm not sure I do either." My cheeks grow warm at the tender curve of her smile. "What do you say we both just accept it and move forward."

"Deal." She laughs to herself. "Most of the time I'm here I just want to run. But then sometimes I wish I could stay forever. Like if there could be some kind of retreat, deep in the woods, you know, some seventy-two-hour purging of my whole goddamned life."

"The time between sessions can be just as important as the sessions themselves. Time to digest, time to assess."

"Oh, believe me, it doesn't stop when I leave here. And then I try to pinpoint what I'm going to talk about when I come back. I make a mental list of each revelation to … present to you. I think if I can organize my thoughts, maybe I can organize my life. Then some new thing comes up and I forget the last one. Or I tuck it away hoping I'm done with it. But that hasn't worked so well." She takes a deep breath and blows it out slowly. "Okay then …" She pulls a book out of her bag. "My sister gave me this when I was about five," she says. "She would read to me before bedtime. I've always kept it on the bookshelf in my bedroom, like a keepsake of my sister, and it's been there for so long I didn't even see it anymore. I mean I haven't actually read it in, well, forever. Not since I was a kid. It's a children's book. *A Light in the Attic*, by Shel Silverstein."

"I'm familiar. I gave all of his books to my nieces and nephew."

"So I was thinking about my sister and I got the book down and I started reading it. Some of the poems are so charming. They're funny and smart and sad, and some of them are really scary—monsters, and horses that eat children, headless people, really gruesome stuff. And check out the photo of this guy, Silverstein! I mean he's downright creepy." She shows me the book jacket and I have to agree. "I was terrified of him when I was a kid and I remember my sister told me, `Don't judge a book by its cover,' and I thought she made that up, and that it was so clever, and when I heard the phrase when I was a little older I thought `wow, that thing she made up really caught on.' Ha!"

She opens the book and begins to leaf through the pages. "So I'm reading it and I'm only a few pages in, and this piece of paper falls out." She finds a folded sheet of pink stationery. "It's a note my sister wrote to me that I'd tucked away when I was seven. I remember the age because it was soon after she was gone and I'd just begun to really read. But I'd forgotten all about it until now." She puts on her readers and opens the page.

My dear little sister, I cannot stay here. I want to be here to protect you but I need to go to protect myself. I hope that you never have to get out, but if you do, I pray that you will find another way. I just can't anymore. I hope that you will never understand why I had to do this, but please trust my decision and know that I love you with all of my heart. Your big sister.

She folds the note.

"I imagined for a long time that she'd run away. That they'd found that boat with the motor running on the shore miles away, and I imagined that she'd stolen it to give herself a head start to wherever it was she needed to get to. I imagined that they never found her body like my parents said they did." She finds the locket against her chest and twists it. "The casket was closed and I was sure she wasn't in it. I thought my mother made it up so no one would know she'd run away, that it wouldn't look good for the family, that's what I told myself. I pictured my sister alive and far from home in some wonderful place, and I thought she would come back someday and we'd be together."

She manages a fragile smile, her graceful crow's feet wrinkling. "And I think I tucked the letter in this book, the book she gave me, because it was a place my parents wouldn't ever find it. It was our secret, my sister's and mine. And even though I finally accepted that she was really dead by the time I was nine or ten, I don't think I knew until now, reading her note after all this time, that the boat on the shore wasn't empty with the motor running because of some accident…It was empty because she let it speed away so she couldn't change her mind. After she jumped. I know in my heart this is true." She pulls the book close to her chest.

I'm not sure what to say. "I'm sorry." My words seem so nothing. "Do you think your parents knew?"

"I think so," she says, quietly but sure. "But I doubt they ever dealt with it or even discussed it. Nothing was ever discussed in our family. You just went on. Pretending. Anything but deal with the truth."

"And what is the truth?"

"That it was him," she says quietly. "That my sister took her own life because of what my father did to her." Sorrow threatens to settle in and she attempts to toss it away. "My father told me that he and my sister had done the same thing. As if to make it seem normal. And I think my mother knew everything all along, consciously, subconsciously, it doesn't matter. And I think she became incapacitated by the guilt for not saving my sister, and she couldn't climb out.

She just lost herself…" She looks away to the window and shakes her head.

"What?"

"Ironic, isn't it?" she smirks. "That she got Alzheimer's and could finally, really disappear. It's what she always wanted." She softens as her shoulders shake, just the once, with a sigh. "I think that her fear of what could happen—the shame, the family falling apart, courtrooms, jail, me ending up with him, who knows, all of the *what ifs*—was greater than her fear of what was actually happening. Greater than everything. Greater than me." Hurt flickers in her black pupils, spreading like smoke over the whites of her eyes. "After my sister died, it was as if she thought that loving me too much would be too…" She searches for the word. "…dangerous."

"Dangerous?"

"Vulnerable, too vulnerable. So, the only way she could show her love, to protect me, was to overfeed me, and lock me in my bedroom, and take me to church, and send me to summer camp, and give me Valium—all the things she did to separate me from him. She did everything she could think of in her mousy, weak, stupid way to make up for not saving my sister."

"Except for one thing," I say.

"She didn't save me either."

"Yes," I say, remaining steady.

Her face bares every wrongdoing that has been poured up her. "It's selfish and cruel and sick. As sick as my father."

"And do you think he knew about the cause of your sister's death?"

"How could he not?" Her brow furrows, her face grows hot. "So how could he still do that with me. *To* me."

"I once had a patient," I say softly. "A man. When he was a boy, he had an older brother who slashed his wrists with a hunting knife his father had given him for his thirteenth birthday. And when the boy turned thirteen, his father gave him the same knife."

"That is so fucked up."

"And the man said he didn't think his father was even aware of the message he was sending. And his mother just went along."

"And that's what happened to me, isn't it? My father gave me the same knife. And my mother just went along."

I want to hold her, to reassure her. But she is too fragile for me to try to break through that wall now and I shudder at the irony: that a person can be too fragile to be held. But when I take in the smooth lines of her face, her kind eyes, her demure posture, I realize that somehow she has not been speaking with the great shock that this newest revelation might have wrought. She is not run over or destroyed. She is in a nearly peaceful moment of this discovery. It's as if she has said something she already knew, this sad, sad epiphany. The lack of surprise is what is surprising. And my heart breaks for her. The sequence of her memory is choked with unaccountable fragments, images with no order, and she struggles to piece them together. Just as I am in my own life.

"When I was little I was so mad at my sister for running away," she says. "And then I was mad at her for dying. And now I am so, so very angry with her for dying that way. For leaving me there alone. With him. With her. We could have saved each other. And I wonder why didn't I just kill myself too, after I was old enough to know how wrong it all was? I could have. I thought about it a thousand times."

I wait for the quiet to settle. And then I say, "But you didn't. You held on. You are here and you're alive and you are strong. You have endured tragedies that would have shattered so many others. That's something for you to hold on to, to be proud of, and help you to see yourself as the woman you truly are. You are a survivor. And I think you're extraordinary. I want you to know that. I think you're one of the strongest people I ever hope to know."

I don't know if she believes me. She attempts to pull herself together. Always pulling herself together. There is a quiet knock and a muffled voice comes from outside the door. "Dr. Dalton." It's Stefani with an *f*.

"Yes?"

"I'm sorry to interrupt." She knows better than to disturb me while I'm in a session. "I just wanted to remind you of the time."

I look at the clock and we're fifteen minutes over. The woman smiles graciously and stands to leave. "That was exhausting," she says with a weak smile. "But it was good. Ha! Now you've got me saying it." When she is almost out, she turns back to me. "Congratulations on getting rid of that stupid iPad tree with all the electronics like a metal octopus. You're making real progress, Doc." Then she winks at me and closes the door behind her.

CHAPTER THIRTY-TWO

Oklahoma City.
I'd been with the revival for seventy-four days. I'd tallied them on the back of a God's Hand cardboard fan. It was the largest venue yet. A real theater, indoors with air-conditioning. I was given the room right next to the star dressing room reserved for Brother Jimmie. Lily slept on my couch and the whisper of her breath was like a breeze in tall grass and I sat beside her to listen. Uncle Darnell stood quietly in the corner and spit on the iron to test it. It hissed and steamed and was the only evidence of his presence.

There was a rap at the door that startled me and woke Lily. Aunty Li and Brother Jimmie barged in, practically floating. The sharp tang of her perfume was like smelling salts. "Big news, honey," said Aunty Li. "We got a local news crew here tonight. KTUV! *60 Minutes* is just around the bend, I can feel it!

"You gotta be your best, boy. Big night!" said Brother Jimmie.

I wasn't sure what my best was supposed to be on this night any more than any other night. What was I expected to do, raise somebody from the dead?

"And tell him what else, Jimmie."

Lily suddenly jumped from the couch. "Hey everybody..."

"Hush up now, Lily, Brother Jimmie's got big news," said Aunty Li.

"But it's real important," said Lily, pulling at Aunty Li's skirt.

"Whatever it is can wait, young lady. Go on Brother Jimmie, tell the news."

Brother Jimmie grinned broadly. His teeth seemed larger than usual. "Word is out, little man. We are talkin' about a tri-state tour in the fall."

Lily gasped with such a sharp intake of air that I thought she might choke. I was confused, tongue-tied. "But I have ... we have school startin' in September."

Aunty Li had anticipated the question. "Honey, you can take correspondence courses, I already checked into it. And what is school for anyway? To learn a trade so you can make a living." She plopped down next to me and gave my thigh a slap. "You already got a trade and you're makin' more than most grownups!"

A chilling thought settled over me and I felt acid rise in my throat. *What if this goes on forever?* I looked past Aunty Li. S*ssssssss* sang the steam from the corner as Uncle Darnell ironed my white shirt, keeping his gaze down. Finally, Aunty Li blurted, "Okay, honey, we'll talk about it later. I know you gotta get ready for the service. Promise me you'll think about it." I nodded. But it would have been easier for me to promise to stop breathing.

Uncle Darnell hung up the shirt, stiff as oak tag, and looked to me with consolation. "Can I get you somethin' to drink? Mountain Dew or ...

"I'm fine, Uncle D, thanks," I said, and smiled to acknowledge our bond.

"Make sure he looks good, Darnell," said Aunty Li. "Sister Sister, you are pretty as a peach. Take your time with those rose petals tonight, sweetie. And smile pretty for the camera."

"That's what I'm tryin' to tell you. Look!" she said, wiggling a front tooth with her tongue, beaming with pride. "Does the tooth fairy know where to find me?"

Aunty Li's eyes grew wide. "Tonight?! Are you kidding me? Stop jigglin' it!" She whipped around to Uncle Darnell. "I am holding you responsible. If that thing falls out before the service, you figure out a way to tack it in with some chewing gum or somethin'. We've got the news here!"

"Come on, Lorelei," said Brother Jimmie, and he opened the door and she sailed away. "Left somethin' for you in the cabinet," he added, winking at me, and he followed Aunty Li out of the room.

My uncle straightened the bow in Lily's hair. "You look perfect. And I am most absotively-positulely certain that the tooth fairy will find you." Lily seemed unconvinced. He paused in the awkward silence that hovered over the room. "I gotta make sure I got water backstage." And he left.

A reflection in the mirror caught my eye and it took a moment for me to recognize that the ghostly pale image was me. I breathed too loudly and stretched my arms too high, and I felt as if I might break. "Hey Bug, why don't you color somethin'," I said, too urgently. "That would be real nice. Take your mind off things."

Lily opened her art pad and colors. She sat. She pondered. "I don't know what to draw."

"How about makin' a picture of something we did lately."

"I can't think of nothin'."

"Okay then. How about something we did a ways back. A good day."

Lily had already drawn the picture of the roller rink for my birthday. It was the last good day either of us could really remember and she sighed and placed the tip of the crayon on the page but it did not move. "I miss Daddy."

"Well, school is startin' soon and we'll be back home in no time," I said. *What home?*

She believed me. She always believed me, and I wondered how long that would last.

"Theo, tell me about the night I was born."

"Aw, Bug, I can't right now. I gotta go out to the people."

"Even if you don't want to?"

"Even if I don't want to," I said, and I buttoned up my shirt.

Lily stared at her blank pad. "Come on, Theo, just tell me the end. The part about where Mama is bein' here with us."

I sat on the couch and invited Lily to my lap with the pat of my knee. She was almost too big to fit anymore. "Well, it's true. She ain't really gone. She's here with us. She helps us. All we have to do is ask."

"And tell me about the special part."

"Mama always told me I was special. And when you were in her belly she would rub it all over and she'd say she knew you'd be special too." I pecked her on the cheek and lifted her off of my lap. "Okay now, shake a leg." I checked myself in the mirror for a last look. Some of the color had come back to my cheeks and I smoothed my hair to the side. Lily grabbed the basket of silk rose petals and started out, then she turned to me.

"Theo?"

"Yes?"

"I wish I could do it for you." And she smiled wide and pushed her tongue against her wagging tooth, then kissed me hard and skipped out of my dressing room.

I sat alone in the crowded space of my thoughts. I looked in the cabinet for whatever Brother Jimmie had left and found a bottle of Ten High bourbon and a glass. I paused for only a moment before pouring a drink and downing it in one swallow, and I liked the burn—the something to calm the sharpening wrench of my belly. I thought to myself how much I didn't want to be there. That I wanted my father to be okay. That I wanted to be home, wherever that might be—nowhere specific was better than this. "Tell me what to do," I said to the empty room, as if someone was listening.

"Theo, quick, hurry!" Lily rushed back in panting and panicked. "Somebody's killing Aunty Li!" She grabbed my hand and dragged me out of the door and down the hall to Aunty Li's dressing room. The screams from inside were alarming and delirious. I tried the locked doorknob, then threw my body against the door, flinging it open.

Brother Jimmie's red face snapped in my direction open-mouthed, captured. His mammoth, blubber-pocked buttocks froze on the sagging sofa and his Cuban heels peeked through the cuffs of his polyester pants gathered below his knees. Aunty Li's head was thrown back over the arm of the sofa out of view, and her body had disappeared beneath the enormity of him, so that the only thing visible were her legs reaching high in the air, framing Brother Jimmie like giant bunny-ear antenna on the top of a TV console. It was truly a missionary position.

I shielded Lily's eyes from the sight. "Get back!" I said, as my aunt's head popped up, her eyes as wide as the preacher's ass. I pulled the door closed. "She's all right, Bug," I said to Lily, and couldn't think of a single explanation for the shrieking that Lily had mistaken for a savage murder, which might have been easier to digest. When I turned around, I found Uncle Darnell standing behind me. His eyes held an unsurprised sorrow.

One of God's Servants rushed down the hall and grabbed me. "We're about ready to start, Theo, soon as I find Brother Jimmie. Have a blessed night." I walked to the wings. The crowd sounded huge. The music blared. Brother Jimmie rushed past me assembling himself and grabbed the microphone on his way to the stage.

"Brothers and Sisters. Welcome to the Hands of God Ministry. I know you been suffering. I know you're in pain. But we surely have some miracles for you tonight!"

Aunty Li ran to me, straightening her dress and reapplying her lipstick. "Theo honey, it isn't what you think," she panted. "Uncle Darnell and me been havin' some problems in a very personal department and Brother Jimmie was healin' me. It's the work of the Lord."

I stared out to the stage, firm.

"We'll talk about this later, sugar," she said, clearing her throat. "It's all gonna be fine. You gotta trust me, sugar. I would never lie to you. Now you just forget all this and go out there and do what the Lord..."

"Leave the boy alone!" It was a voice I'd never heard before. It was low and bold and brave. It was my Uncle Darnell. Aunty Li turned around so sharply that I realized she hadn't recognized it either. "I'm in charge of Theo now," he notified her. "You do what you gotta do, Lorelei. You sing your silly songs and you parade around in your flashy dresses and you screw your preacher, but you leave the boy alone." His eyes fixed on her like a bayonet. She did not move.

Brother Jimmie energized the crowd. "To get the spirit flowing, please welcome a servant of God, Miss Lorelei Unwin."

The band played her musical introduction. Aunty Li put on her most winning smile, grabbed the microphone and took to the stage, singing:

Something good is coming to you today
This very day, let us all pray
Something good is coming to you today
Jesus Christ is coming your way

I was numb and cold. Uncle Darnell rested his sure hand on my shoulder. Lily joined me, grabbing a fist full of fake petals. When my aunt finished her song, Brother Jimmie continued, "You've heard about this boy. You've heard about the healings and the glory. And you are here tonight to witness the miracle for yourself. Please give thanks to God Almighty for Theodore Dalton."

Lily walked ahead of me sprinkling my floral pathway. *Step touch. Step touch.* The spotlight hit me and I did not flinch. I was long used to it. Through the haze I could see the masses. It must have been more than a thousand. Each night more and more had come. I knew that some were there to be healed, but many just to watch. I had become a spectacle. I tried to remember myself, who I was before this place, this life, as if it had all been forever ago. And I knew I could never return to that Theo again; the one before the bits of lies and ceaseless expectation had accumulated like grit in a skinned knee until it becomes scarred and calloused. That Theo was gone.

I walked to the edge of the proscenium, raised my hands and the band cut off. The crowd quieted, expectant. I stood silently and looked out among them, taking in the largeness of their anticipation. The danger of it. I padded down the set of stairs and through the congregation. My hands had become accustomed to the ebb and flow of their power as I began touching the people, holding them, one by one. But I knew I couldn't reach them all and so did they. Ever so slowly, they began squeezing in, encroaching, closer and closer. A man, pale and desperate, pushed his way past a young woman on crutches, reaching out to me, and she would have none of it. "You wait your turn!" she fumed, lifting a crutch like a weapon.

Everything started to move more swiftly, as if time had switched into fast-forward, and I began to feel the muscle of the crowd and the weight of its intention. My hands remained open as if in the act of healing, but I couldn't maintain their heat, their purpose. There was pushing and pawing, the urgent press of strangers, fighting to be nearer to me—the medicine man—the medicine boy.

A flashbulb flared in my eyes and I heard the mechanical buzz of a Polaroid camera. I felt the tug of someone ripping my hand from one person and placing it on themselves. Hands were laying on *me*. Even more than the constriction of the mob was the magnitude of its sickness, which swarmed me like angry wasps, stinging, swallowing me. I sucked in air and held it too long and then let it out raggedly. My hands cramped, recoiling into clawed fists. Someone tore my shirt. Another grabbed my hair. I was overtaken by a flood of faces and arms and voices and hands and mouths and eyes and my vision blurred like a windshield in a hard rain. I grew hot, then cold, and my limbs grew numb. I felt my knees crumble and my body go slack.

I knew that I was on the floor, I could feel the cool of it. But I couldn't open my eyes. A fog of noise surrounded me—the throng of screams and blowing whistles. The band began playing a spirited hymn.

"Boy, can you hear me?" I thought I heard in the muddy babble, and I felt someone pressing their fingers against my neck just under my chin.

I lay limp and disconnected for what could have been minutes or hours. Suddenly, I felt the sensation of hands crawling beneath me. One arm sliding under the bend of my knees and the other under my shoulder blades. Strong arms lifting me, cradling me, and I struggled to raise my eyes to my liberator, but my heavy head would not obey. I knew, even in my bewilderment, that it couldn't be Brother Jimmie. I felt steady footsteps beneath me. The smell was familiar and comforting; the shape of the arms that held me was intimate, native, and I knew.

My father carried me out of the place and I could feel the crowd parting to let us through.

CHAPTER THIRTY-THREE

I lay in the hospital bed. I could hear the dull beeping monitor keeping time like a metronome to remind me that I was not dead. And more than that, I knew that it was my father's hand holding mine, and that it was my sister whispering a song in my ear:

... All through the night
Guardian angels God will send thee,
All through the night
Soft the drowsy hours are creeping,
Hill and dale in slumber sleeping
I my loved ones' watch am keeping,
All through the night.

I felt my father reach across me and take my sister's hand, and they let them rest on my chest. I heard footsteps enter the room. My father said, "Punkin, why don't you go outside the room for a bit while I talk to the doctor," and I heard her pad away.

A man's voice told my father he wasn't sure what could be done. He rattled off the report of his analysis, my mind grasping every few words: "his white cell count suggests leukemia...riddled with ulcers...his creatinine levels are high...his glomerular filtration numbers could mean kidney failure … heartbeat is irregular …" I felt the doctor come closer and stand over me. "None of this makes sense," he said. "The boy has arthritis in the joints of his knees and his hands. It's unheard of for a thirteen-year-old." He placed his hand gently on my arm. "Mr. Dalton, your son is not getting better. And I need to be honest with you. I'm not sure he's going to."

I wanted to tell them I was there.

The doctor promised he'd be back soon and that he wasn't giving up, and then I heard him leave. My father sat beside me and stroked my arm. And then I felt it. Another presence in the room. "Hey there, you little shit." It was Frank. And he knew to speak to me. Directly to me. "You got a regular prayer vigil goin' on in the lobby. Candles and whatnot. People tryin' to return the favor." He lifted my limp hand and kissed my palm. "I been missin' you, boy," he said. I wanted to open my eyes. I wanted to say that I missed him too. "I been thinkin' it's been too long since we had a good talk in my fancy trailer." And I smiled without smiling.

Sometime later—an hour, a day, three—my sister came to me. "Sookietwo and me met a lady," she said. "I was coloring a picture and a lady sat beside me but I didn't even see her sit and she was really pretty and she said what's that you're coloring? and I said a picture, and she said a picture of what? and I said a picture to make my brother feel better and she said may I see? and I showed her my drawing pad and I told her I *was* gonna draw a picture of cool stuff we already did but I decided to make a picture of a bunch of stuff we're *gonna* do when you waked up.

"And I showed her the picture and I know you can't see it but here's us fishin' but I won't put the worms on the hook `cause that's your job and the lady made me laugh `cause she said she don't like to do that neither, and I showed her this part here where we're gonna ride the Tilt-A-Whirl when the fair comes `cause this year I'll be tall enough, and then this part of the picture where we're eatin' cotton candy and she said she liked that I drew a pink one for me and a blue one for you."

I could hear the paper crumple as she moved it for a different angle. "And then I showed her this part here where we're playin' hide and seek and I told her how I always find you right away but I think I'm gonna wait a little while from now on so you don't feel bad, and this is us readin' and I told her how you help me sometimes `cause I still get my p's and my q's mixed up, and she really liked it a whole lot and I told her it's my best picture I ever made ever."

I could see the drawing in my mind as she continued in a breathless stream.

"And she said it was beautiful and she was sure you would like it very much and I asked her if she was visitin' somebody and she said yes, her daughter, and I asked her if her daughter was sick and the lady said her little girl is gonna be fine and she's goin' home today as a matter of fact, and I told her I wasn't sure what's wrong with you but you ain't talkin or movin' and she said she bets you know how much I love you.

"Oh, and then I told her your name is Theodore and that you're special, and she said she was sure you are, special I mean, and then she said she was sure that I'm special too and I told her that's what my mama said but I never met her `cause she died when I was born and she said she bet that my mama was always watching over me and I told her that's what you said. And then Daddy called me in here and he said he was gonna go get some coffee and get me an Orange

Crush and when I looked back out to tell the lady goodbye she was gone."

I felt my sister crawl into the bed and curl herself into me, tucking her head beneath my chin as she had so many times before, and I could smell the sweetness of her. After a while I felt her shift, turning to face me, then place her hands on me gently. One on my forehead and one on my chest. She let them stay there, pressing into me. And I felt their warmth. And then I knew what she was trying to do. And I imagined: *We are doing all the things she'd drawn in the picture: fishing, the fair, hide-and-seek. All the things that lay ahead of us, my sister and me.*

And I felt the twitch of the muscles in her hands and then the heat flowed from her palms. And it stirred in me from the center of my chest and it expanded, moving out and out like liquid. And I felt my body swell and tingle like so many pin pricks stinging and flaring from the inside out, and it flowed in me and I swam in it.

And then I sensed the tiniest flutter of my eyelids and I could feel the tip of my tongue peeking out to moisten my cracked lips. Then my eyes opened to a squint and I took a shallow breath and coughed. And I breathed again. I could feel the blood rising in my cheeks and I opened my eyes more fully just as Lily opened hers.

And in Lily's face I saw my mother. At last I saw her. The milky softness of her pale cheeks, the way her eyebrows wryly snaked, the tenderness of her lips, her green eyes ringed in black, spots of gold dancing within them, liquid warm and gleaming. Familiar. These were my mother's eyes. And in that moment, I knew she was alive in Lily and in me.

And then my little sister smiled, broad and generous, but for the empty spot where a front tooth used to be. "Mama was right," she said. "I'm special too. Do you want to see the picture I made for you?"

Session 17

"I went to see my mother," she says, biting her lower lip. "I hadn't been to the nursing home in a long time. Not since I started coming here."

"That couldn't have been easy, knowing all you know now."

"I was ready," she says firmly. I was ready to tell her how much I hated her. I actually prepared the words even though I knew she wouldn't understand anything I was saying. But I wondered if she could, you know, hear me on some level. Like she was in some sort of coma but she could take it in. They say in the very late stages of Alzheimer's when the person can't even speak that there may be some sort of a core there. And I was hoping there was—some essence of her buried somewhere in that tiny fragile body. And I hoped that she could take it in enough for me to hurt her. Really hurt her."

"What did you say?"

She sets her jaw, determinedly. "She was sitting by the window staring out at the sky. I pulled up a chair next to hers. And I asked her why she never protected me. I said, 'I am your daughter. Why didn't we leave? Why didn't you get me out? What could you have possibly been afraid of that was more important than me? I was a little girl. Your little girl. You were the adult.'" She wipes her nose with the back of her hand and resumes bravery. "I said, `You conspired with my father by doing nothing. You may as well have planned it together.' I didn't yell. I thought I would, but I didn't. I told her that my life is a fucking nightmare because of her and my father. I told her that I haven't had a decent relationship or even a real friend for my most of my life. I told her I can't even be touched by another human being because it hurts. Because it physically hurts. And that I've been just so—so sad, for so long. For as long as I can remember."

Her chin trembles. She closes her eyes tightly. She is not in the room, she is with her mother. "And she turned to me and just stared with her milky, hollow eyes. And I wanted to punish her. A part of me wanted to lay her down and put a pillow over her face. I wanted her to die. And she sat there so frail and empty. And I actually waited for her to say something even though I knew she couldn't."

"What would you have wanted her to say?"

"I don't know. That she loved me. That she was sorry. That I should have been more important to her than anything, anything in the world. That she should have told someone, the police, social services, one of her fucking priests, anyone, even if she thought I would defend my father. Even if it meant the end of our family that wasn't a family. That she should have saved me."

She becomes very still. I want to hold her.

She whispers. "And then I wondered why *I* didn't say something. After I knew...that it wasn't normal, that it wasn't something daddies did with their little girls. Why didn't *I* tell someone?—a friend, a counselor, any of the people I thought she should have told. Anyone." She lowers her head and shakes it, and her voice breaks. "Why didn't I tell *her*..."

I wait and wait more. Then finally, I say, "Why do abused women stay with their husbands? Why do raped women not accuse the one who raped them? Why don't all those little boys in the Catholic Church come forward when they are kids, when it's happening, instead of years later? Why do children who are beaten still look for comfort from the ones who beat them? Why do *dogs* keep coming back after they've been kicked, time and time again, for some sign of affection from the one who assaults them?"

"I know why," she says faintly. "Because we are powerless. Because of the shame, the fear, even the hope. The goddamn hope. Because on some sick level the person or the fucking dog thinks they deserve it. Or is complicit, somehow." She becomes furious. "And me, I actually *was*. I *was* complicit! I didn't fight or cry or even say no. I thought I was saving my daddy. My father. The word daddy makes me sick now."

"You weren't complicit. It was what you knew. It was your *normal* for a very long time. You were ... you were resigned."

She leans forward, elbows on her knees, and rests her forehead on clenched fists. "I was ready to tell her how much I hated her. How much I've hated her practically my whole life. I could taste the words in my mouth and I was determined to say it all." Heartbreak swells, then anger. "The coldness, the Valium, the food! The fucking food! That she locked me in my room!" She sits up, erect. "And I looked at my mother, so pathetic, as if the light was out of her soul, like a dying animal, and I knew the light had been out of her soul for as long as I could remember. Like mine. And I leaned in close to her and I said it. I said `I've hated you. And I've loved you. And I've spent my whole life not being able to tell the difference."

She leans back into the sofa and her shoulders fold like a flower wilting in the noon sun, and she sits for minutes. I am amazed that there is not one tear. Then, finally, "It's funny, you know," she says. "There was a moment, a split second, I thought I saw something in her. A flicker of presence. But I don't believe it was really there. It was just in my mind because I was looking so desperately for it. Who knows? I won't ever know."

"What if I told you it doesn't matter?" I say. "What if I say you did your part? You did what you needed to do. And there is nothing, nothing in the world she could have said that would have changed or explained anything at all. And in a way it's probably better. A friend of mine used to call it *action without the hitch*. You do your part and the rest is none of your business."

A peace comes over her. She clears her throat and smiles. "I have something to tell you." She summons fortitude. "A week from Tuesday will be our last session."

I am stunned, bewildered, even alarmed. I compose myself. "Of course, you can do whatever you want, but I don't think this is a good idea. You've come a long way but there's still a great deal to do."

"I know. And I'll continue to do it. But I'm moving. I've known this for a week now but I couldn't say it to you."

"How did this come up? Where are you moving?"

"San Diego. I got a job. A real job. I'm going to work at this small publishing house. When I say small, I mean small, as in specializing in essays and poetry. The ad said they needed strong communication and organizational skills, attention to detail, a multi-tasker. I knew it was a long shot but I applied, and I went down for an interview and, well, they said yes." She carries a sense of pride I've not seen in her before.

"Congratulations," I tell her, still swimming in the news. "I think that's fantastic."

"It's not the other end of the world, but it's too far to commute."

"When do you go?"

"Two weeks. It doesn't pay a fortune but it's something I want to do and I don't want to pass it up. I'd appreciate it if you can help me find another therapist. Maybe somebody you know and trust."

"Yes, of course." I don't know what to say and I can't tell if I'm more upset by her not seeing me or me not seeing her.

"Do you think I'm lying? Like before?"

"No."

"Do you think I'm ready?"

"Yes."

"It's a *good* thing. I have to start sometime, being in the world."

I think of Frank. What he'd said to me, and it's as if he is speaking through me. "You put it out there, you say 'yes', and you don't know what's going to happen. And it's terrifying. But if you say 'no', you know damn well what's gonna happen."

"Not a goddamn thing."

"Not a goddamn thing. So you take the chance."

"You say 'yes'."

She pulls a piece of paper from her purse.

"I presume this isn't a packing list," I say.

She laughs. "I guess maybe it is in a way." She takes out her readers and adjusts them on her nose until they sit evenly. "I'm not saying this is good, but here goes."

> I know how it feels to gaze at the sky
> To spread my wings, only to never fly.
> When the earth grows cold and desire dies.
> Secretly, desperately, yearning to rise.
>
> But in the stillness there is a stirring
> as I stumble past the past.

In the quiet there is courage
to try again at last.

I will stand up; I will be free.
I will live the life that's meant for me.
I will soar and I will sing,
I'll embrace whatever love may bring.

I'm healing from the yesterdays
that tied me to the ground.
I've only got a broken wing
And it won't keep me down.

I will miss you,
but I don't need you.
Not in the way I have
when you steadied me on wobbly legs
and set me forward.
Not rushing blindly to, nor turning from tomorrow.
Now I can make my own way
without you there to push me through.

I wish you days of love and hope.
I wish you swift and unpredictable winds
to carry you to places beyond your imagination.
Thank you, my dear friend.
You have touched me.

Chapter Thirty-Four

It was Sunday, and I would go back to church when I was ready, if I was ever ready. Since the "miracle" of my recovery had been reported, the congregation was eager to exalt me. But I'd been the center of too much for too long—more than enough to last a lifetime. And on this day Henry and I ran hell-for-leather along the dirt road in a frenzy of infinite relief, jumping and yelping and buoyant. We heard the squawking call of a crow and called back to it. I was allowing myself to be a boy again.

It was peculiar, I thought, that I'd seen more towns in Oklahoma than anyone I knew, more than anyone should, unless they sold encyclopedias door to door. And it was good to be home. Well, not home exactly, but in a place I knew where I was. I didn't know what would come, where I would live, what my family would do, but I knew that today was better than yesterday and that was enough for now.

"How long you gonna stay at that motel?" asked Henry, jumping over a ditch where water once ran but was now cracked and flaked. I followed him and it became a sport, hopping back and forth over the ditch.

"My daddy's waitin' to see about the insurance before he decides if we're gonna rebuild or move to another house."

"Do you miss your stuff?" he asked, tossing a rock at a tree stump.

"I don't know. My mama's stuff, I guess. Not like I ever looked at it, but I knew it was there." I stopped to watch a horned toad sunning itself on a rock and Henry crouched down next to me.

"You ever gonna tell your daddy about that will and the Whites?"

"Prob'ly not."

The clouds grumbled a warning and Toby White and his crew appeared from around the bend. They'd been to church, of course. Henry muttered under his breath. "You can't time this shit." Then loudly, "Well, speak of the devil. And I mean that sincerely."

I stood solidly, my eyes fixed on Toby, as the rest of the gang circled Henry and me like a wagon train. Toby remained silent as the others heaved their usual taunts.

"Well, if it ain't Jesus Christ himself."

"Wanna come down to McAffee Pond and show us how you walk on water?"

"Ooh, I can't see," said Hammer Pullman as he blindly searched with his hands. "Help me, Theo!"

"Ooh, I got blue balls. Hey, Theo, wanna suck my dick?"

Toby stepped forward. "Hey guys, knock it off. We got better things to do."

I neither flinched nor budged. Then I stalked around the interior of the circle, glaring at each of their repugnant faces. "You been chasin' me since second grade," I said, calmly. "I ain't afraid of you no more. Go ahead. Hit me."

"Who wants to go first?" yelled Jerry Carmichael, acne blazing, as he stepped to me, nose to nose.

My head slumped forward with its full weight, then lifted slowly, mouth gaping, until it rose high enough for all to see that that my eyes had rolled back in my head. The gang of boys gawked at me with apprehension as my shoulders

345

began to twitch, jostling my head in every which way, my mouth contorting wordlessly, my hands flinging into the air until my entire body convulsed. Then the sounds came— strange, cryptic, unassignable. *"Abell-be-in-coo-ma-ka-meesh-flomp!"* I rambled in a low ominous tone. The boys stepped back in terror. The sounds came louder and faster. *Sinka-locca-poca-dia! Ma-kan-ish-totuto-reg-ima-pa-pa!* I spun in a circle, my hands waving as if shooing away a colony of bats. And then I suddenly stopped, smiled broadly, and sang, *E-I-E-I-O!!*

Henry burst out laughing. "You guys are such imbeciles," he said. And I saw Toby smile.

"You think so, midget?" said Hammer. "I'll take both of you down!" He lunged for me but Toby jumped in and threw him to the ground.

"Lay off!" he commanded.

"What's up with you, man?"

"Nothin'," said Toby. "It just gets old. Grow up, jerkoff."

Hammer got to his feet, dusted himself off and the crew walked away, befuddled, their puffed-up chests deflated.

Toby shook his head. "Don't pay them no mind. They're assholes."

"You should find some new friends," I said.

"Maybe I will."

We exchanged knowing looks and Toby joined his brood, at least for the time being. And I watched my almost half-brother something-or-other walk down the road and out of sight.

Henry knew it was time let me go to where I needed to go. We promised to meet later in the day, maybe at McAffee pond, and we slapped the scarred palms that connected us for life. Then Henry sprinted off and through the field until the trail of crushed grass was all that remained.

I resumed my path. I wasn't sure what I was going to say to Frank or how to apologize, and decided I would know when I got there. Suddenly, there was a rustling in the golden forsythia on the side of the road and it stopped me in my tracks. A young buck stepped out of the brush. His reddish-brown coat trembled with muscle and his antlers were still in velvet, knobby and soft, spokes reaching and bent inward, like hands.

I froze, not wanting to scare him away, but the animal knew I was there. The buck strode to the center of the road and stopped, turned its regal head to look to me, black eyes shining, and waited a long wait. Then he gracefully walked to the other side, his carriage high and hooves silent. Then he pulled back on his hind legs and sprung over the gully, and disappeared into the pasture.

I gazed at where the deer had stood; where he had looked deeply at me, into me, seeming to know something about me that I hadn't known about myself. Then I knew. *This was where it had happened,* I was nearly sure of it. I'd walked this road a thousand times since I was old enough to venture on my own and I'd never recognized it until now. This was the spot that had forever altered my life, my heart, my hands, all of me. I closed my eyes and saw it all: the sudden swerve, the jarring crash, glass shattering, metal tearing. The crackle of my bones. The silence and the rain. My mother's voice.

"Help me, Theo."

"I don't know how."

"Try. You're my big boy. Can you walk?"

"I think so."

"Run, Theo. Run and get help!"

I opened my eyes and looked to where I'd run that night for help, just up the road, to a plain white house with black-shuttered windows that was no longer there. To a place where Frank had once lived before it was burned to the ground, and where his trailer now stood.

I arrived at the gravel drive and Frank appeared in his doorway holding an envelope in his hand. "Hey there. I was just takin' this into town," he said.

"Town? For real?" I called out, amazed. "Shouldn't we call the newspaper or the local news?"

"Don't be a smart ass!" yelled Frank.

I knew that he would say nothing of our time apart, of having been right when I had come to him. What was done was done. That was his way. He walked to the truck jangling his keys.

"You know, I can take it into town for you," I offered.

"No, sir. I can do it, but you can come along if you want." He stuffed the envelope in his baggy jeans pocket and it appeared at his feet on top of his boot and he laughed. He checked his other pocket and found another hole. "Guess a person don't need no pockets if he ain't got nothin' much to put in 'em. Hold onto this for me," he said, and he got in the truck. I glanced at the letter before pocketing it. It was addressed to Frankie Kotori. Frank's son. And a long, complicated address in France. "Well, what are you waitin' for, boy? Get in!"

The drive was a quiet one. I thought that most people made too much noise and it wasted the quiet. Aunty Li, Brother Jimmie, Pastor Flynn. Always so much to talk about and so little to say, tossing out words like apple cores left to rot by the roadside. I was grateful Frank didn't feel the need to fill the space, but it sat on me like a burden.

"I'm sorry," I finally said.

"For what?" he asked, keeping his eyes on the road.

"For when I was so mad that day. Before I left. I said things."

"Everybody gets mad, son." He messed up my hair to pledge his forgiveness. "And you said the truth. I didn't like hearin' it much but you said the truth."

The air was moving, slowly at first, since it hadn't moved for a very long time and wasn't used it. Sooty gray clouds moved too, spreading, poking like fingers across the sky.

"And..." my breath shook with the jumble of the road.

"Bring it on, boy." Frank pulled a Lucky Strike from the pack with the corner of his mouth and lit it, took a long pull, and slowly exhaled.

I gathered courage. "It was your house I ran to that night of the accident, wasn't it? It was you who called the ambulance. And saved me and my daddy and my sister."

"I didn't save nobody, son. You're the one done the running. You're the one done the saving. I just made the connection."

I let his words settle on me. "How long you known it was me?"

"I expect I knew first time I saw you."

"'Cause of my hands?"

"Well, sure. But even before that. I knew when I saw you up in my hackberry tree taking the hit from those boys throwing rocks so you could protect them baby birds."

"How come?"

"Just did." He blew a stream of smoke out of the corner of his mouth. "That's why you're on this earth, Theo. To give folks second chances. To be the connector. You just gotta learn to protect yourself, too."

We passed the McMorrow place and I saw Miss Patsy grazing in the field and smiled to myself. "What about you, Frank? Why do you think you're on this earth?"

"Hmph. That's a mighty good question, son. I've spent a lot of years trying to figure that one out."

"And?"

"I reckon I'm here … to make a different kind of connection. You and me, we ain't so different." The truck staggered along.

"I'm done." I said.

"With what?"

"All of it. I can't do it no more. And I'm glad."

"Hmmm. Well, I guess that's that," he said, his voice even. "There's other ways to give folks second chances."

We drove into town and found a parking spot in front of Judson's Drugs. The clouds fell low and the sky erupted with an echoing boom, as if men with guns were nearby. I looked up, anticipating something, and together we walked past the place where Vinita always sat, but was empty now.

"You can change your mind, you know," said Frank.

"I know."

People we passed stared wild-eyed, as if two camels were wandering through the streets of Dalton. A young couple holding hands even parted to steer clear. Frank muttered, "You think it's you or me?"

"Guessin' it's both. Quite the pair, the two of us."

Rain came. And the world stopped. Everyone, everyone on the street abandoned whatever they were doing—shopping, gossiping, scolding children, even driving—and looked upward to the heavens, holding out their palms as if accepting a gift. The cool sweet sprinkle bathed our faces and it was the only time I could remember when everyone smiled at the same moment. And then the world resumed, but kinder.

Frank and I passed the church. I wanted to tell him about the cow but I'd save that story for another time. The post office was just across the street and we waited on the curb for a car to pass. I noticed that Frank was slightly trembling. "Action without the hitch," he whispered to himself, and he took a deep breath.

As we started across Dalton Boulevard, the rain began to fall harder, drops as big as pennies.

Then, from nowhere, a speeding car careened toward us, brakes screeching, skidding on the wet pavement. Frank pulled me out of the way but was too late to dodge the hit himself. There was a thud, his body thrown over the hood of the car and tossed into the air, landing on the side of the road, limp and bloody and broken.

"No!" I ran to him.

The driver jumped out of his car. "Oh my God, oh my God! Shit! Somebody call somebody!"

I threw myself to the ground and covered Frank like a cloak, sobbing, wiping drizzle from his face. He lay motionless, his chest barely rising and falling. Blood trickled from the back of his head and mixed with the rain, soaking into the muddy red clay that was earth. A crowd gathered and a man stepped forward.

"Stay away!" I commanded.

I laid my hands firmly on Frank and turned my face to the sky, clenching my teeth, the rain beating against my closed eyes. I desperately tried to imagine our future together, but instead, only memories flashed through me like pictures of a dream, the vastness of their number surprising me.

"Don't you leave me!" I wailed. "You can't leave me!"

Frank peered at me affectionately, his breath shallow. "It's okay, son."

"Try! Try goddammit!" I cradled his heavy head. "It takes both of us, remember? You have to want to stay. You have to want it. Please want it!"

A siren sounded in the distance, dissonant and cruel. I closed my eyes again and pressed down hard on Frank's body, my hands open and hot, searching my mind for the images that would bring him back. When I opened them, Frank was gazing at me, his eyes like black stars. "I'm already healed, boy," he said with a weak tender smile. "And besides—it ain't none of your business."

A sound crawled around in his throat like a whistle and Frank fell silent. I took his face in my hands. And when I removed them, the scar was gone. And I wept.

CHAPTER THIRTY-FIVE

The weather had passed and the sky was pale. I stepped over the foundation of what had once been Frank's house, *the* house, and into his trailer, still wearing his blood on my white T-shirt that had melted into a soft pink from the rain. I sat in his broken-down Lay-Z-Boy, a spot previously forbidden. It smelled of Lucky Strikes and Coors and Frank. I felt my chest ache, actually ache, and I understood where the word *heartbreak* came from, even more so than when my mother had died. I was older now and understood too much.

I looked around the room at the meager possessions of a big life and the impermanence of it struck me hard: the Paris café print, the wall-mounted Winchester, the Golden Nugget ashtray, the hot plate, "The Seven Rites of Cheyenne" book, the always bowl of half-shelled peanuts. I studied the singed World War II snapshot of a proud young Frank with his compatriot, and the tarnished-framed photograph of him with his once family.

Suddenly, I remembered the letter. I pulled it from my pocket and smoothed it flat on my knee, running my fingers over the name. Frankie—the softer sounding version of Frank. I found an open edge and carefully ran my thumb under the seal to open it and delicately unfolded its contents.

Dear Son,

It has been a lifetime, your lifetime, since I seen you. I tracked you down and I see you kept my name and I hope that means something. Your mama made it clear she didn't want nothing to do with me and my shame has kept me from trying to reach you all these years. But you're a man now. 18 if my math is right. You was just a baby when I went to Korea and left your mama alone with an infant son in a country that wasn't hers and no family to help her. Nothing fair about that. I don't know what you been told about me, but for the record, I was in prison for killing a man.

"Is it true? Did you do what they say?"
"Depends on what they say. But probably."

That man was like my brother. We had served in the same battalion in WWII in France where I met your mama. And then we was together again in a new war and all I wanted was to be home with your mama and my new baby boy. I'd seen enough torment for one lifetime. And it was right after the Second Battle of Seoul and hundreds of us was dead and over a thousand wounded. And my buddy was tore up bad. Half his body blown up. So bad I knew he wasn't going to make it. And he begged me, he said Frank, please help me. He said please make it end, I can't take no more. But I couldn't help him and I couldn't heal him. So I did the only thing I knew how to do to make it end. I did what I'd want him to do for me. I shot him. I shot him with my pistol right there in the field hospital.

"But what if I could have saved her?"
"Then she'd be alive."

And the MPs come after me and I fought hard. I should have just let them take me but I couldn't see straight, I couldn't think straight. I went bat shit crazy. And they wrassled me down and I got sliced up in the belly and across my face deep.

"I can make it go away."
"I don't want it to go away. Some
things shouldn't be healed."

As soon as I was able they shipped me off to Leavenworth. Your mama didn't have much choice but to take you back to her own family in France. She didn't want no contact with me and I didn't blame her one bit. She just wanted you to be safe and grow up proper.

"And she had to decide.
And Mama told them to save me."

I studied the law and got me an attorney to take my case and after 10 years I got an appeal and they called it temporary insanity from war trauma, and they let me free. But I was mad. Mad at everybody and everything. Mad at myself. And when Vietnam started up it just gave me something to aim my mad at. And the local folks burned down my house and tried to run me out of town but I wouldn't give them the satisfaction. And I wasn't willing to come to you. I wasn't willing to give up the mad. I had to stew in it until I could finally let it go piece by piece.

I come a long way since I been out of prison but there's a part of me that ain't never really been free. Not until now when I'm writing this letter. What I'm trying to say is that even though we don't know each other, I ain't never stopped loving you. I don't expect your mama to ever forgive me but I hope you can try.

"Do you talk to them?"
"They ain't much interested in talking to me."

I want to be a part of your life but if you don't want to I understand. There's this boy. He makes me think about what I missed by not being your daddy. And he told me to practice what I preach and get off my ass which I should have done a long time ago.

"You say 'yes', and you don't know what
the hell's gonna happen.
But if you say 'no', you know damn
well what's gonna happen.
Not a goddam thing."

*Love,
your dad*

I folded the letter and slid it back into the envelope. I would mail it in the morning along with a note I would write myself. I spotted Frank's arrowhead necklace on the coffee table and I picked it up and explored its cool beveled edges. Frank always wore it always, but not that day. I thought perhaps he'd grown tired of protecting himself. I wrapped the chain around my fingers so that the stone lay in my palm, then I held it tightly and put it in my pocket.

I stepped outside the trailer. The sun sliced through the ceiling of clouds and the clean breeze tasted like honeysuckle. I looked up to the tree where I'd hidden that first day and I remembered the baby birds. And I smiled.

SESSION 18

She changed her session time to my last appointment so she could spend the day taking care of the details of her move—cable, electricity, gas, internet, all the endless hours of phone-on-hold essentials of a life ahead. She enters the room with a paper grocery bag and brings it to her lap as she takes her seat. "I brought something." She pulls a heavy box from the bag. It is wooden, walnut colored, with a heart crudely carved on the lid. It is the box. The one from her father.

"So, I'm packing and packing and I knew exactly where this was, but I kept avoiding that upper shelf in the closet. And since I knew I was coming here today, I waited until an hour ago to get it down so I could open it here. With you."

"Sounds like a good plan."

"Come," she says, patting the cushion next to her. "It'll be easier to show you."

I've never sat on the sofa with a patient. It feels awkward to cross the border, yet right. My knee nearly brushes against her but I catch myself. She opens the box. Its hinge is slow. The green felt lining is grazed and worn. Inside are dozens and dozens of items. A hundred? Two hundred? Curios and trinkets, coins and jacks and gadgets and knickknacks. Lipstick, cheap metal rings, plastic bracelets, gemstones, a pocketknife, a yo-yo, marbles, gold chains, perfume samples, colored pencils, stickers, a watch. Souvenirs, each one representing each act. Each one a prize.

She lifts a handful and splays a sample of an entire childhood. "Go ahead, touch them."

I don't want to. I don't want to touch anything he has touched. But I place my hand inside the box and lay it on the things. It is too real. I am disgusted and I want to crush them.

After a moment, I pull my hand from the box and I stand. "Did you drive here?"

"Yes."

I grab my jacket and keys. "Do you have anything planned after we're done?"

"No. Packing. No."

It is dusk. I park my car and walk up the wooden stairs built from railroad ties, splintered and worn, with pockets of sand gathered in crevices. The salty air makes me wrinkle my nose. I see a sign reading "Santa Monica – Route 66 – End of the Trail." I'm sure it's been there forever, but I've never noticed it before. The pier is nearly empty; on week-nights, there are never many people left after the shops and burger stands and rides have all closed.

I'm guessing I've arrived first, but as I walk past the car-ousel, I can see her silhouette against the setting sun. I go to her and resist touching her shoulder. "Hi. You beat me here!"

A pelican hops over the quay as if too lazy to spread its wings. "It's getting chilly," she says. "I'm always surprised how nippy it can get by the water, even in the summer."

"Do you have it?"

She points to the box sitting on a green wooden bench. I go to retrieve it and turn to see her, eyes closed, her face tilted toward what is left of the golden sun, the wind flooding her hair. She is beautiful. I almost don't want to interrupt the picture because I know I'll never see it again. She catches me looking at her and I turn away and see the Ferris wheel across the pier. I don't know how I could have passed it without noticing before, without thinking. It takes me by surprise and I know that I've shown it. She looks to where I am staring and spots it herself. It sits ominously unlit and empty and still.

"All right then," I say. "Are you ready for this?"

"Yes."

I walk to her with the box and I open it. She looks fixedly at its contents before slowly gathering a small handful. She cast her eyes to the smoky horizon and it's as if the pull of the tide draws the words from her. "This is for hurting me," she says, and throws the things into the ocean. Pieces of shiny metal sparkle against the surface as they disappear. She takes another small handful.

"This is for tricking me." She tosses it away.

And then another.

"This is for making me trust you."

And another.

"This is for violating me."

And another.

"This is for the secrets."

And another.

"This is for stealing my childhood."

And another. And another. And another.

"This is for making me think no one else could love me."

"This is for betraying me."

"For degrading me."

"This is for all the fear."

"The shame."

She pulls the box from my grasp and empties the rest of its contents into the water.

"This is for destroying me."

She tosses the box into the sea and it floats, drifting, bobbing, until it takes on water and sinks.

Her mouth opens in a silent shout. She holds onto the railing, gripping, anchoring herself, and it comes. Finally, it comes. The vast sorrow. And it overtakes her, and she wails and chokes and her shoulders shake and her body convulses and I fear she cannot breathe.

I have never in my life wanted so desperately to hold someone. Not doing so is against everything in me that is human. I think of my childhood, standing and watching my house burn down and being helpless to do anything about it. But the memory pales next to this agony. This is a human being. A person I have grown to care about, and yes, even love. And her pain cuts into me. I grab the railing, my fingernails pierce the chipped white paint, and I stand beside her as she gives in to the catastrophe of her lifetime.

When she calms, her breath gasping in little spurts, she lifts her head and wipes her cheeks dry and we stare at the sea, pockmarked and ever-changing. The wind picks up and a seagull swoops near us.

"There's one more thing," she says. She reaches behind her neck and unclasps the locket she has worn every day since I first met her—the locket her father had given to her sister and then passed on to her. She holds it tightly in her hands and pulls them to her forehead, as if praying.

"This is for my sister," she whispers. She throws it high into the air and it sails against the setting sun and into a cresting wave that overtakes it.

Chapter Thirty-Six

It was morning and my father and Lily and I sat on the curb across the street from where our house used to be. Most of its remains had been hauled away, leaving a shallow bed of ashes, broken glass and the foundation of the fireplace with blackened bricks scattered around the base like dominoes. A single skeletal wall of charred two-by-fours stood stubbornly in an act of defiance.

Within the ash were the possessions of our lifetimes: mine, my sister's, my father's, our ancestors', and the last of my mother's. I wasn't quite sure what I was supposed to feel—as if my guilt wasn't enough. There was an emptiness and a heaviness. But there was something else. Something clean.

"Daddy, can I go across the street?" asked Lily.

"Just don't get in the soot, punkin," said my father. Lily looked from right to left and skipped away. She found a long branch and poked at the char of a fallen beam, and I thought it strange and beautiful to watch her so alive against the death. The future chipping at the past.

Uncle Darnell had promised Lily he'd bring Sookie to visit as soon as there was a place to visit, or as soon as he'd found a place for *us* to visit him, having left Aunty Li for good when I was in the hospital.

I felt the tension of my father about to speak. "You know it was my fault, don't you?" he said, staring straight ahead. "The fire."

I stared ahead too. "I wasn't sure. Coulda been me. Well, because of me."

"It wasn't you. And I was wrong for lettin' you think that for even one minute." He took in a great breath and his chest rose and remained there, still, until he finally let it go. "I think maybe I did it on purpose without really thinkin' about it."

I squinched up my face. "What? How do you mean?"

"I been holdin' onto a lotta shit, son," he said with a skidding sigh. "A lotta shit. And I been angry for a long time. About this town, about things I thought shoulda been different than they was. About failin' your mama, about when she died. Even about your sweet little sister. Sometimes I couldn't even look at her. Or you … or even that goddam antique furniture for chrissakes. That goddam furniture," he said laughing. "I hated that goddam furniture."

"I hated it too," I said. "I hated that goddam furniture."

My father softly shook his head side to side, then measured me with his eyes: the size of my hands, the breadth of my shoulders, my length of my feet, as if assessing who I would grow into. I looked back at him, wondering the same thing about myself. And I supposed he decided I was old enough.

"I got somethin' I wanna say," he said, uneasy, like trying to speak the words he'd rehearsed but unsure if they were the right ones. "When the accident happened and Lily was born and your mama died and you and me was in the hospital, the doctors said they might be able to fix your hands, but it would be a lot of surgeries and it was real expensive. And I didn't have no money and your mama was gone, and I had a new baby I didn't know what to do with. And I told them I couldn't do it, the surgeries. And I didn't tell nobody. Not even your Aunt Li. She already hated that your mama ever married me in the first place—thought I wasn't worth nothin'—and after the accident I couldn't say I disagreed. So I couldn't bring myself to ask her to help me."

The air closed in with apprehensive reckoning, but I didn't speak. A fury rose up in me like a fever but it did not overtake me as I thought it should; and it occurred to me that I didn't wish for my hands to be restored, and it perplexed me.

He continued. "I mean, what kind of father don't figure out a way to get his son's crippled hands fixed, no matter what? So these years later when my leg just up and got better like some kinda miracle, I thought it was gonna make everything different, but it didn't. Somethin' wasn't right about me walkin' straight and your hands still not working like they was supposed to." He paused, then, "And that was you who done that wasn't it? Fixed my leg."

Neither of us shifted our gaze from across the street, but I placed my hand on my father's shoulder and he reached across his chest and covered it. "Anger is an ugly thing, son. It holds onto you like a grip, tight around your chest, and the more you try to break away, the tighter it holds on 'til you can't breathe, 'til you're the one holdin' on to it and there ain't no difference between you.

"So with the fire," he said, measured. "With the fire, maybe I was tryin' to do somethin' in my sleep—drunk—that I wasn't brave enough or man enough to do otherwise." I let my hand fall and I turned to him. "So now," said my father, "I was thinkin' now maybe we ain't got nothin' to hold us here. No house, no job." *No Frank, I thought. And Henry would move on from Dalton, but we would be bound forever and I knew that was true.* "And we can just get outta here. Outta Dalton all together. Maybe somewhere up north where the sun don't beat you down. Colorado or

Nebraska. And we can just be a family in a town where we ain't got no history and there ain't no statues lookin' down on us, and we ain't got nothin' we're supposed to be or supposed to do. Me and you and Lily startin' over fresh. And I could even open my own shop, I could do that. *George's Auto Repair.*" He placed his hands over mine. "And we could get your hands fixed." My father looked to me as if for permission.

"That sounds real nice, Daddy," I said, "but you know I can't take that money from that preacher, and I don't see how..."

"Well, I'm gettin' to that. I knew everybody thought the church folks set the fire on account of your healing, on account of a gift so big I can't even begin to understand. And it woulda been easy to just let it be, but I wasn't, I *couldn't* sacrifice you one more time. My son. Not ever again." He shook his head in shame.

Then, "I talk to your mama sometimes. I tell her I'm sorry, I tell her I'm scared, I tell her lots of things. But I ain't never listened to find out if she was talkin' back to me. And when you and your sister was gone and it was just me sittin' in that damn motel, I said to your mama, `I don't know what to do. I need you to help me and tell me what to do.'"

"And what happened?"

"I listened. I can tell you at first I was scared outta my boots but I knew I wasn't gonna feel right, I knew I couldn't look you in the eye unless I did what she told me to do. Unless I come clean. So, I told Rance Bradley the truth, that it was me who started the fire with a cigarette probably fell on the floor when I was drunk. And he said that's what they call negligence and there ain't no insurance coverage for that."

"So what are we gonna do?"

"Just listen, son. As soon as I told old Rance what really happened it was like there was somethin' lifted from me. Like somethin' new was possible."

"But if we ain't got...?

"So here's where it gets downright crazy. After I left Rance I went straight to the bank to see what we had so I could try to figure out what we was gonna do 'cause everything, all the records, burned in the fire. And then the goddamndest thing happened." My father smiled a strange, squinty smile. "There was a lotta money in that savings account."

"How much is a lot?"

"*Two hundred thousand dollars.* Actually, two hundred and one thousand, four hundred and thirty-two dollars." He waited for shock or excitement from me. Instead, I looked at him with a kind of puzzlement, and then a bent, easy smile crept over my lips.

"Where you reckon the money come from?" I asked.

"Hell if I know." He shrugged and laughed.

"Maybe," I said, "maybe Mama inherited it from somebody."

"She woulda told me."

"I guess we won't never know."

But I knew. And I knew that it was necessary for everyone, especially Melva White, for it to be given, and that it was necessary for everyone, especially myself, for it to be accepted.

I turned back to the ash and dust. Lily was standing under the sycamore tree in what had been our backyard. It was scorched on one side but it would survive. "Theo, come here! Hurry! Quick!"

I got to my feet and my father followed suit, heartily waving to Lily. I took a step forward and suddenly, without thinking, I turned and hugged him—an act I could not have carried out had I planned it. And I realized I'd not done such a thing since I was Lily's age, grabbing his towering legs when I was only so high, before Mama was gone. I drew him close and he let me, giving himself to my pull. And he wrapped his arms around me and drew me closer and rested his chin on my head, and I felt the gentle weight of him. And we held ourselves there, suspended. I breathed in his distinct smell, one that I would recognize in a crowd of a thousand, and had. *He's my dad,* I thought. *He's my dad.*

He gently pulled himself away and placed his hands firmly on my shoulders and took me in, head to toe, and his eyes grew soft and proud and the corners of his mouth peaked. "Look at you. Look at my boy. I think you're gonna be taller than me."

"Hurry up, you guys!" cried Lily. "It's-a emergency!"

I ran across the street and around the perimeter of the foundation to find Lily holding the branch like a staff, staring at the ground. A baby sparrow, quivering and injured, lay on a patch of grass still damp from morning dew. I crouched down and stared at it carefully and Lily kneeled by my side. It was plump and neckless, brown and gray and white breasted, flicked with spots. Its frightened black eyes glittered. And it was broken. And I knew what it felt like to be broken and I knew what it felt like to be healed. And I lifted the fledgling carefully in my cupped, crippled hands, and they fit around it just so, as if they'd been shaped to hold it. But I couldn't bring myself to do what needed to be done. There had been too much hurt, too much pain. And whatever gift I'd possessed had served its purpose and I was done. With all of it. Frank was gone, and I couldn't swallow the burden of expectation, or bear the ache of my failure one more time. I placed the baby bird in Lily's hands and I vowed to myself that I would never heal again.

THE LAST SESSION

We sit across from each other. She tells me about her new apartment and how sunlight pours into the living room, and the colors she will paint the walls and the furniture she has bought—the lamps and bedding and dishes and all the details of starting over. The newness and cleanness of it. She tells me she's excited about her new job.

I assure her that the therapist I've set up for her is a brilliant man and a friend, and that I trust him completely. "Here's his name and contact," I tell her, handing her a slip of paper. "He's expecting your call."

She examines it. "Doctor Henry Hardy."

I glimpse at the faded *X* on my palm. "I think he'll be very good for you. And he also uses horses as part of therapy. I know you'll like him."

There is a silence that some might call awkward if they didn't know better. There have been so many silent moments between us in this room, many of them fraught with tension and fear. But this is not that. It's the kind of quiet that comes from two people not having the need to fill the space with sound for the sake of itself. Like it had been with Frank and with Henry.

"We only have a few more minutes," I finally say.

"I know."

"I'd like to give you something." I unclasp the arrowhead necklace from around my neck and hand it to her, dangling, and the chain pools in her palm. "I've worn this for a very long time and I want you to have it."

"But it belonged to your friend."

"And it belongs to your friend. You don't have to wear it..."

She draws it around her neck and I laugh when I see it on her. "It doesn't suit you! Way too masculine and pointy and just wrong. You're much too... too beautiful to wear something so, I don't know, rugged."

At first she is taken aback by my compliment, but then she smiles contentedly and accepts it. She pats the arrowhead against her chest. "I'll keep it handy when I'm nervous," she says. "I know if I'm putting myself into the world I will, inevitably, be touched. I think I'm ready but it scares me."

"What is it that scares you the most?"

She contemplates. "I guess it's that I don't know who I am without this... what's the word... *definition* of myself. It's all I've ever known."

"I understand. I think you know that about me. In my own way."

"Yes."

"And the unknown is scary."

"Maybe something good."

I nod. "Good."

"It's a precious word, that one," she says warmly.

I look at the clock and she follows my eyes. It's time.

We rise, together, several feet apart, and we look to each other knowing that these are our last moments together. Perhaps forever. Probably forever.

I take a step toward her. And I reach out to her and she steps into my arms and I hold her. And nothing bad happens. Nothing hurts. Nothing burns. She pulls me closer. And I wait for my fingers to strengthen and elongate and my hands to grow hot—the feeling I have not known since I was thirteen years old and is finally welcome, once again. "Imagine your future," I whisper in her ear. "Create images in your mind. See yourself free. Healthy. Deserving. Enough. See yourself as who you want to be."

But my hands do not change. The heat does not come. There is no need.

"I will miss you," I say.

"I will miss you."

"I'm always here."

"I know…"

We let go at the same time, neither of us wanting to be first. She gathers her things and moves to the door, then she turns back to me. A last goodbye I think. "By the way, she's a good kid."

"What? Who?"

"Stefani."

"Who?"

"Your receptionist. She has three Chihuahuas and she's going to night school to be a nurse and her boyfriend just proposed to her. You should get to know people, Doc," she chuckles, offering the playful, wicked smile I've grown so attached to. "Oh, and one more thing. That accent you think you've lost? It's charming. I wouldn't want you to lose it completely." I watch her until she disappears at the end of the hall.

"Stefani," I call out. "I need a few minutes before my next appointment."

I close the door and take in my room. I see the clean and I remember the clutter. I sit in my chair. And I think of fathers and sons and fathers and daughters. Mothers present and not present; alive and dead or somewhere in between.

Sisters. And that nothing, and no one, is one thing. Not my father nor his father's father before him, not my aunt, who returned to Georgia and I never saw again. Not my uncle, who'd spent the last twenty years of his life with a man I grew to call Uncle Dan. Not Brother Jimmie, Mrs. White nor Toby, not dear Sookie, no one, not even Henry or my mother or my Lily. There is no good and bad. Black and white is easy. Gray is not. Fog is gray, and at times it is hard to see through it.

And I cry tears with no sound. And I miss my mother. And I forgive my father. And myself. Not so much for the things I've done, but for the things I've been unable to do. I think about all I've come to, secrets discovered and uncovered, gifts and the burden of them, and all that has come to pass and how one thing could not have happened without the other—how each person, each incident, each misfortune, no matter how large or small, brought me, her, everyone to this place. I think of the gift of this woman and how she has touched me, and I smile at the irony of the thought.

I consider the substance of all things lost and all things found. And how grief and mourning and anger are the necessary precursors to bravery; the forefathers of courage; the ignition of change. They shake us into what needs to be done if we let them inform us rather than define us, just like Frank had said. *Frank.* I will miss him always and always with all of myself, but only in proportion to having loved him with all of myself, so I cannot wish the loss away, or any of anything away.

I look at the blue of my room. And I close my eyes, and I still myself, and my aching, happy heart. And I imagine. For her. For myself.

I imagine for myself.

ACKNOWLEDGEMENTS:

During the four years that this book evolved, draft after draft, I am humbled by the encouragement and talents of so many people: Jen Bergstrom (for telling me I should be writing fiction), Doug Veith (for getting me out of my block and inspiring me to write what I know), Bruce Newberg (for saying "where's the 3rd act?"), Christine Pepe (for her meticulous eye and flawless instincts as my editor), Mitchell Ivers (for asking the important questions and serendipitously leading me to the right path), Laura Brugnoli, Marc Olmsted, Diann Duthie, Michelle Lafitte-Zabel, Jennifer Giancola, Bridget Moynahan, Noelle Kahwaji-Karaki, Craig Dorfman, Carolyn Harris, and my dear, recently departed father, Bill Harris, for their invaluable reads, notes and guidance. I am grateful to the doctors and psychologists who advised me along the way. My deepest thanks to my husband, Danny Jacobsen, for his unwavering support and insight, and to my son, Cooper Harris-Jacobsen, for his patience and understanding when Dad didn't surface for hours on end and dinner was inevitably late. I would also like to thank Frank Abdo, wherever he may be, who inadvertently inspired this book over thirty-five years ago and led me on quite the personal adventure. Most of all, heartfelt thanks to my agent, David Forrer at InkWell, who believed in this story and in my writing enough to make me really work for it, and whose tireless enthusiasm got us this far. You are the best of the best and I am honored to call you my friend.

Sam Harris was born in Sand Springs, Oklahoma. He has a multi-hyphenate career in entertainment. He is the author of the critically acclaimed memoir *Ham: Slices of a Life*. He lives in Los Angeles with his husband and their son. Visit www.samharris.com or follow him on www. twitter. com/samharris, Instagram @ samharrismusic, and www. facebook.com/samfans.

COVER DESIGN BY DIANN DUTHIE

AUTHOR PHOTOGRAPHY BY DANNY JACOBSEN

Made in the USA
Middletown, DE
13 October 2020